Éric Noël

AF886488

Understanding Audio Mixing

Knowing How, Understanding Why

MusiquePROD.com

Understanding
Audio Mixing

Knowing How, Understanding Why

Éric Noël

Reddac
1615 Avenue du Lac-Saint-Charles
Québec, Quebec G3G 2W5
Canada
info@reddac.com

Published by Reddac
Translated from French by Éric Noël
Original Edition Copy Editor: Carole Noël
Cover Design and Layout: Reddac

Legal deposit: Bibliothèque et Archives nationales du Québec and Library and Archives Canada, 2026

ISBN : 978-2-9818249-7-4

To Samuel and to my family for their constant support, and to my sister Carole, whose expertise, sound advice, and encouragement helped me persevere in this ambitious project.

Table of Contents

Preface

IN THE LIFE of a musical group, there inevitably comes a moment when someone says, “What if we made an album?” In the case of the band in which I was the guitarist at the time, the idea came up in 1997. Obviously, relying on anything other than our own means to finance and carry out the project was out of the question. So the project was handed to me.

It must be said that I have always been fascinated by music production. As early as the mid-1980s, armed with a mighty beige Mac SE, MIDI software, a sound module, and two SM58 microphones, I was putting together demos of my compositions. Everything was laid down on a cassette multitrack recorder that gave me four tracks of pure happiness. Four tracks! Talk about sharpening your sense of priorities!

Being in a band playing pubs and bars also means learning to make the cheapest rented gear possible work. In the early 1990s, I was regularly tasked with choosing, renting, and, of course, transporting that sound reinforcement equipment to the venue. As a result, I often found myself behind a console that seemed to be held together with duct tape. Those were the days!

During those same years, I was also a technical assistant in the Department of Communication at Université Laval. One of my tasks was to introduce students to the operation of recording equipment so they could produce a soundtrack for their... slide show! Basic explanations of the console, the ABCs of sound recording, the rudiments of mixing, razor-blade tape editing: nothing too frightening.

All this charming preamble to say that I seemed to be the obvious person to bring our ambitious album project to completion. So I took the plunge by expanding my embryonic home studio with the latest editing software, Cubase VST, and a few additional microphones.

At the end of that first adventure, I had to face the fact that making an album requires more than equipment and a few setting recipes picked up here and there. It requires knowledge. A great deal of knowledge! Knowledge of recording, acoustics, mixing, production, arrangement, and even crisis management and psychology. I then threw myself wholeheartedly into acquiring these concepts by every means possible: experimentation, meetings, books, the Internet, DVDs, and so on. More than a passion, it became a true obsession!

Today, I have been running a home studio for more than twenty-five years, where I produce, record, and mix musical projects. Since 2014, I have also had the privilege of teaching studio production, work from which I derive enormous satisfaction and which keeps me aware of the challenges involved in this wonderful profession.

The "How," but Above All the "Why"

When it comes to mixing, we tend to focus much more on how to do something than on why we do it. The emphasis is on the "how": how to compress drums, how to place reverb on the vocal, how to set the equalization of an acoustic guitar, and so on. However, we very rarely examine the "why" behind these interventions. Why do we compress drums? Why do we place reverb on the vocal? What is the equalization of the acoustic guitar meant to accomplish? Yet these are the questions that matter most.

I also find that far too much importance is often placed on the equipment, rather than on the know-how of the person operating it. In truth, no device or plug-in can guarantee the success of a mix by its mere presence. All tools have their particularities, their strengths, and their weaknesses. Although they can make certain tasks easier to accomplish, their effectiveness still depends mainly on what the user is trying to achieve with them.

Throughout this book, mixing techniques are presented in relation to the goals they help achieve. Without neglecting the "how," we will focus above all on the "why." Since everyone has their own devices, software, and plug-ins, the settings will be explained without reference to any particular model. You will therefore be able to put the techniques discussed into practice using the equipment you already own.

I should also add that I am not sponsored in any way by manufacturers of audio equipment or plug-ins. Any products shown or mentioned in this book are used strictly to illustrate the subject being discussed. Although most of these tools are well known, they should not be interpreted as recommendations.

Much More Than Settings

The music industry has undergone many changes over the past few decades. The popularity of streaming platforms has completely transformed how people listen to music. More than ever, mixers must use strategies to capture and hold listeners as their attention spans steadily grow shorter. We will, of course, discuss some of these strategies and how they can help make a mix more engaging for the listener.

Mixing your own music is one thing; working on other people's projects is another. When clients trust us with their projects, we become part of a much broader process, with its deadlines, budgets, and the many people involved. This is when technique gives way to much less tangible notions such as trust, communication, understanding, and negotiation. Many mixers, in fact, say that this part of the work is as important as, if not more important than, the technical side. Yet it is very rarely discussed in books on mixing or music production in general. We will therefore address these aspects, particularly during the crucial stages of presenting the mix to clients, dealing with revisions, and finalizing the project.

I designed this book to come as close as possible to the kind of work I would have liked to have on hand at the start of my journey. I have covered all the concepts that I believe are essential to know in order to succeed in mixing. They will help beginners build a solid technical foundation and avoid the pitfalls that can slow their progress. Intermediate and advanced mixers will find new ways to look at techniques they already use and, I hope, inspiration for discovering and experimenting with new ones.

I hope this book helps you on your own mixing journey.

Éric Noël

1
WHAT IS MIXING?

AT FIRST GLANCE, mixing seems easy to define: you take a set of individual audio elements and combine them to create a stereo track. While this view is correct in many respects, it is nonetheless a rather reductive vision of a far more complex art. In truth, finding a definition of mixing that accounts for all its subtleties is no simple task. Still, I will venture to propose the following:

> *Mixing, the final link in the musical creation process, aims to draw out a piece's full potential—both technically and emotionally—in order to move the listener, capture their interest, and hold their attention.*

Let us briefly explore each element of this statement.

"The final link in the musical creation process"

Even though mixing is carried out largely autonomously, it is nonetheless part of a much broader creative process. The mix engineer therefore seeks to achieve the best possible result while contributing to the project's original vision. In this respect, the mixer is part of a team.

"To draw out a piece's full potential"

The mixer is also in service of the song. They strive to get the most out of the elements provided and assemble them in order to achieve the most effective whole possible.

While a good song does not guarantee a good mix, a bad song greatly complicates the task. Certain shortcomings in the arrangement or recording can limit a piece's possibilities. Whether or not we have the ability or freedom to mitigate these shortcomings, the objective remains the same: to draw out a piece's full potential—whatever the extent of that potential may be!

"Both technically"

The mixer must, of course, eliminate purely technical problems they are able to address (background noise, phase issues, editing problems, etc.). A large part of this work takes place during the preparatory stages of the mix. We must also ensure that we do not create new problems along the way. Each intervention should therefore be motivated by a clear objective, its result evaluated carefully, all while maintaining a healthy gain structure.

"And emotionally, in order to move the listener"

Although these technical considerations are important, we must never lose sight of the fact that music's primary purpose is to convey emotion to the listener. Emotion should always take precedence over technique. At times, what appears technically incorrect may in fact be the best way to serve the song.

This is particularly evident in how pitch correction is applied to the lead vocal and, to a lesser extent, in adjustments related to tempo.

Although technical considerations are important, we must never lose sight of the fact that music's primary purpose is to convey emotion.

Along the same lines, whether the mix was created using a DAW's basic processing tools or with an outrageously expensive analog console, whether you spent 30 minutes or 30 days on it, or whether your frequency analyzer displays the most ideal distribution imaginable—none of this matters to the listener. The one and only thing that reaches them is emotion.

By keeping this reality constantly in mind, our mixing decisions—from how we balance the elements to the types of processing we choose—will be guided by the desire to move the listener.

"To capture their interest and hold their attention"

Music is no longer consumed in the same way. Streaming platforms now provide access to an almost unlimited musical catalog. Listeners can browse this vast repertoire and, if a track does not appeal to them, move on to another with a single click.

In this context, capturing the listener's interest is no longer enough—it must be sustained throughout the entire piece.

It is therefore up to the mixer to employ strategies that keep the track engaging and prevent the listener from pressing the dreaded "next" button. We will examine some of these strategies later on.

2
THE ESSENTIAL COMPONENTS

EVEN THOUGH MIXING requires a good deal of creativity, it remains a technical task that calls for specific equipment. This chapter therefore explores the essential components of a digital mixing studio intended for professional or commercial use.

2.1 Essential Components

2.1.1 THE COMPUTER

The computer is the conductor of everything connected to it, whether through physical cables or virtual connections. Since computer power continues to grow exponentially, a mid-range computer—laptop or desktop—is now perfectly adequate for mixing. That said, it is wise to ensure that its hardware configuration will properly meet the specific demands of mixing.

PC or Mac?

The choice between PC and Mac matters little. Of course, each operating system has its own workflow, but either will deliver excellent results. Your personal preferences and, as we will see later, your DAW will guide your decision.

The Linux operating system should, however, be avoided, as very few mixing applications are available on that platform.

Regardless of the operating system used, better results are achieved by dedicating the computer exclusively to audio production. Removing unnecessary applications and limiting background tasks will ease the load on the processor and free up disk space.

Configuration

A mid-range computer is perfectly adequate for mixing.

Mixing software and plug-ins are often resource-hungry. A mid-range computer will likely offer a sufficiently fast processor, but it will generally benefit from additional RAM. By maximizing the available memory, you will be able to handle projects with a high track count without constantly running into your computer's limits.

Audio files also require significant storage space, as do sample libraries, virtual instruments, and drum replacement software. A large-capacity internal drive is therefore highly recommended.

Finally, your software and needs will evolve. It is therefore preferable to choose a computer with memory expansion capabilities. It is also wise to review the types and number of connectivity ports available and, if necessary, acquire an adapter or docking station to handle all required hardware connections.

2.1.2 THE DAW (Digital Audio Workstation)

All DAWs are cross-platform and run on both Mac and PC. The only exception is *Logic Pro*, which runs exclusively on Mac.

The range of available software is vast, which can make selection difficult for beginners. If you seek advice on discussion forums, you will quickly notice that recommendations vary from person to person. Preference for one DAW over another generally stems from two reasons: loyalty or necessity. Someone may be devoted to *Ableton Live* simply because it was the first DAW they mastered. Another may have started with *FL Studio* and later migrated to *Logic* because a collaborator uses it.

Over the years, certain software has become firmly established among professionals. In addition to *Pro Tools* by Avid (probably the most widely used), *Cubase* by Steinberg, *Logic Pro* by Apple, *Live* by Ableton, and *FL Studio* by Image-Line are all considered reliable industry standards. *Studio One* by PreSonus is also increasingly present in the industry.

Other software such as *Reaper* and Bitwig Studio have found their place among those seeking a more affordable solution.

Although their interface design, workflow, and purchase cost differ, all are powerful and offer the full range of features required for mixing. Once again, your personal affinity will guide your choice. Regardless of the software used, the key is to thoroughly learn its environment and capabilities so you can work without constantly consulting the manual.

2.1.3 THE AUDIO INTERFACE

The audio interface is the device that links the computer to the outside world. It converts sound from analog to digital at the input stage and from digital to analog at the output stage. Beyond this crucial conversion task, it also allows you to connect monitors, headphones, microphones, instruments, analog gear, and more.

The interface connects to the computer via USB or Thunderbolt cable, or via a PCI card. Although most interfaces work with both PC and Mac, it is important to ensure compatibility with the version of the operating system in use.

For mixing done entirely in the computer, your audio interface should include:

- 24-bit / 96 kHz conversion capability
- At least one monitor output
- At least one auxiliary output
- At least one headphone output

If you contribute to arrangements as a musician or producer, XLR microphone inputs, phantom power, line inputs (1/4" TRS), and an instrument input (Hi-Z) may also prove useful for recording.

2.1.4 EXTERNAL HARD DRIVES

In computing circles, one often hears that if a file is not backed up on three different media, it simply does not exist. This is equally true in audio production. It is therefore essential to have at least one external hard drive for backups.

In fact, a second external drive is far from excessive, particularly if you mix for clients. Losing one of your own projects is frustrating enough—imagine the disaster if it were a client's! With two external drives and therefore two backups on separate devices, you significantly reduce the risk of facing such a situation.

Cloud storage is also an excellent solution for keeping a copy of critical folders. Although more expensive than physical drives, it allows automatic synchronization and, above all, increases data security by storing it outside your studio.

2.1.5 MONITORS

Monitors are the loudspeakers you use to hear your mix. Since most mixing decisions are based on what comes from these speakers, they are undeniably a crucial piece of the puzzle.

One of the main qualities of a studio monitor is its ability to reproduce the frequency spectrum evenly. The absence of coloration is essential for identifying problems and avoiding skewed judgment during mixing.

Unlike hi-fi stereo speakers, studio monitors are not designed to "sound good," but to "sound true."

Unlike home hi-fi speakers—no matter how "high fidelity" they claim to be—studio monitors are not designed to "sound good," but to "sound true."

Passive or Active

Any speaker requires amplification to produce audible sound. Monitors referred to as "passive" use an external amplifier; "active" monitors include a built-in amplifier.

Active monitors offer several advantages over passive models. Most obviously, they eliminate the need for additional equipment in the studio setup. Furthermore, because the internal amplifier is specifically designed to optimize the performance of the monitor that houses it, it eliminates the tedious search for the ideal external amplifier.

Technical Specifications

First, it is important to take manufacturer specifications with caution. The impressive results listed are typically obtained in anechoic chambers—environments far removed from normal listening conditions.

In reality, perfectly neutral monitors do not exist. Even if they did, the room and the listener's position relative to the monitors would greatly influence frequency representation.

Choosing Monitors

Monitor size is a frequently debated topic. It is easy to become lost in conflicting opinions and overly technical or subjective information.

However, one fundamental concept must be understood: the performance of any monitor will always depend on how it is positioned and on the acoustic environment in which it is heard.

In most home studio scenarios, the location of the listening position and computer screens largely determines the remaining space available for monitors. Proper positioning should therefore always take precedence over type, shape, power rating, or woofer size. The goal is to choose a monitor format that allows optimal placement without compromise.

Proper monitor placement should take precedence over their type, shape, or power.

Because of their vital role in decision-making, purchasing monitors represents a significant investment. One must be prepared to allocate a substantial budget. That said, within a given price range, brand preference ultimately becomes a matter of taste.

It goes without saying that purchasing a pair of monitors without listening to them first is unthinkable. The best method is to bring songs from various genres that you know well to compare models in-store. Try to identify which ones allow you to clearly distinguish each instrument and reveal nuances in the sound. Although it will not be your own listening environment, you will gain a solid sense of what best suits your taste and budget.

As with your DAW, the key is to know your monitors well. Take the time to listen to a great deal of music to become familiar with your listening environment, so your mixing decisions are better informed.

2.1.6 HEADPHONES

Headphones offer a completely different perspective on mixing. They remove the room's acoustics from the equation.

During editing, they provide a microscopic approach that helps detect background noise, clicks at edit points, and other anomalies that might go unnoticed on monitors.

According to many, their exaggerated stereo image makes them particularly useful for evaluating the precise placement of instruments in space and the balance of ambience effects, especially reverb and echo.

This romanticized representation—both in detail and stereo imaging—exists without the natural effects of room acoustics. It can therefore limit translation to other listening environments. Spatial simulation plug-ins have been developed to mitigate this issue by simulating studio or room acoustics in the headphone signal. Although they do not replace real monitors, they can often improve the headphone mixing experience and enhance translation.

It must also be considered that even the best headphones quickly become uncomfortable and place significant stress on the ears. This makes it physically difficult to sustain sessions as long as those conducted on monitors.

While it is entirely possible to achieve good results using only headphones, monitors remain the primary reference for mixing decisions. Headphones nevertheless provide a complementary soundscape that can be useful in many situations.

While it is possible to achieve good results using headphones, monitors remain the preferred reference for mixing decisions.

Choosing Headphones

If headphones are used only occasionally for mixing, there is no particular advantage to lightweight, fully sealed models. A more substantial model can be chosen with emphasis placed on sound quality.

As with monitors, "studio" models are preferable to "hi-fi" models due to their more uniform frequency representation.

If you are required to mix primarily on headphones, a model that includes its own spatial simulation plug-ins can enhance your decision-making.

2.2 Useful Additions

Beyond the basic equipment, certain tools and accessories can enhance your mixing process.

2.2.1 ADDITIONAL MONITORS

When mixing, it is always beneficial to evaluate your work on multiple playback systems. It is therefore practical to equip your studio with speakers closer to what consumers use—not high-end products, but rather typical household devices.

A pair of small computer speakers, a portable stereo, or even a laptop can serve as excellent occasional references. Their limited frequency response and near-mono stereo image provide a brutally honest reproduction that emphasizes what truly matters: midrange frequencies and the center channel.

Given that an incredible number of people now consume music using earbuds, it would be negligent not to consider what this large audience hears. A standard pair of earbuds will complement your listening arsenal well.

Rest assured, the majority of your mixing decisions will be made on your studio monitors. However, these additional speakers allow you to judge how your mixes translate "in real life" and can reveal shortcomings that are often easily corrected.

2.2.2 A FREQUENCY ANALYZER

A detailed frequency analyzer is extremely useful in mixing. Beyond providing an instant visual overview of the frequency distribution of a track or entire mix, it facilitates the identification of more specific issues. Resonance, sibilance, background noise, or excessive low end quickly become evident on the analyzer's display.

Some analyzers also graphically display the stereo field. It then becomes easier to assess the overall width of a mix or finely balance two instruments positioned on opposite sides of the stereo image.

2.2.3 DRUM REPLACEMENT PLUG-IN

Today, it is difficult to produce mixes comparable to commercial releases without a good drum replacement plug-in. It is common practice to enhance or even replace certain drum elements—usually the snare and kick—with samples.

Adding samples to acoustic drum tracks allows you to supplement the sound with characteristics absent from the original recording. For example, the depth of a kick drum can be increased by layering a sample rich in sub-bass frequencies, or a snare can regain bite by adding a sample with strong attack.

Replacement samples can also resolve issues that are difficult to address using conventional techniques—for example, an excellent drum performance compromised by a poor recording. Since samples are recorded individually, they are not subject to bleed and can therefore help when bleed makes the original recording difficult to use.

Adding samples to acoustic drum tracks allows the sound to be enhanced with characteristics absent from the original recording.

Samples may also stabilize volume and attack. This technique is widely used in metal to ensure each kick drum hit is equally loud.

One of the main qualities of a good replacement plug-in is its ability to avoid introducing latency between the original sound and the sample. Ease of use, as well as the quality and variety of the accompanying sound library, must also be considered.

2.2.4 VIRTUAL INSTRUMENTS

It can sometimes be useful to add sonic elements to enhance a mix. As with drum samples, these additions are often motivated more by practical than artistic reasons and can take many forms. An ambient synth pad may be inserted to add depth, a special effect to emphasize the transition between two song sections, or a doubled bass line to strengthen a chorus. Having access to a varied collection of instruments becomes a valuable asset.

2.2.5 MICROPHONES AND ACCESSORIES

It is increasingly common for the person responsible for mixing to also wear the producer's hat, particularly in smaller-scale projects.

Although not essential to mixing itself, basic recording equipment can prove very practical for quickly adding complementary elements (hand percussion, sound effects, simple vocal harmonies, etc.) by recording them on the spot.

2.2.6 CONTROLLERS OR CONTROL SURFACES

Even though all audio parameters in a DAW are accessible directly on the computer screen, DAW controllers or control surfaces make it possible to physically manipulate some of the most common settings, particularly faders. In this sense, they bring back part of the instinctive character associated with analog mixing.

These devices, which resemble mixing consoles, connect to the computer to transmit and apply the adjustments performed on them. Although most are compatible with any DAW, some are designed to integrate with a specific software, enhancing usability.

3

STUDIO ACOUSTICS

THE CHARACTERISTICS OF THE ROOM we are in contribute enormously to what we hear. The walls, floor, ceiling, and the objects furnishing the studio interact with one another and influence every component of the sound. As fundamental as the quality of our equipment may be, the acoustic attributes of our working environment have a direct impact on our ability to make informed mixing decisions.

The acoustic attributes of our working environment have a direct impact on our ability to make informed mixing decisions.

Acoustics studies the properties of sound and its interaction with the environment in which it propagates. Since this discipline is a science in itself, an in-depth explanation of its principles falls outside the scope of this book. However, it is important to introduce certain basic concepts in order to better understand its effects on our perception of sound.

When it comes to designing a room dedicated to music production, two branches of acoustics are of particular interest: soundproofing and room acoustics.

3.1 Studio Acoustics

3.1.1 SOUNDPROOFING

Soundproofing aims to reduce the transmission of sound from one environment to another. For example, when soundproofing a studio, we generally seek to eliminate noise coming from outside. In doing so, we also limit the amount of sound leaving the studio and reaching adjacent rooms.

In soundproofing, mass and density are our best allies. This is why it is common practice to increase the thickness of the walls of a room in order to provide as much resistance as possible to sound waves.

Air is essential to the propagation of sound. It's simple: no air, no sound (the soundtrack of the film *Gravity* deserves recognition here for respecting this fundamental rule of acoustics—something rather rare in science fiction movies!). Therefore, we strive to minimize air leaks, particularly in structural openings such as doors and windows. Weatherstripping similar to that found around exterior doors and windows is often used for this purpose.

Unfortunately, human beings need to breathe to survive! That is why ventilation systems are sometimes installed to allow air exchange—and thus ensure our survival in this austere environment!

One may have walls of sufficient density and seal all air leaks without necessarily achieving proper soundproofing. Sound also has the property of propagating through structural vibration via the materials that compose them. In professional studios, the most common strategy to address this concern is to reduce the number of contact points with the building's main structure by placing the studio inside a self-supporting room. This type of construction is referred to as "a room within a room."

3.1.2 ROOM ACOUSTICS

Since soundproofing mainly aims to defeat sounds coming from outside the room, it ultimately has very little impact on what happens inside it. Thus, a room may be perfectly soundproofed and still have dreadful acoustics.

Even when perfectly soundproofed, a room can still have dreadful acoustics.

Room acoustics studies how sound propagates within an enclosed space and how partitions and objects influence the room's sound. At the heart of this field lies acoustic treatment, which focuses on ways to promote uniform frequency distribution within a room and to control its reverberation time.

3.2 Acoustic Improvements

In a perfect world, studios would all be installed in rooms with ideal dimensions, no parallel walls, and no windows. In real life, however, things are often quite different, and we usually have to work with the characteristics of an existing room. In many studios—particularly home studios—it is not feasible to reduce the room's space by tripling wall thickness or modifying wall angles. Nor can we simply get rid of noisy neighbors! The goal is to achieve optimal acoustic quality without compromising our working environment.

When browsing certain websites dedicated to studio acoustics, one might get the false impression that it takes a seasoned acoustician and an enormous budget to obtain a room worthy of mixing a triangle solo! Yet simple actions can often tame many of a room's acoustic problems. But what aspects should we focus on?

3.2.1 LISTENING POSITION PLACEMENT

The position of the source and that of the listener within a room create a complex set of fluctuations in the frequency spectrum. The placement of the listening position therefore requires the utmost attention—even before considering the installation of acoustic treatment devices.

Even before considering acoustic treatment, the placement of the listening position in the room requires the utmost attention.

Along the length of the room, the listening position should be offset toward one end so that the rear wall is farther away from the listener. The ideal location for the listener is approximately one third of the room's length.

Regardless of the room's shape, it is advisable to center the listening position along the width of the room so that the monitors are equidistant from the side walls.

If the room does not have a regular shape and includes different angles, choose a location where the walls on each side of your monitors are similar in shape.

Listening position placement scenarios within the room.

3.2.2 MONITOR PLACEMENT

Once the listening position has been determined, the monitors can be installed more precisely. Ideally, they should be placed on stands independent of any other structure. Although many types of isolation foam are available on the market to place between the speaker and its support, these often expensive products generally have no tangible effect on sound quality. The expenses involved in a mixing studio are numerous; as long as the monitors have their own stands, it is wiser to invest elsewhere for better returns.

The placement and orientation of the monitors must be determined with great care.

When using nearfield monitors, it is generally recommended to leave some space between the rear of the monitors and the wall directly behind them. This can help reduce the impact of wall reflections on the sound.

The monitors should be arranged to form an equilateral triangle with the listening position. A distance of approximately 1.5 meters (about 5 feet) between each of the three elements (the two speakers and the listener), measured from the tweeter, is generally a good starting point. It is nevertheless wise to consult the manufacturer's recommendations.

The apex of the imaginary triangle should be located between 30 and 60 cm (about 12 to 24 inches) behind the listener's head. The speakers should be aimed toward this point. If the speakers are aimed directly at the listener or are too close to one another, the ideal focal area (the sweet spot) will be smaller. A slight movement of the head would then be enough to alter frequency distribution and distort the stereo image.

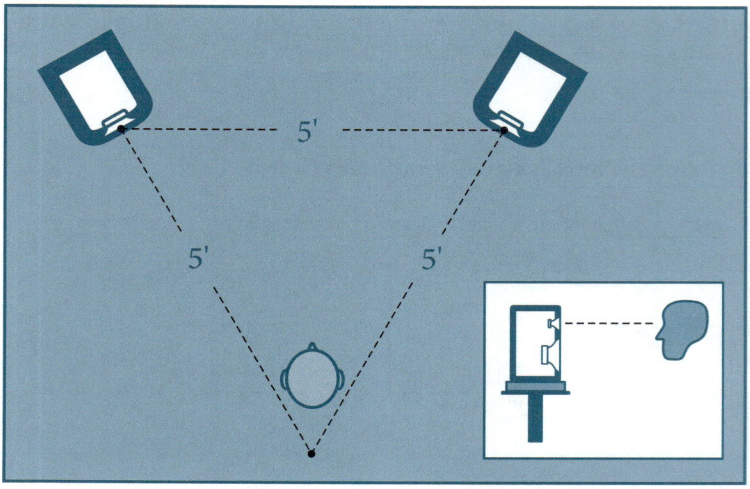

Monitor placement.

Each tweeter should be at the eye level of the seated listener.

Obviously, nothing should be placed in the path of the imaginary lines connecting the monitors to the listener—an important point to consider when using two computer screens side by side.

To adjust the orientation, place a small hand mirror on each of your monitors' tweeters. When you can see your face in each mirror, your speakers are correctly aimed.

3.2.3 ACOUSTIC TREATMENT OF PRIMARY REFLECTIONS

One of the main objectives of studio acoustic treatment is to achieve the most neutral sound possible at the listening position. Reducing the room's influence on the sound facilitates decision-making and maximizes the chances that mixes produced in this environment will translate more easily to other listening contexts.

A basic step in acoustic treatment is therefore to limit direct sound reflections from the walls. These primary reflections create numerous phase issues that alter not only frequency distribution but also the accuracy of the stereo image.

There is a very simple trick to identify the areas to treat. Sit at the listening position and ask someone to slowly slide a mirror across the wall. As soon as you see one of the monitors appear in the mirror, mark the wall with chalk. When the monitor disappears, make another mark. Repeat the process while scanning the wall vertically.

After scanning all the walls and the ceiling, the chalk marks will precisely indicate the areas where the walls reflect the sound from the monitors directly toward the listening position. All these areas will require absorption material.

3.3 Acoustic Treatment of the Rest of the Room

If your listening position is properly placed, your monitors correctly arranged, and your primary reflections treated, you should already have fully functional acoustics at the listening position. Even though you have already accomplished a significant portion of the work, paying attention to the rest of the room will further enhance the acoustic quality of your space. Here are a few concepts to help better manage the acoustics of your mixing environment.

3.3.1 ABSORPTION COEFFICIENT

Suppose we throw a bouncing ball forcefully into an empty room. It will bounce frenetically from one partition to another until it loses enough velocity to stop. Of course, this loss of speed will vary depending on the surface it strikes. A wooden floor covered with carpet, for example, will slow it down much more than a concrete floor. A brick wall will slow it down much less than one made of drywall. The time it takes for the ball to stop is therefore directly governed by the materials that make up or cover the room.

If your listening position is properly placed, your monitors correctly arranged, and your primary reflections treated, you have already achieved fully functional acoustics at the listening position.

A sound emitted in a room behaves in much the same way as our ball. It bounces from one partition to another, gradually losing volume until it becomes inaudible. The speed at which it loses volume depends on the composition of the room's surfaces. The interval between the emission of the sound and the moment it fades away is called reverberation.

Our analogy is, of course, only an image of a more complex process. Sound does not behave as uniformly as our bouncing ball. Materials distribute the loss of volume differently across each of the frequencies that make up the sound. Some, for example, will slow down low frequencies, while others will not impede them at all.

The acoustic properties of the materials that compose the partitions therefore affect not only the duration of sound propagation but also the distribution of frequencies within the room. A material's absorption coefficient indicates how it reacts to each frequency range of the sound. It is expressed in sabins (named after the physicist who developed this scale), and its value ranges from 0 to 1. For a given frequency range, a coefficient of 0 indicates that the material reflects everything that strikes it, whereas a value of 1 indicates that the frequency is completely absorbed.

3.3.2 REVERBERATION TIME

We now know that a sound takes a certain amount of time to become inaudible and that this duration depends on the room's dimensions and the materials composing its partitions. But why is this factor so important to the acoustic quality of our working environment?

Because a room's reverberation has a direct influence on the intelligibility of a source and on our ability to localize it. By adding to what our monitors project, it colors not only the frequencies we hear but also alters our perception of the stereo image.

One might think that completely eliminating a room's reverberation would yield a better representation of sound. Such spaces, called anechoic chambers, have been created to perform precise acoustic measurements of certain devices in an environment where reverberation is totally absent. The data found in audio equipment specification sheets are often collected in such rooms.

However, such an environment is physically intolerable for human beings. One clearly hears the sound of blood circulating through one's veins and the air entering and leaving one's lungs. The slightest movement reveals the sound of one's joints. To date, no one has been able to remain in an anechoic chamber for more than 45 minutes without becoming completely disoriented and subject to hallucinations! A true nightmare!

A certain degree of reverberation is therefore necessary to ensure natural hearing and to make the working environment pleasant.

Calculating Reverberation Time (RT60)

In acoustics, the duration of sound propagation in a room after the sound source stops (in other words, its reverberation) is represented by a value called RT60. Expressed in seconds, this value corresponds to the time required for the reverberation level to drop 60 dB below that of the sound source. For a mixing studio, for example, we generally aim for an average RT60 between 0.3 and 0.4 seconds.

A room's reverberation time depends on its dimensions and on the materials that compose or cover its partitions.

It is true that, based on the room's dimensions, the absorption coefficients of its partitions, a mathematical formula, a calculator, and a great deal of goodwill, it is possible to estimate a room's reverberation time. But to be perfectly honest, it is rarely necessary to embark on such a detailed analysis. Many common acoustic problems are easily identifiable and can often be addressed through simple, targeted actions.

That said, if this type of analysis interests you, you will find numerous tables online listing the absorption coefficients of common building materials. These data can provide insight into your room's acoustic characteristics. There are also software tools capable of measuring the duration and frequency distribution of a room's reverberation. Although such measurement is not essential, it can help you better choose the type and amount of acoustic treatment to use and experiment with its placement.

3.3.3 COMMON ACOUSTIC PROBLEMS

Many of a room's acoustic characteristics are intrinsically linked to its physical dimensions. Its proportions impose a regular path on sound, generating both accumulations and cancellations of certain frequencies.

Many common acoustic anomalies are easy to identify because of their predictable nature.

As a general rule, acoustic treatment aims to disrupt the natural trajectory of sound waves, particularly those directed toward the listening position. To create this "chaos," materials are used that either absorb the waves or diffuse them along a more random path. Here are some common acoustic anomalies whose predictable nature makes them easy to identify.

Flutter Echo

If you have ever clapped your hands in an empty room, you have probably heard that strange sound somewhat resembling the twang of a metal spring. This is known as flutter echo. This type of resonance occurs when sound literally bounces back and forth between two parallel surfaces. Although it may originate from two walls, it is more often the result of reflections between the ceiling and the floor. Since the audible portion of this sound lies in the mid frequencies, it is essential to eliminate flutter echo near the listening position.

It is possible that by treating the primary reflections, you have already eliminated much of the flutter echo. If not, diffusion panels will help attenuate the problem.

Standing Waves

Standing waves (standing waves or modes) are also the result of a wave traveling back and forth between surfaces. Unlike flutter echoes, which are rather localized, standing waves cause one or more frequencies to be constantly overrepresented throughout the room.

Standing waves are directly related to the room's dimensions.

Standing waves are of three types: axial (involving two surfaces), tangential (involving four surfaces), and oblique (involving all surfaces).

The frequencies affected by standing waves are directly related to the room's dimensions and the distances separating its partitions. It is purely mathematical. There are countless websites that allow precise calculation of the three types of standing waves present in a room based on its dimensions. The main challenge in treating these waves lies in the fact that they are located at the lower end of the frequency spectrum.

What must be understood is that the lower a frequency, the longer its wavelength. For example, a 114 Hz wave has a length of approximately 3 meters (about 10 feet). Absorption and diffusion panels are of no help in taming such a wavelength. Another method must be used: bass traps.

Without going into detail, the principle behind bass traps is to cause a particular frequency to resonate in order to reduce its energy. The frequency becomes trapped, and its diffusion in the room is attenuated. The construction method and dimensions of the trap determine which frequencies will be attenuated. It is therefore possible to design a model that directly targets the standing wave to be treated.

Bass traps are often installed in the corners of the room, since these are the areas where low-frequency energy accumulates the most.

f you are handy and your budget is tight, dozens of detailed construction plans for absorption panels, diffusion panels, and bass traps are available online.

3.3.4 ACOUSTIC TREATMENT PLACEMENT STRATEGY

A suitable mixing room relies on a proper balance between absorption and reflection. In a room with too much absorption, the engineer will tend to add too many high frequencies, making the mix overly bright. Conversely, mixes produced in a room with too many reflections will sound dull in other listening environments.

A common way to address this issue is to concentrate absorbing material in the section of the room where the listening position is located and to reduce the amount on the more distant walls. This is the principle of "live end dead end."

Thus, the area containing the most disturbing direct reflections—near the monitors—is controlled, while the more distant areas, where reflections are less problematic, preserve the room's ambience.

3.3.5 RECOMMENDATIONS

Eliminate Resonant Vibrations

From an acoustic standpoint, everything in the room matters. It is essential to remove anything that can vibrate in response to the monitors. It is therefore difficult to keep a piano, an acoustic guitar, or even a drum kit in the room where you mix. The same applies to objects that may produce parasitic noise (a poorly mounted picture frame, a metal filing cabinet, a heating

The live end, dead end strategy, in which more absorption is applied in the section closest to the listening position (dead end) and less in the section farther away (live end).

baseboard, etc.) and those that may vibrate due to loose screws or bolts.

A simple way to identify objects that vibrate sympathetically is to play low frequencies at high volume in the room. Anything that vibrates will quickly become audible and can then be located and corrected.

Take Advantage of Furnishings

One mistake to avoid when dedicating a room to mixing is emptying it of all furniture. Not only do furnishings make your environment more pleasant, they also help alter the natural trajectory of waves in the room.

There can hardly be a better diffuser than a bookshelf filled with books of different sizes—or better absorbers than a couch!

Of course, these pieces of furniture also reflect sound. If possible, place them behind the listening position rather than on the sides so that they affect the room more uniformly.

In the same vein, a simple rug can help tame flutter echo in the room. Thick curtains will reduce reflections from windows.

Lower the Volume

Many renowned engineers do most of their mixing work at a volume low enough that one can hold a conversation in the room without raising one's voice.

One advantage of working at a moderate volume is limiting the influence of acoustics on the sound at the listening position. Surrounding objects no longer have sufficient level to make their vibrations audible, the impact of standing waves is reduced, and wall reflections lose amplitude. All this simply by turning the output volume knob to the left rather than to the right!

We will see later that working at low volume offers numerous advantages that go well beyond acoustics.

4

CABLING, ROUTING AND GAIN STRUCTURE

If you've been involved in the music world for some time, you undoubtedly know someone who believes that audio quality is largely attributable to the quality of the equipment. Unfortunately (or rather, fortunately), that's not the case! Even the best audio gear imaginable does not allow you to dive headfirst into mixing without possessing some of the fundamental notions we rely on daily. That is the purpose of this chapter.

Cabling, routing, and gain structure are not the most exciting topics—I'll grant you that! However, these concepts are essential to preserving signal integrity, speeding up the mixing process, and improving the quality of the final result.

4.1 Analog Cabling and Connectors

All analog cables, regardless of their connectors or purpose, are either balanced or unbalanced. This is a basic principle that must be clearly understood.

4.1.1 UNBALANCED CABLES

A mono unbalanced cable carries the signal using two conductors: one for the signal and the other for ground. This type of cable therefore uses connectors with two contact points.

Cables used to connect an instrument (guitar, bass, keyboard, etc.) to an amplifier belong to this family, as do those used for common household connections, such as hi-fi speakers, CD or Blu-ray players, and so on.

Mono Unbalanced Cable

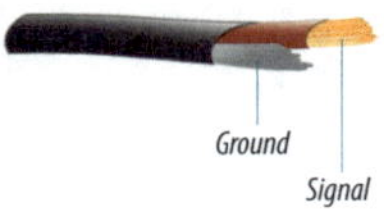

Some unbalanced cables can also carry a stereo signal. In that case, three conductors are hidden beneath the outer jacket: one carries the right channel, one the left channel, and one serves as ground. Headphones, mobile phones, and other consumer devices use this type of cable.

All unbalanced cables are susceptible to radio and electrical interference. This sensitivity increases with cable length. In the studio, we therefore try to keep them as short as possible. It is also preferable to keep them away from power adapters, electrical wiring, computer screens, and other potential sources of interference.

Stereo Unbalanced Cable

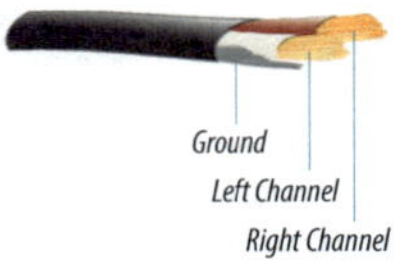

4.1.2 BALANCED CABLES

A balanced cable uses three conductors to carry a mono signal. One wire carries the signal, another carries the same signal but with reversed polarity, and the third serves as ground. The connector therefore has three contact points.

This type of cable takes advantage of a property of polarity whereby the amplitudes of two perfectly identical signals add together when they share the same polarity and cancel each other out when their polarities are opposite. Thus, in a balanced cable, interference reaches both signal conductors simultaneously. However, since the polarity of one conductor is inverted at the input of the cable, any interference picked up along the way is canceled out once the two signals are restored to the same polarity. At the output, we obtain a signal free of impurities. Ingenious, isn't it?

Because they are not subject to interference, balanced cables can be used over long distances. In live sound reinforcement, for example, they are used to carry signals from the stage to a console located at the back of the venue.

In the studio, balanced cables are used for microphone connections and to link various analog components together (preamplifiers, monitors, DI boxes, etc.).

The property of electrical polarity is put to use in balanced cables.

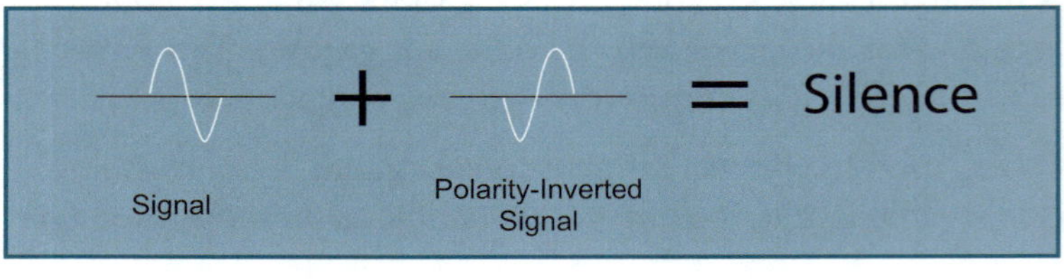

Naturally, their ability to preserve signal integrity encourages us to use them whenever possible. Even if some monitors, for example, accept an unbalanced connection, it is preferable to eliminate the risk of noise by using balanced cables.

Balanced Cable

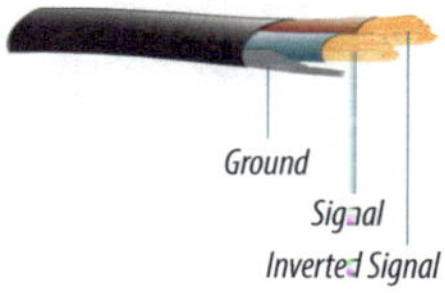

4.1.3 RECOMMENDATIONS

Choose Good-Quality Cables

With analog cables, conductor gauge and connector quality have a direct impact on durability and signal integrity. Of course, the number of cables required to operate a recording studio can quickly drive up costs. That said, studio cables have a much easier life than those used on stage. I therefore suggest opting for effective, reasonably priced cables. In short: don't buy the cheapest, don't buy the most expensive—aim somewhere in between.

Learn to Solder

Soldering simple analog cables requires neither extravagant equipment nor advanced skills. A basic soldering iron and a spool of solder will suffice to repair defective wires. If needed, you can quickly find online wiring diagrams for connectors that require more attention, such as XLR or send/return cables. This will allow you to extend the life of your cables and troubleshoot when necessary.

The connection panel, known as a patchbay, allows connections between devices to be made in one place.

4.2 Digital Cabling and Connectors

The computer now plays a leading role in audio production. Computer cables are commonly used to connect audio interfaces, keyboards, control surfaces, and other devices to the computer. Since we are all familiar with USB, USB-C, and Thunderbolt cables, let us instead focus on digital cables that carry audio data.

Unlike analog cables, digital cables transmit information in the form of data. There can therefore be no signal degradation. The advantage of digital cables is that they are just as binary as the information they carry: they either work or they do not! Moreover, once connected, they are rarely handled. Since the quality of a cable's components has very little impact on signal quality, there is no need to spend a fortune on digital cables.

You will find a list of the most common digital cables and their functions in the table entitled "Common Digital Cables and Connectors."

COMMON ANALOG CABLES AND CONNECTORS

The **XLR** cable features male and female connectors with three contact points. Most of the time, it is used to establish balanced connections, whether for connecting microphones or linking equipment together (monitors, for example).

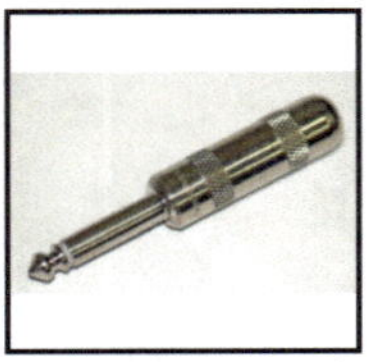

The **TS** cable (Tip, Sleeve) contains two conductors and carries a mono signal. In its most common version, it uses 1/4-inch connectors. It is primarily used to connect instruments (guitar, bass, keyboard, etc.) to an amplifier. Being unbalanced, it is susceptible to interference. For connecting equipment, a TRS cable should be used whenever possible.

The **TRS** cable (Tip, Ring, Sleeve) features connectors with three contact points. In its 1/4-inch version, it is commonly used to establish balanced mono line-level connections between devices.

The TRS cable can also carry an unbalanced stereo signal. In this case, one conductor carries the left channel, another carries the right channel, and the third serves as ground. The TRS connector is, of course, the standard connector for headphones.

Many consumer devices (iPod, tablet, computer, mobile phone, etc.) can be connected to studio equipment using a variation of this cable featuring a 1/8-inch TRS plug on one end and two 1/4-inch TS or RCA plugs on the other.

Certain processing devices require a send/return connection, in which one conductor of a TRS plug carries the original signal and another returns the processed signal. The third conductor serves as ground.

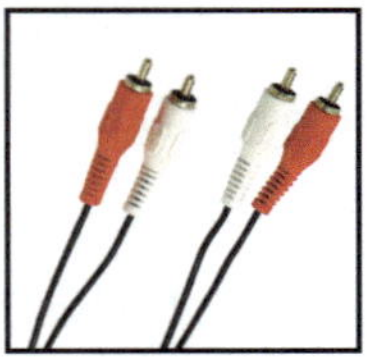

The **RCA** cable is mainly used for connecting consumer devices such as CD players, DVD players, or turntables. It is unbalanced and therefore susceptible to interference. In the vast majority of cases, it carries a consumer line-level signal.

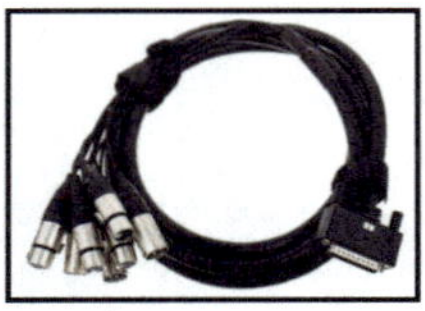

The **SUB-D25** cable transmits analog audio using a 25-pin (D25) connector.

The compact size of the D25 connector allows multiple audio channels to be connected to audio interfaces or large-format analog consoles without cluttering the device. One of the many variants of the SUB-D25 cable, known as a breakout cable, is then used to split the D25 connector into individual cables with common connectors (XLR, TS, TRS, or even RCA).

COMMON DIGITAL CABLES AND CONNECTORS

TDIF (Tascam Digital Interconnect Format) transmits eight channels of digital audio through its 25-pin connectors.

TOSLINK is an optical digital connection. When used with the S/PDIF protocol, it carries two channels of digital audio. When used with the ADAT protocol, it can transmit up to eight channels, depending on the resolution.

S/PDIF (Sony/Philips Digital Interface Format) transmits a stereo channel using the S/PDIF protocol. Although an S/PDIF connector resembles a standard RCA connector, the cables are not interchangeable. An S/PDIF cable is designed for digital transmission, which a standard RCA cable cannot perform.

The **AES/EBU** cable (developed jointly by the Audio Engineering Society and the European Broadcast Union) uses the AES protocol to transmit a stereo digital signal. Although it uses the same type of connectors, it should not be confused with a standard XLR cable, as a standard XLR cable cannot reliably transmit digital data.

MADI is a protocol capable of transmitting up to 64 channels of digital audio, depending on the resolution..

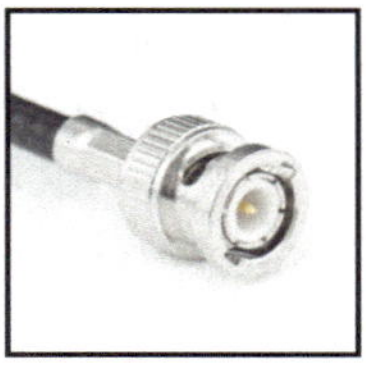

BNC is a coaxial cable used to carry word clock signals, ensuring sample-rate synchronization between digital devices.

MIDI (Musical Instrument Digital Interface) is a communication protocol commonly used to transmit information to a keyboard or to carry data from various types of controllers.

4.3 Analog Inputs and Outputs

There is hardly anything less intelligent than a cable! It has no idea what signal it carries, let alone what that signal is used for. For example, an XLR cable is commonly used to connect microphones, but it can also be used to establish a Line connection with a loudspeaker or a preamplifier. You have also likely noticed that TS and TRS cables can be used in many different ways. It is therefore not the cable or its connectors that determine the characteristics of the signal it carries, but the port into which it is plugged. That is, in a way, what gives it its very purpose in life!

As long as the connection is viable, the quality of a digital cable has no impact on signal integrity.

At its most fundamental level, what flows through our cables and devices is simply an electrical signal. This is why concepts such as impedance and voltage determine the type of inputs and outputs we must use when making connections. There are four types of analog inputs and outputs, each with its own characteristics.

Mic Level
As the name suggests, a mic input is primarily used to connect microphones. Unsurprisingly, these inputs feature a female XLR connector.

Microphones transmit a very low-level signal, generally between 0.001 and 0.010 volts. Since most consoles and audio interfaces are designed to operate at professional line level, a preamplifier is built into each mic input to increase the signal's strength.

It is not the cables that determine the characteristics of the signal, but rather where they are connected.

Mic inputs are also used to deliver phantom power, a 48-volt electrical current required for condenser microphones and certain DI boxes.

Phantom power is usually activated via a clearly labeled switch. On some consoles or audio interfaces, each input has its own switch, while on others, the selector distributes phantom power simultaneously to several adjacent inputs. In the latter case, special care must be taken to avoid inadvertently activating phantom power on a channel where a ribbon microphone is connected. This type of microphone can indeed be damaged by phantom power. Fortunately, this is not the case for other microphone types.

Professional Line Level
Virtually all professional audio equipment operates at professional line level. If you plug a microphone into a line input,

there is a strong chance that you will receive no signal at all, since its level is far too low. Similarly, if you plug an instrument directly into a line input, you will likely obtain a noisy signal with little definition due to the significant impedance mismatch.

This is why signals that do not meet the impedance and voltage characteristics of line level are, in one way or another, brought up to that standard along their path.

On consoles and audio interfaces, line inputs and outputs are primarily used to connect devices together. They most commonly use TRS connectors. Some preamplifiers and processing units establish line connections using XLR connectors. To avoid confusion, inputs and outputs are usually clearly labeled as line level. It is therefore important to verify the type of signal involved and make the appropriate connection.

Many devices allow either a 1/4-inch or XLR plug to be connected using a single combo connector. In many cases, the signal level to be used (Mic, Line, or Hi-Z) is selected via a switch. In the absence of such a switch, the XLR portion of the connector is automatically set to mic level, while the 1/4-inch portion operates at line level.

Consumer Line Level

Of course, many of the devices that surround us—CD, DVD, Blu-ray players, turntables, etc.—feature inputs or outputs labeled "Line."

However, consumer line level operates at a lower nominal level (−10 dBV) than professional line level (+4 dBu). If a consumer device is connected directly to a professional line input, the signal will need to be significantly amplified, which will often introduce background noise. Many consoles and audio interfaces include a few inputs (often labeled Aux In) designed specifically for connecting consumer devices.

Some DI boxes and preamplifiers also allow consumer line level to be cleanly boosted to professional standards.

Consumer devices are most commonly connected using RCA connectors, although some older equipment may feature TS

THE PREAMPLIFIER

Essentially, a **preamplifier** is used to raise a microphone's level to line level. Consoles and any audio interface therefore include an internal preamplifier for each of their XLR inputs.

External preamplifiers perform the same function, but are primarily used to impart a particular tonal character to the sound. They may be tube preamps, solid-state preamps, or hybrid designs. The unit's output typically features 1/4-inch or XLR connectors, which are used to connect the preamplifier to a line-level input on an interface or console.

An **external channel strip** is also a preamplifier. However, it offers expanded functionality (equalizer, compressor, etc.) reminiscent of what is found on a console channel.

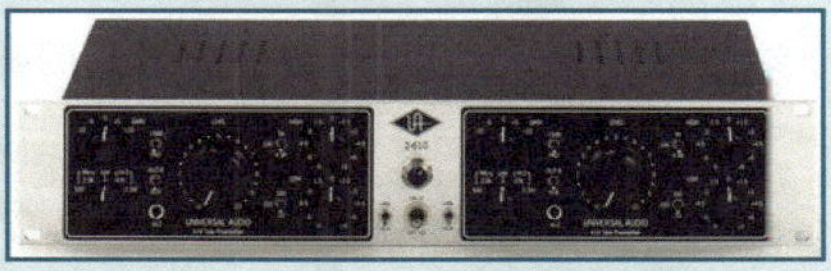

Universal Audio's 2-610S dual preamplifier.

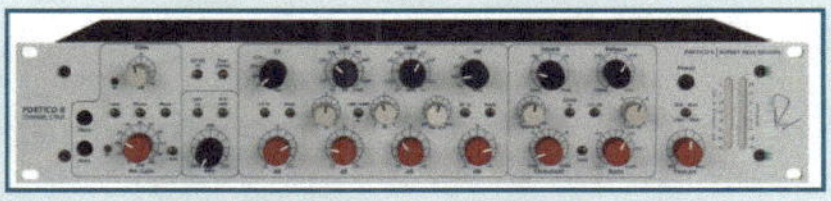

Rupert Neve Designs' Portico II Channel channel strip.

connectors. Consumer connections are never balanced, so it is advisable to use the shortest cables possible.

Hi-Z or Instrument Level

Musical instruments designed to be used with an amplifier, such as electric guitars, basses, and many analog keyboards, produce signals whose characteristics differ from the previous categories, particularly in terms of impedance. For this reason, most audio interfaces include at least one Hi-Z input (sometimes labeled "Instrument" or "Inst"), which allows an instrument's signal to be received directly and brought up to professional line level. Unsurprisingly, the input connector is typically a 1/4-inch TS jack.

4.4 DI Boxes

Since a Hi-Z input establishes an unbalanced connection, it is practical only when a reasonably short cable can be used. Obviously, this is not always possible. Moreover, many analog consoles do not include this type of input.

To address such situations, a direct injection box (more commonly called a DI box or simply a DI) is used to convert the signal coming directly from an instrument into one that matches the characteristics of a microphone input. In essence, a DI performs two main functions: it transforms a high-impedance signal into a low-impedance signal and allows a balanced connection to be established. The signal can then be transmitted over long distances using an XLR cable.

Passive or Active DI?

Although it accepts most sources quite well, a passive DI is particularly effective with instruments that feature active electronics, as it can handle higher input levels.

An active DI requires either a battery or phantom power to operate. Its lower noise floor compared to a passive DI allows it to capture lower-level signals more cleanly.

Connecting and Adjusting a DI

A DI box consists of two sections. The input section receives a standard 1/4-inch instrument cable. The output section allows two connections to be made.

First, an unbalanced 1/4-inch output, usually labeled "Thru," carries the original instrument signal to the amplifier and any effects pedals used by the musician. The other connector, an XLR output, sends the converted signal to a microphone input.

DI boxes generally offer additional features, the most common being a ground lift switch, which can reduce electrical interference within the unit, and a pad switch that lowers the signal level at either the input or the output of the direct box. Some models accept signals from consumer devices via RCA, 1/4-inch stereo,

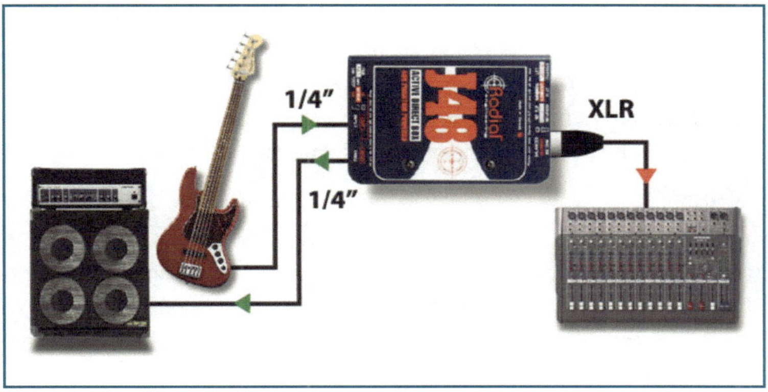

Here, an instrument cable connects the bass to the DI, and a similar cable carries the original signal to the amplifier. The DI's output is also sent to a console's microphone input via an XLR cable. Note that the connection between the DI and the amplifier is optional.

or 1/8-inch stereo (mini-jack) inputs. More advanced DI units may include features reminiscent of a microphone preamplifier. One may therefore encounter frequency equalization controls, gain adjustments, and sometimes even a compressor.

4.4.1 RECOMMENDATIONS

Be Cautious with Built-In DIs

Some amplifiers include a built-in DI or an output labeled "Line Out." However, it is rarely possible to determine exactly where the signal is tapped in the amplifier's internal signal chain without consulting the user manual. On some models, the original instrument signal is sent to the line out; on others, it may be the signal after preamplification, and sometimes even after the amplifier's equalization stage.

Furthermore, the quality of the components used in this output varies greatly from one model to another. It is therefore often much wiser to use an external DI box. This ensures that you know exactly where the captured signal originates, while eliminating the risk that unwanted noise from the amplifier's internal circuitry will find its way into your signal.

4.5 Reamp Boxes

A reamp box is used to convert a line-level signal into a high-impedance signal similar to that of an instrument. This device allows us to route the signal from an already recorded track to an amplifier in order to perform what is known as reamping.

The connections are simple. The input receives the line-level signal via an XLR or 1/4-inch connector, and the output sends a Hi-Z signal that is connected to an amplifier or effects pedals using a standard instrument cable.

Instrument reamping typically takes place in two stages. First, the signal coming directly from the instrument is recorded through a DI box or a Hi-Z input. A reamp box is then used to route the signal from that recorded track to an amplifier. One or more microphones are placed on the amplifier to capture the amplified sound.

Although this technique was originally designed for reamping bass or guitar recordings, there is nothing preventing us from using it on other types of tracks (vocals, synthesizers, drums, etc.). Reamping is a very interesting avenue to explore in order to expand processing possibilities and create special effects.

Advantages and Disadvantages of Reamping

Reamping offers several advantages when recording instruments. Since the signal is recorded with the intention of being reamped later, the quality of the amplifier recording during the performance is of little importance. Ultimately, our main concern is to provide an inspiring sound to the musician. It is even possible to complete the initial recording without amplification, which is often the case when recording bass.

In the same spirit, when recording multiple musicians simultaneously, reamping allows us to place the amplifier or amplifiers outside the main room in order to completely eliminate bleed between microphones.

Because the recording of the amplified sound takes place after the performance, reamping allows us to experiment with different types of amplifiers, effects, and microphones in order to achieve the sound that best suits the song.

It is also possible to assemble a flawless performance from the

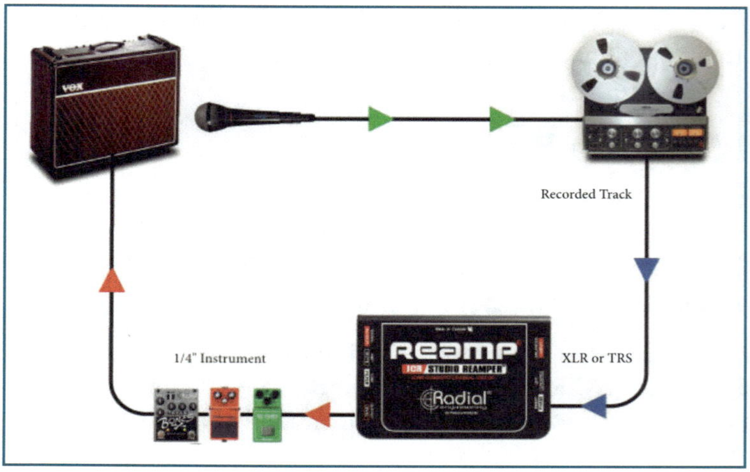

To perform reamping, the signal is first recorded directly from the instrument through a DI. A reamp box is then used to route the recording to an amplifier, optionally passing through effects pedals. The amplified sound is finally captured using microphones placed on the amplifier.

direct takes before re-recording, which greatly facilitates editing and makes transitions completely transparent.

However, reamping inevitably adds an additional step to the production process, since each selected take must be re-recorded in real time. It also delays decisions that could have been made during the initial recording stage, which is rarely advisable. The use of reamping should therefore be the result of a deliberate and well-considered decision.

Despite its interesting possibilities, reamping adds an additional step to the production process.

That said, recording a direct track in addition to the amplified track is often a good idea, whether or not reamping is planned. First, the direct track can serve as a safety net in the event that the amplifier recording proves unsatisfactory. Furthermore, attacks and chord changes are much easier to identify on the direct track than on the amplified one, especially when the amplifier sound is heavily saturated. When necessary, the direct track can therefore serve as an editing guide, whether or not it remains audible in the final mix.

4.6 Routing

Suppose you need to travel across town to meet with a producer and a singer-songwriter to define the overall mixing direction of an album project.

Since the weather is beautiful, the producer chooses to drive his magnificent convertible to the meeting. The singer-songwriter (environmentally conscious and, let's admit it, on a tighter budget) winds through the streets on a bicycle. As for you, you decide to take public transportation. You first board a bus to reach a subway station. Unfortunately, the subway line does not go directly to your destination, so you must transfer to another train before finishing the rest of the trip on foot.

Everyone arrives at the agreed time—a first! Admittedly, the producer is slightly windblown after his convertible ride, but he sports a sun-kissed glow that the songwriter eyes enviously while catching his breath. As for you, you are fully prepared for the meeting, having listened to the album's rough mixes three times during the commute.

Each of you used a completely different route to reach the same destination. Like our travelers, an audio signal can move through our equipment in various ways. Routing allows us to define the path a signal will take in order to reach the destination or destinations to which we want to send it.

To explore the fundamentals of routing, we will use a simple analog console as our model. Since the operation of DAW software is largely inspired by this type of device, you will quickly recognize many similarities in terms of terminology, signal flow, and routing possibilities.

4.6.1 SIGNAL FLOW WITHOUT INTERVENTION

Several years ago, when I taught introductory courses on analog console operation, some of my students (most of whom had never approached a console before) came close to panic at the sheer number of knobs on the surface!

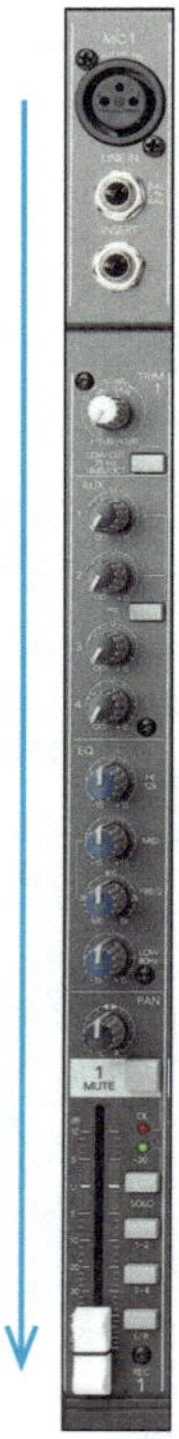

Without any routing intervention, the signal flows through the channel strip from top to bottom before being directed to the master bus.

At first glance, an analog console can indeed look like the cockpit of a spacecraft. However, upon closer inspection, one quickly realizes that this sea of knobs is essentially the repetition of the same strip of controls, known as a channel strip. A 24-channel console therefore contains 24 identical strips arranged side by side. Ninety-six channels: 96 strips. If you were feeling anxious, you should already feel some relief!

One of the advantages of analog consoles is that, as a rule, the signal travels from top to bottom. Without any routing intervention, it enters through the input section at the top of the console, passes through the various sections of the channel strip, and ends its journey at the output fader located at the bottom of the channel.

Once the signal has completed its path through the channel strip, it is automatically directed to a section of the console known as the output bus, or master bus. The output bus is the final stage a signal passes through before leaving the console. Regardless of the features included in this section, it typically contains two faders—called master faders—that control the console's overall output level.

DAW mixers function in exactly the same way. The signal flows from the top of the channel strip to the bottom and ultimately ends its journey in the output bus. A DAW mixer channel strip and its various sections are illustrated on page 54.

4.7 Routing Modifications

In many cases, this straight path limits our processing options. Fortunately, certain techniques allow us to divert the signal from this route. This is the very essence of routing.

4.7.1 INSERTS

The first point at which we can alter the signal's path is called the insert. An insert allows us to divert the signal to an external processing device—or to a plug-in—in order to reintroduce the processed signal back into the chain. What is essential to understand is that, when using an insert, the entire original signal is replaced by the processed signal.

The insert is therefore primarily intended for applying overall processing to a track. Equalizers, compressors, gates, de-essers, and various saturation tools are typically placed on inserts.

Analog consoles often have a limited number of inserts. When multiple processors must be applied through a single insert, the devices are connected so that the signal passes through them in the desired order.

In a DAW environment, each mixer channel includes a series of insert slots. The desired processing plug-in is selected from the drop-down menu of the chosen insert.

It is important to keep in mind that the signal flows through the inserts from top to bottom. The first insert feeds into the second, which feeds into the third, and so on. As we will see later, the order in which inserts are placed greatly influences the outcome of the processing and has significant implications for gain structure.

It is also possible to place effects on inserts, such as reverb, modulation, or delay. However, this approach generally complicates matters rather than simplifying them. First, an effect inserted on a given track is not accessible to other tracks, which may force us to duplicate it multiple times within a mix. In addition, effect plug-ins (reverb, for example) typically require substantial processing power. Managing effects through individual track inserts can therefore quickly overload the computer's processor in large sessions.

Another limitation is that the balance between the original signal and the inserted effect must be adjusted within the plug-in itself using its mix or dry/wet control. The plug-in must therefore be opened each time we wish to modify that balance. It goes without saying that the more we rely on this method, the more cumbersome effect management becomes.

In short, before inserting an effect on a track, we must ensure that it is intended exclusively for that track and that it will require minimal adjustment during mixing.

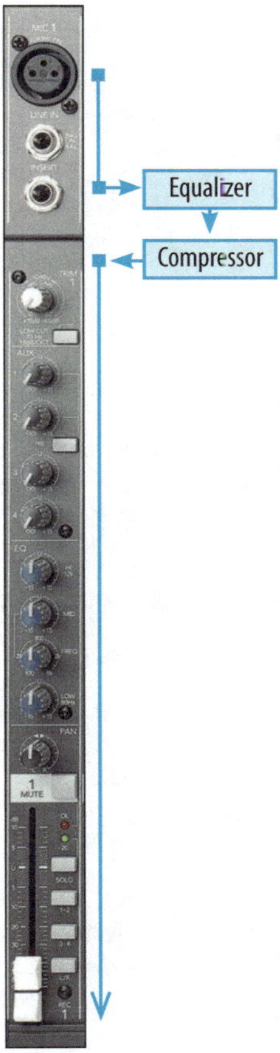

Here, the signal leaves the channel strip through the insert jack. It passes through an external equalizer and then an external compressor before returning to the channel to continue its path toward the output.

THE CHANNEL STRIP OF AN ANALOG CONSOLE (MACKIE 1642 VLZPRO)

The Input Section
This is often where the phantom power switch is located, as well as, when applicable, a selector allowing the type of input to be chosen (Mic, Line, or Hi-Z).

Mic Input

Line Input

Insert: allows an external processing device to be inserted into the signal path and, in this case, reintegrated into the chain using a send/return cable.

Gain or **Trim:** adjusts the input level.

Low-Cut (High-Pass Filter): note that this control is more commonly located in the equalization section.

The Auxiliary Section
This section diverts a portion of the signal to an auxiliary output. Auxiliaries are numbered and generally operate in pairs. They are typically used to route the signal to an effect (such as reverb) or to prepare a monitoring mix.

Pre/Post-Fader Switch: determines whether the signal sent to the auxiliary is taken just before the output fader (pre-fader) or after it (post-fader).

The Equalization Section
Depending on the type of console used, this section may be more or less complex. At a minimum, it usually includes high and low frequency shelf filters and a bell-type filter with adjustable gain for the mid frequencies.

High-Shelf Filter

Mid Frequency Selector

Mid Frequency Level

Low-Shelf Filter

Pan: positions the sound along the left/right stereo axis.

Mute: silences the channel.

The Output Section
This section controls the final parameters before the signal leaves the channel. It determines the output level using the fader, as well as the signal's position in the stereo image and its destination.

Solo: allows only the selected track or tracks to be heard.

Output Destination: This set of selectors determines where the signal is routed. It may be assigned to the master bus (here labeled "L/R") or to one of the subgroups ("1–2" and "3–4").

Fader: sets the output level.

4.7.2 SENDS

Unlike an insert, which affects the entire signal of a channel, a send diverts a portion of that signal to a secondary destination without altering the original signal. Every send includes a level control that determines how much of the signal is routed out of the channel.

In analog audio, a send routes part of the signal to an independent output called an auxiliary or bus. It is relatively uncommon to see the term "send" explicitly labeled on a simple analog console. Instead, one typically finds a section labeled "Aux" or "Aux Send" that performs the same function. Regardless of the terminology used, this section of the console is normally where the balance sent to stage monitors or studio headphones is created.

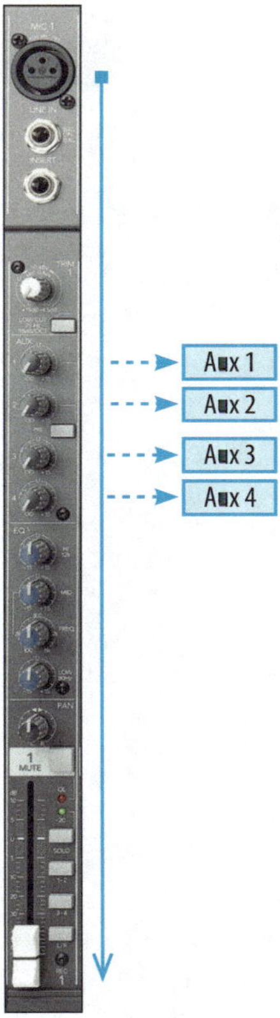

This console's sends allow a portion of the signal to be routed to four auxiliary outputs.

In a DAW environment, although it is possible to manage monitoring directly within the software, it is often easier to handle this at the audio interface level. Instrument signals are then routed to the headphones before entering the computer. This prevents software latency from creating a delay between the original sound and what is heard in the headphones.

Because a send does not alter the original signal and makes the effect accessible to all elements of the mix, it is the preferred method for managing mix effects. Reverb and delay are, with few exceptions, almost always used with this type of routing.

On an analog console, if we want to apply a reverb to multiple tracks, for example, we connect the outputs of two auxiliary sends to the input of a reverb unit. The output of that unit then returns to the console through one or two channels.

In a DAW, using a send generally requires creating an auxiliary track, bus, or effects track (depending on the software) in order to define a new audio destination. The desired effect is then inserted on that channel. Once created, this destination becomes available from the send menus of all mixer channels.

Naturally, if any portion of the original signal is passed through the effect's output—even a small amount—the output level of the processed tracks will vary according to the send level. This does not make mixing any easier. It is therefore essential to set the mix or dry/wet control of the effect to 100% so that the auxiliary or effects track outputs only the processed signal.

Many analog consoles and most DAWs include a selector that allows a send to operate in either pre-fader or post-fader mode.

A DAW CHANNEL (CUBASE)

The Routing Section

This is where the signal's source and final destination are determined. The available options are displayed in drop-down menus.

Input: selects the audio interface channel from which the signal is received.

Output: defines the signal's destination (master bus, subgroup, etc.).

The Insert Section

This section allows one or more processing plug-ins to be inserted into the signal chain. It also provides access to the full range of tools included in the software.

Insert: allows processing plug-ins to be inserted. The signal flows from top to bottom.

Equalization: opens the software's frequency equalizer.

Channel Strip: opens the various processing tools available in the software (gate, compressor, saturation, etc.).

The Send Section

This section diverts a portion of the signal to an effect, an auxiliary, or a subgroup. The available options are displayed in drop-down menus.

Send: routes a portion of the signal to a destination. Although sends are post-fader by default, they can be set to pre-fader using a keyboard command.

The Output Section

This section controls the final parameters before the signal leaves the channel. It determines the output level using the fader, as well as the signal's position in the stereo image.

Pan: positions the sound along the left/right stereo axis.

Mute ("M") and **Solo** ("S"): Mute silences the channel, and Solo allows only the selected track or tracks to be heard.

Meter: displays the output level. The number at the bottom of the meter indicates the maximum level reached in dB.

Fader: sets the output level. The number below the fader indicates its position on the scale.

The Automation and Recording Section

Automation: Read ("R") plays back automated data, and Write ("W") records it.

Record: the speaker icon routes the signal to monitoring, and the circle enables recording for the track.

The Identification Section

Identification: displays the track number and name. A color or icon can also be assigned to the channel for easier identification.

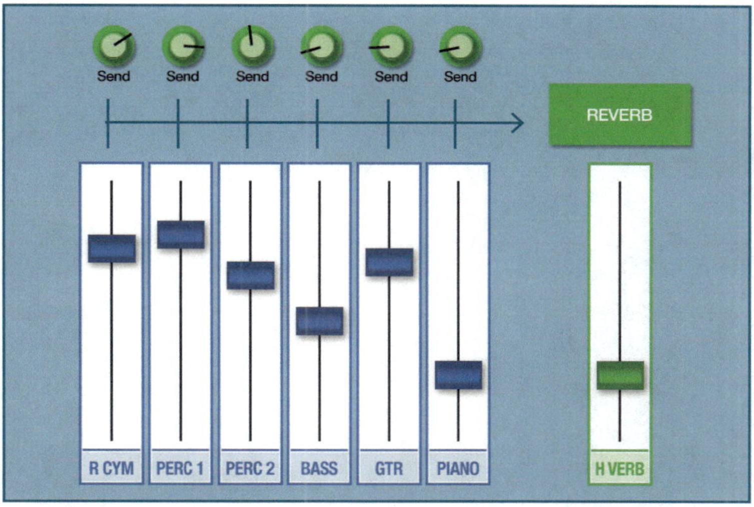

In this example, post-fader sends route the tracks' signals to a reverb. The amount of reverb applied to each track is controlled by its send level.

Pre-Fader and Post-Fader Sends

Unsurprisingly, in post-fader mode, the signal is routed to the effect after the channel's output fader. The send control then determines the proportion of effect relative to the original signal (dry/wet), and that proportion remains constant regardless of the track's volume. In most cases, this is the most effective way to manage effects.

In certain situations, however, we may want the amount of signal sent to the effect to be independent of the track's volume. This is precisely what happens when a send is set to pre-fader mode. Because the signal is tapped just before the output fader, the send control alone determines how much signal reaches the effect. For example, by increasing the send level on a track, we

THE SEND AND THE STEREO IMAGE

The positioning of elements within the left/right panorama when using sends requires some clarification.

First, it should be noted that very few DAWs offer a dedicated panning control for sends that allows us to define their position in the stereo image. This is even less common in the world of analog consoles. We must therefore understand how this position is determined according to the routing being used.

When a send is set to post-fader mode, the position of the routed signal mirrors that of the track itself. For example, consider a track being sent to a stereo reverb. If the track's pan control is set to the right, its reverb will also tend toward the right. In this case, the send can be described as post-fader and post-pan. This is the default behavior of most DAWs and analog consoles.

Things become slightly more complex in pre-fader mode. Since the sends do not take the track's pan setting into account, the routed signal is automatically placed at the center of the stereo image. They can therefore be described as pre-fader and pre-pan. This significantly limits our options, especially when preparing headphone mixes, for example.

To recreate the stereo image, we first create two mono auxiliary (or bus) destinations. The pan control of the first is set to the left, and that of the second to the right. A send is then assigned to each of these auxiliaries. From that point on, the level of the first send places the signal on the left, and that of the second places it on the right. The sound can therefore be moved across the stereo field by varying the balance between the two send levels. This type of routing, very common in the analog domain, works just as effectively in a DAW environment.

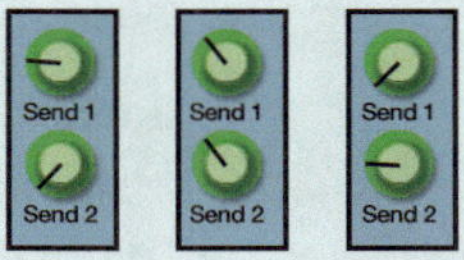

Left *Center* *Right*

In this example, pre-fader sends feed two auxiliary outputs used for monitoring during recording. The left/right balance is established using the sends. Notice, for example, that Guitar 1 is heard only in the left side of the headphones, since Send 2 is turned down.

Because the sends are pre-fader, the position of each track's fader has no influence on the headphone mix. As we can see, the monitor mix contains more piano and less guitar than the main output mix.

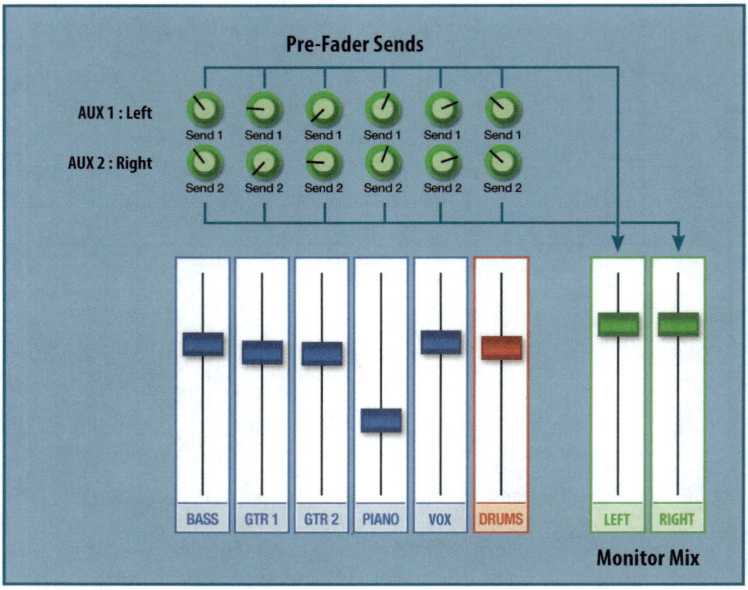

can hear the effect applied to it even if that track's fader is completely lowered.

Pre-fader sends are also extremely useful when setting up monitoring during recording. They allow us to create one or more headphone mixes tailored to the specific needs of each musician during tracking.

4.7.3 SUBGROUPS

A subgroup allows us to modify the usual routing of one or more tracks by adding a shared point along their signal path. Instead of going directly to the output bus, the selected tracks are routed to a common destination where they can be processed and controlled as a whole.

A subgroup allows multiple tracks to be processed as a whole. It is a powerful tool for simplifying and accelerating the mixing process.

On an analog console, assigning tracks to a subgroup is done by routing the output of a channel to what is called a bus. Buses have their own faders and are typically arranged in pairs to allow stereo operation. At the bottom of each channel strip, there are as many assignment buttons as there are bus pairs on the console. For example, on a console equipped with four buses, there will usually be one selector for buses 1–2 and another for buses 3–4.

An additional button, often labeled "L/R" or "Master," may also be present to indicate that the channel's output is routed directly to the main output bus. If this button is absent and none of the bus assignment buttons are engaged, the signal follows its normal path to the output bus.

On a simple analog console, subgroups are typically used to simplify volume management. Suppose, for example, that a mix includes eight drum tracks. After establishing the internal balance between those tracks and assigning them to a bus, it becomes possible to adjust the overall drum level using the fader of that bus rather than manipulating each individual drum track fader.

In a DAW, the method used to create a subgroup varies depending on the software, but it generally requires creating (or at least activating) a channel that will serve as the subgroup. A new output destination then becomes available to the project's tracks.

Unlike most simple analog consoles, a DAW subgroup channel is virtually identical to a standard track. It can be mono or stereo, depending on the need, and includes its own inserts, sends, pan control, and fader. In addition to controlling overall level, we can therefore apply processing or assign effects to the entire group.

For example, by assigning all backing vocal tracks to a subgroup, we can apply compression, equalization, and a shared effect without having to perform these tasks individually on each track. It goes without saying that the subgroup is a powerful tool for simplifying and accelerating the mixing process.

Most DAWs also allow a subgroup to be routed to an auxiliary send or to another subgroup, which opens up additional processing and management possibilities.

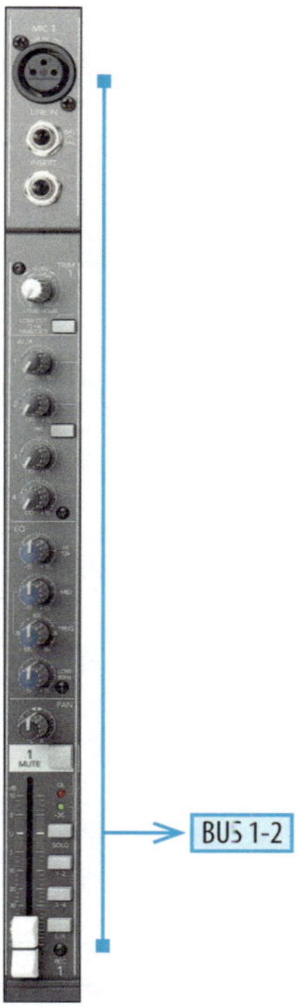

On an analog console, a track is assigned to a subgroup using the assignment buttons located at the bottom of the channel strip.

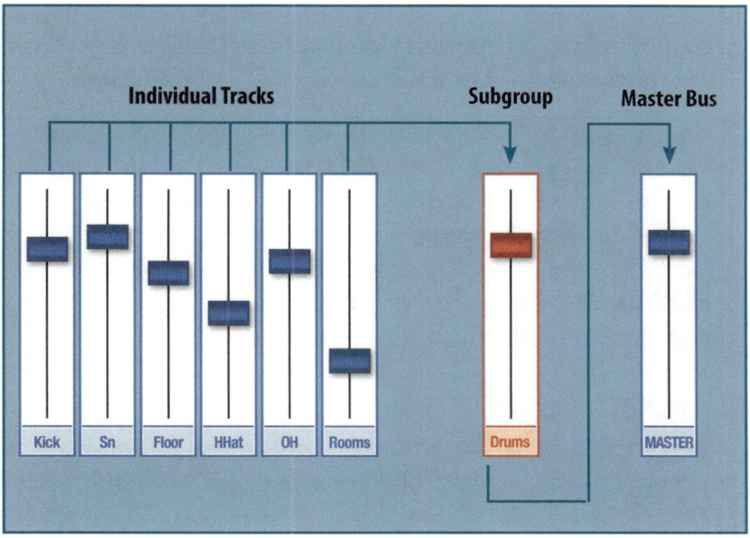

Here, the drum tracks are routed through a subgroup where they are managed as a whole before reaching the output bus.

Although routing tracks to a subgroup is typically done via their output assignment, it is also possible to use a send for this purpose. This approach is particularly useful when applying parallel processing to a group of tracks—a technique we will explore in later chapters.

To conclude, throughout this book, the term "subgroup" will refer to the type of routing described above.

4.8 Gain Structure

You are mixing a song and everything is moving along smoothly. After several minutes of intense work, you suddenly realize that your faders are barely open. They are all languishing at the bottom of the console! Fine adjustments now require so much effort that you can hardly breathe as you climb the steep slope of Mount Mixing! Take comfort: we have all experienced this situation. It simply means that you have overlooked a fundamental concept in audio handling: gain structure.

Gain structure aims to preserve signal integrity by maintaining an optimal level from input to output.

When mixing, the level of a signal is modified multiple times along its path, whether through the insertion of a processing tool or as a result of routing. The concept of gain structure aims to preserve signal integrity by maintaining an optimal level from the signal's entry into the chain all the way to its exit at the final stereo bus.

Furthermore, once a signal's input level has been set at the beginning of the chain, it should not need to be amplified later on, regardless of its routing or the processing devices it passes through. Although this rule is less strict in a DAW environment for various reasons, it promotes a valuable working habit.

A proper gain structure ensures the best possible signal-to-noise ratio and prevents unwanted saturation. It allows us to get the most out of our routing choices and processing tools, whether virtual or hardware-based. Respecting the principle of gain structure also helps us avoid the frustrating situation described above by keeping our faders near their nominal position, where fine adjustments are easier to make.

4.8.1 INPUT LEVEL

When mixing, it is important to understand a fundamental concept. The gain control of a console or audio interface sets

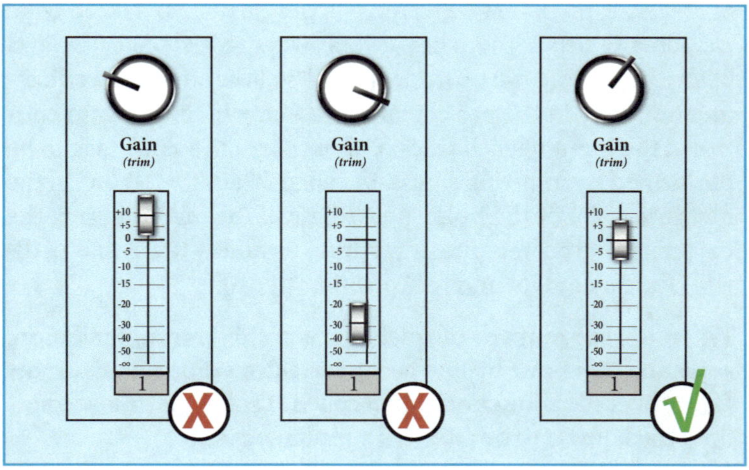

To maintain proper gain structure, the input level must be set using the gain control while the output fader remains at its nominal position.

the input level of a channel, while the fader at the end of the signal path determines its output level. The same applies in DAW software. In other words, the gain control affects the track at the beginning of the chain, before any processing. The fader, on the other hand, controls the level at the end of the channel, after all processing. Although their respective roles are unambiguous, I must admit that this fundamental distinction sometimes escapes beginner users.

To properly set a signal's input level, the fader should first be placed at its nominal position (0 dB), and the gain control adjusted until the optimal input level is achieved. In analog systems, this level is displayed either on the channel's input meter (if available) or on the output bus meter. In a DAW, it will typically appear on the audio interface meter or on the track's input meter within the software.

The gain control sets the level at the input of a channel, while the fader determines its output level.

In a purely analog recording context, an input level as close as possible to 0 dB provides the best signal-to-noise ratio. It is, of course, common practice to exceed 0 dB deliberately in order to achieve saturation.

Digital systems, however, do not offer the safety net of analog saturation. If the digital zero is exceeded, the signal clips, which will likely render it unusable. In a digital recording context, our primary gain structure concern is therefore the level entering the audio interface. We must take advantage of the wide dynamic range of digital systems and aim for a level well below zero. An input level between −10 and −15 dB is more than sufficient to preserve signal quality, whether the signal comes directly from the source or from a processing device applied to it.

Sometimes, tracks are delivered with levels that far exceed what we actually need. There are several ways to reduce their level before beginning the mix. Most DAWs allow amplitude adjustment directly in the project window. Some include a gain control at the input of each track. Others allow the same task to be performed by inserting a plug-in called "Gain" or "Trim" in the first insert slot of the track. Regardless of the method used, the objective is to achieve meter readings around −10 dB to −15 dB with the fader at its nominal position (0 dB).

When a large number of tracks exceed this recommendation, adjusting them one by one becomes tedious. Fortunately, most DAWs include a function (often called "Link") that allows multiple track levels to be adjusted simultaneously.

The output level of virtual instruments also deserves attention. A quick glance at the preset list of most virtual instruments reveals that their levels often approach digital zero. The simplest solution is to reduce the output level within the instrument itself.

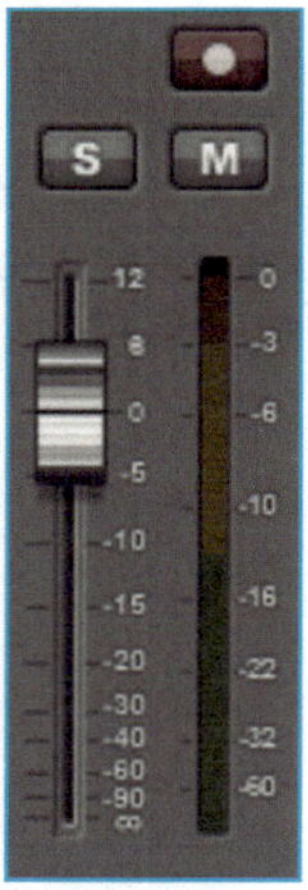

By examining this Pro Tools fader, we can see that its scale is not linear. Fine adjustments become increasingly difficult as the fader moves away from its nominal position (0 dB).

4.8.2 OUTPUT LEVEL

Because it is used to establish the balance of a mix, the fader is undoubtedly the most powerful mixing tool at our disposal. It is a graduated control that sets the output level of a channel or bus. Faders are located at the bottom of both analog and digital mixing consoles.

Faders have a characteristic that should not be overlooked. If you look closely at their scale, you will notice that in most cases it is not linear. This means that moving the fader by a given distance will produce a completely different result depending on its position along the scale. For example, a 1 dB change requires a much greater physical movement when the fader is near the top of its range than when it is near the bottom. As the fader value decreases, fine adjustments become increasingly difficult.

The best way to avoid this loss of precision is to maintain a proper gain structure throughout the mix. This keeps the faders near their nominal position, where they offer the greatest range of control.

4.8.3 MANAGING TRANSITIONAL LEVELS

Routing changes often alter the gain structure. The signal level must therefore be reassessed at each point along its new path.

Inserts

When a signal passes through a processing tool, its output level will very likely differ from its input level. This is especially true since many manufacturers deliberately add a few extra decibels to the output level of their presets in order to impress us.

One way to maintain a proper gain structure is to aim for similar levels before and after processing whenever possible. Ideally, when the plug-in is bypassed, there should be no significant perceived change in level. Not only does this habit help preserve gain structure, but it also ensures that our perception of the processing's effectiveness is not biased by a level increase—a perceptual bias we will discuss in a later chapter.

One way to maintain proper gain structure is to aim for similar levels before and after processing.

Some plug-ins include a function that links input and output levels to maintain consistent volume. However, it is still worth verifying by ear, as in some cases the processed signal may remain slightly louder than the original.

Analog-Modeling Plug-Ins

Plug-ins that emulate analog equipment require special attention. Their algorithms are typically designed around the behavior of the original hardware when driven at typical analog operating levels. To get the most out of such emulations, we must feed them a level comparable to what the physical device would normally receive. This may require temporarily adjusting our digital gain structure.

If the emulation includes an input control, it should be used to set the appropriate level. If not, we must ensure that the plug-in receives the expected input level by adjusting the track gain or the output level of the preceding plug-in.

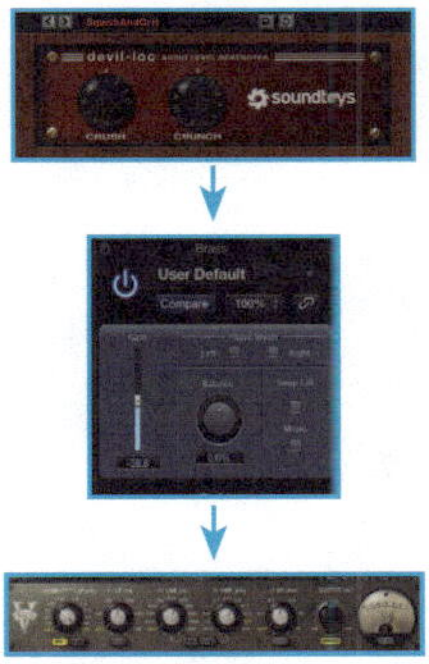

Devil-Loc by Soundtoys does not include an output control. A gain plug-in in Logic is therefore inserted afterward to bring the level back to a usable range for the next plug-in in the chain.

The output level of an analog-modeling plug-in must also be monitored carefully. Because these plug-ins often replicate the saturation produced by analog equipment when driven, the output control is sometimes integral to the character of the sound. In such cases, it cannot simply be used to correct the level without altering the tone. When necessary, the level can be adjusted after the emulation by inserting a trim plug-in or by modifying the input level of the next insert in the chain.

Sends

When it comes to sends, signal integrity is often more closely related to the quality of the processing device than to the amount of signal being sent to it. If the effect generates background noise, we must send enough level to mask it.

In this example, the levels of the individual tracks should be increased to bring the subgroup fader closer to its nominal position.

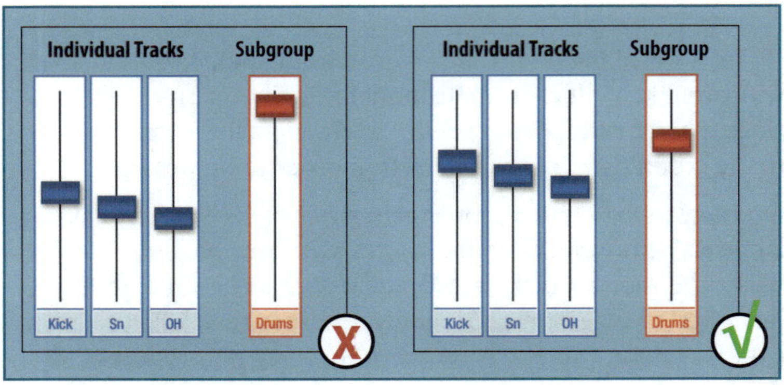

In a DAW environment, this issue rarely arises. Instead, we focus on adjusting send levels so that the fader of the effects channel remains as close as possible to its nominal position.

Subgroups and the Output Bus

When a group of tracks is routed to a subgroup, the first step is to establish the internal balance among the group members. Because individual levels are summed, attention must be paid to the level at the input of the subgroup. We must avoid unintended saturation caused by excessive input level and, as mentioned earlier, avoid having to amplify the signal later if the level is too low. The simplest way to achieve this is to set the subgroup fader at 0 dB and adjust the internal balance accordingly.

In essence, the output bus is simply a subgroup that receives all elements of the mix. In analog audio, the same principle therefore applies to managing the level entering the master bus. A level that is too low or too high may alter the behavior of processors inserted on the output bus.

In a DAW, the input level of the output bus can be adjusted as needed using its gain control or by inserting a trim plug-in in the first insert slot. In addition to reducing the overall mix level, this approach allows us to avoid readjusting effect balances, parallel processing levels, automation moves, or any other elements tied to individual track levels. The same method can, of course, be applied to subgroups.

It is true that the way DAWs process audio internally provides greater headroom than analog systems. That said, gain structure must still be monitored throughout the mixing process. A good rule of thumb is to work as though you were operating in an analog environment.

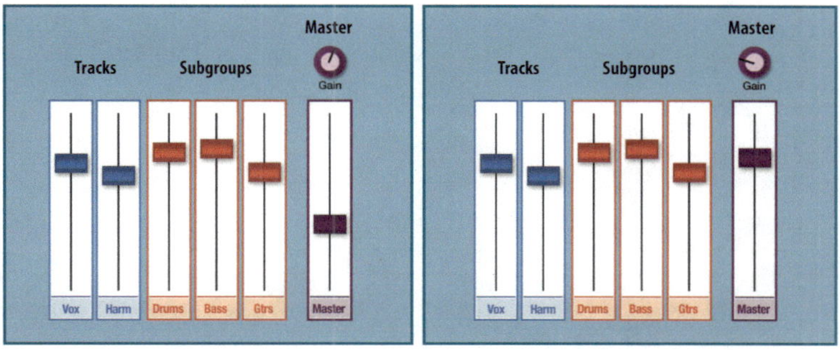

On the left, the input level at the master bus is too high, even though the track and subgroup faders are properly set. The simplest solution (on the right) is to reduce the gain at the output bus input, thereby avoiding the need to readjust every track in the mix.

5
THE MIX PREPARATION STAGE

BEFORE YOU EVEN START THINKING about mixing a song, there are a whole lot of tasks to get through. Track management, editing, and solving the technical problems in a recording or performance all demand a lot of attention and make up a good portion of the total time spent mixing a song.

The initial stage of the mixing process is probably the most technical in the strict sense of the term. Most of the time, seasoned mixers have one or more assistants who handle much of the preparatory work for each song they receive.

The preparation stage is often overlooked by aspiring mixers. Yet it is a determining factor in the success of a mix.

The goal of the prep work is to allow the mixer to focus on mix decisions without having their train of thought constantly interrupted by purely technical issues. These tasks are often neglected by aspiring mixers because, let's be honest, they're not very glamorous! Still, track preparation is a determining factor in the success of a mix.

The method proposed here assumes that you're mixing on a freelance basis. Even if you only ever mix your own music, it's important to proceed with the same rigor as if you were mixing for someone else. Try to detach yourself from the project and approach it as if a client had handed it to you.

5.1 Getting Familiar with the Project

Backup Copy

As we'll see, the material you receive will go through several transformations before mixing begins. The first task is therefore to create a complete backup copy of the project as it was delivered, so that you always have access to the original files.

First Listen

Even before you hit play, loading the song into the DAW already provides a good deal of information. At first glance, the number of tracks in the project gives you an idea of how extensive the prep work is going to be. The name of each track tells you what instruments are present in the song.

The Rough Mix

Songs are often accompanied by a reference mix, or rough mix. Although the quality of this mix can sometimes leave something to be desired (after all, the client hired you, right?), it often gives you a general idea of the direction the producer (or the musicians) wants to take the song. It also clarifies the musical style, the overall vibe, and gives valuable indications about the balance of levels and the importance of different instruments in the various sections of the arrangement.

If a rough mix is provided, it should be the first thing you listen to.

If a rough mix is provided, its should be the first thing you listen to. Since the first listen often sets the tone for everything that follows, it's important to write down your first impressions and your observations (positive or negative) about level balance, spatial placement of instruments, use of effects, and so on. All this information will prove very useful in the steps to come.

Listening to All the Tracks

Once the rough mix has been analyzed, it's time to listen through all the tracks. No fuss, just hit play and listen!

Chances are the balance of levels will be all over the place, but that's not the point. A few quick level adjustments will make the song evocative enough for you to evaluate how much prep is needed and what kinds of challenges lie ahead.

5.2 Converting the Tracks

The resolution of the delivered audio files (bit depth and sample rate, expressed in bits and kilohertz respectively) can vary from project to project. The next step is therefore to convert all the material, if necessary, to a resolution that's appropriate for mixing.

For audio material, a resolution of 24-bit at 48,000 Hz (24/48) is the ideal format for mixing. This recipe offers extended dynamic range while keeping the file sizes reasonable. In addition, using this resolution is required if the song is eventually going to be mixed in Atmos format.

That said, if a project is delivered in 16-bit at 44,100 Hz and there are no plans for a spatial version, there's no significant advantage to changing its resolution. You can work with the tracks in the format in which they were delivered.

Once the conversion is complete, you should listen through the project at its new resolution to make sure the process hasn't altered the integrity or timing of the tracks.

MIDI Files

Sometimes MIDI files are delivered along with the audio. In that case, it's a good idea to ask the client to export these as audio tracks themselves.

And if you're working on your own projects, it's essential to convert all your virtual instrument tracks to audio before mixing. First, because doing so will free up your computer's CPU; and second, because it creates a clear separation between the creative phase and the mixing phase

The Zero Point Backup

Creating another clearly labeled backup copy marks the end of the track conversion stage. This will become the zero point you can always return to if something goes wrong.

5.3 Organizing the Tracks

5.3.1 NAMING THE TRACKS

These days it's quite common for a song to have a hundred tracks or so. Unfortunately, depending on the discipline and working method of the person who handled the recording, the names assigned to these tracks can range from very precise to downright cryptic.

The purpose of track identification is to speed up navigation during the mix.

It's essential to listen to each track individually and give it a name that clearly describes its content. The entire point of this identification process is to speed up navigation during the mix. So there's no room for ambiguity! Names like "Alex1" (who on earth is Alex?), the ever-original "Spatial Destruction," or the classic "Audio 48" are simply unacceptable.

Using Abbreviations and Suffixes

Using abbreviations reduces the number of characters in a track name and speeds up navigation. For example, a rhythm guitar track might be labeled "GTR RTM"; the snare drum "Sn"; the main vocal "VOX," and so on.

Suffixes are also useful for distinguishing between different tracks of the same instrument or multiple mics on the same performance. For example, a guitar solo recorded with three

THE MYTHS OF THE DIGITAL SIGNAL[1]

Myth 1: The Higher the Sampling Rate, the More Faithful the Audio

Audio sampling rate (44.1, 48, 96 kHz, etc.) is often compared to video frame rate. However, audio works very differently.

Sampling rate determines only the range of frequencies represented. It must be at least twice the value of the highest frequency to be reproduced[2]. Thus, a sampling rate of 44.1 kHz (the standard for audio CDs) faithfully reproduces all frequencies up to 22.5 kHz.

That said, the human ear, at its very best, perceives sounds from 20 Hz to 20 kHz. This has been established for decades. Most people reach their upper limit somewhere between 15 and 17 kHz. Using sampling rates higher than 44.1 kHz therefore adds nothing audible, since the entire audible spectrum is already fully represented.

Myth 2: Information Between Samples Is Lost

Another widespread notion claims that a digital signal does not account for what lies between samples, resulting in errors in timing and frequency reproduction. To minimize these supposed problems, one would need to increase the sampling rate.

Despite the common stair-step image of the digital signal displayed in every DAW, the final reconstructed signal is a waveform just as precise and continuous as an analog one. Even though sound is sampled at discrete intervals, the position and content of the original signal remain intact.

Myth 3: The Greater the Bit Depth, the More Faithful the Audio

To understand the impact of bit depth, one must first grasp how analog-to-digital conversion works. The signal is first sampled, and each sample is assigned a value. These values are then processed in a way that generates background noise similar to the hiss produced by analog media (for example, the noise of a tape machine).

The margin between the level of this background noise and the maximum signal level is known as the dynamic range.

Bit depth therefore governs only one thing: dynamic range. It has no direct relationship to the quality of sound reproduction.

In 8 bits, for example, the total dynamic range is 48 dB. In other words, any waveform above –48 dB will be faithfully reproduced.

In 16 bits, the noise floor sits at –96 dB, which is so low that it is inaudible even at very high listening levels. At 24 bits, there is enough dynamic range to represent as faithfully a fly buzzing in the back of the room as a jet taking off in your living room!

Myth 4: Levels Should Be Set as Close as Possible to 0 dB Without Exceeding It

This method, entirely appropriate in the analog domain, is harmful in the digital domain.

First, because the dynamic range of digital audio is ridiculously large compared to analog. A well-preserved cassette tape has a bit-depth equivalent of about 9 bits — though 6 is often more realistic. Our beloved vinyl: 11 bits on its best day. The finest studio tape machine: 13 bits, perhaps a bit more if you are willing to add distortion. All of these media offer less dynamic range than the 16 bits of a standard digital CD.

Second, because digital does not offer the same safety net as analog: distortion.

In analog, exceeding 0 produces distortion that adds warmth and roundness — one of analog's strengths. In digital, if you exceed 0, you get an unpleasant crackle known as digital clipping.

Moreover, many transients are too fast to be accurately displayed by a VU meter (the actual level of a snare drum hit, for example, can easily exceed the meter reading by 10 dB).

For all these reasons, it is far more appropriate to aim for –12 dB or –15 dB rather than pushing levels close to 0. At 16 bits, even at these levels, the noise floor still sits more than 80 dB below the signal.

Conclusion

The 48 kHz / 24-bit combination is the optimal format for working with audio intended for commercial release. It provides ample headroom for level management as well as full frequency representation. Higher sampling rates and greater bit depths do not improve sound quality; they simply increase computer workload and create unnecessarily large files.

[1] *Inspired by Sampling Theory For Digital Audio by Dan Lavry, Lavry Engineering Inc., 2004 (26 pages), and the demonstrations presented in the videos Episode 1: A Digital Media Primer for Geeks and Episode 2: Digital Show & Tell by Monty Montgomery (xiph.org).*

[2] *This principle is expressed in the Nyquist–Shannon theorem.*

microphones might become "GTR Solo A," "GTR Solo B," and "GTR Solo C."

If a part or group appears several times in the same song, you can add a number at the end of the name to distinguish between occurrences. To continue the previous example, if the song has a second guitar solo, you might label it: "GTR Solo A2," "GTR Solo B2," and "GTR Solo C2."

The exact abbreviations and suffixes you choose don't really matter. What matters is that you establish a coherent system and apply it consistently across all your projects.

Using Colors or Icons

Most DAWs allow you to color a track or assign an icon that illustrates its content. Using this feature also speeds up navigation, especially in projects with a large number of tracks.

5.3.2 LAYING OUT THE TRACKS

For many mixers, the order in which the tracks of a project appear on their console or in their DAW is so systematic that it's almost a reflex. For some, for example, there's simply no way the kick drum or the main vocal can appear anywhere other than track 1.

What's more, every studio has its own particular setup. Using a console, an analog summing box, or even a specific DAW strongly influences how tracks are laid out.

A rigorous and clearly organized track layout in the DAW is a simple way to ensure greater fluidity in the mixing process.

With an analog console, tracks are traditionally laid out from the center toward the ends in order of importance. Tracks that require the most manipulation—particularly the lead vocal and the drum tracks—are assigned to channels closest to the mixer so they're always within reach. That way, the mixer doesn't have to move around to make adjustments and their head stays at the ideal listening position (sweet spot), allowing for more accurate decisions.

Obviously, these ergonomic constraints don't apply to mixing "in the box." At the computer, tracks can be laid out however the user wishes.

Even so, a clear, rigorous layout of tracks in the DAW is a simple way to ensure smoother mixing. In general, tracks are grouped by instrument. In a DAW, the most important elements are placed first to make them faster to locate.

The 33 tracks of this instrumental piece were renamed according to their content. Suffixes were added to distinguish elements recorded with multiple microphones and repeated occurrences of those elements in the song. The tracks are now grouped into folders by instrument class. In this example, the use of subfolders also helped define the role of the different guitars.

Instruments with multiple tracks (drums, guitars, percussion, vocal harmonies, etc.) are placed in folders (if the DAW allows it) in order to lighten the track overview in the main project window.

Again, the idea is to proceed so systematically that you almost develop an obsessive habit of always laying out tracks in the same order, no matter the project. That way, your attention is fully devoted to mix decisions rather than hunting for elements.

5.3.3 CREATING AN "UNUSED" FOLDER

Before moving on to editing, it's a good idea to create a folder in the editor to hold all the tracks that won't be used in the mix.

You can move into this folder any original tracks that have been exported, processed, or rejected during editing. This folder lets you clear the mixer and editor of tracks that are no longer needed, while still keeping access to their original content.

5.4 Preliminary Editing

Now that the tracks are clearly identified and laid out in the project window, you can start the editing work. In the first phase, you'll focus on the purely technical aspects of the audio files. There's no particular order for these operations. What matters is that the entire project is processed track by track.

5.4.1 DELETING UNUSED SECTIONS

Empty Sections

As mentioned earlier, tracks delivered to a mixer often come as a single region running from the very beginning to the very end of the song, to make alignment easier in the editor. Some sections may therefore be completely empty. These sections should be cut and deleted. That way, it becomes possible to visually pinpoint active audio regions at any point in the song.

It's also common to discover drum tracks that contain nothing but bleed. This is often the case with one or several tom tracks that simply aren't used in the song. If they don't contribute to the overall ambiance, mute these tracks and move them to the "Unused" folder to avoid cluttering the editor and mixer unnecessarily.

Background Noise

The count-off, the squeak of fingers on a guitar or bass, the rustle of turning pages, or the movement of a music stand are often audible at the beginning and end of a performance. These noises should be removed using the handles at the start and end of the region.

In addition, a musician's movements, headphone bleed, amplifier hum, or even microphone preamp noise are constantly picked up during recording.

If they don't contribute positively to the vibe of the song, it's appropriate to get rid of sections of background noise between performances. Cut the region to isolate the noisy sections, then delete them.

5.4.2 ADDING FADE-INS AND FADE-OUTS

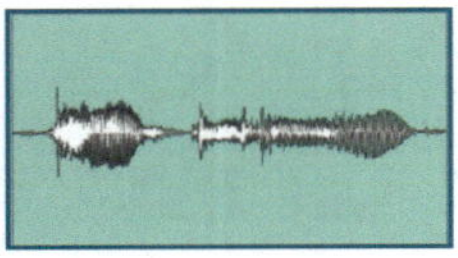

Hard cuts must be eliminated and replaced with fade-ins at the beginning and fade-outs at the end.

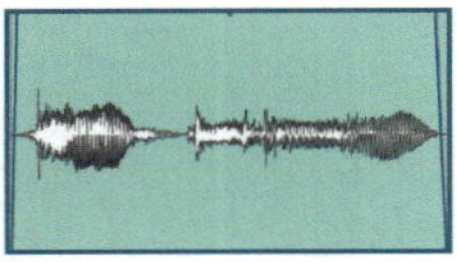

Tracks are often delivered with hard cuts at the beginning and end of the recording. It's also common for a single track to have been divided into multiple regions, each with hard cuts of its own. These abrupt entries and exits in the audio can cause clicks on playback and must therefore be eliminated.

Every region must have a fade-in and a fade-out, regardless of its length. Care should be taken not to chop off the transients at the start of the audio, and to preserve as much as possible of the natural decay at the end.

Even though this job is mind-numbingly repetitive, especially on large projects, it's not advisable to rely on automatic fade functions (auto-fades). It's rarely possible to define a fade length that suits all regions. What's more, the exact placement of fades needs to be set with precision—something that's done more effectively by ear or eye than by any algorithm.

In short, automatic fades are an act of faith that usually cause more problems than they solve. Better to avoid them.

5.4.3 CHECKING CROSSFADES

Sometimes the delivered tracks already contain crossfades. These edit points are easy to spot in the project window. You should check each one to make sure it's seamless.

In some cases, you won't be able to adjust the fade itself. A bit later on, we'll look at some strategies that can help get rid of clicks caused by bad crossfades.

5.4.4 SPECIAL CASES

Background Noise

When it comes to background noise, you need to exercise some judgment. The film industry has long understood that back-

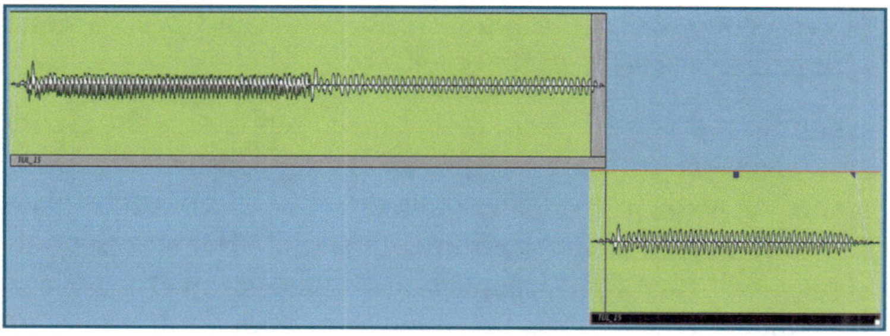

Edit points, such as crossfades, must be checked to ensure they are seamless.

ground noise plays an important role in recreating the illusion of a space. Recordings of an empty room—called room tone—are commonly added to studio-recorded dialogue to smooth over edits and make the ambience more realistic.

In analog recording, the hiss from tape machines and processing gear offers a similar advantage. This is one of the reasons why developers often add a noise component to analog-emulation plug-ins.

Systematically eliminating background noise is not always desirable.

Given how dense today's productions can be, this approach is less common than it used to be. Still, background noise can help "glue" tracks together and contribute to ambience and continuity, often lost when recording track by track.

It can therefore make sense to keep some of this noise in more spacious mixes or projects with lots of overdubs. In other situations, background noise doesn't add anything positive to the overall sound and needs to be controlled.

It's often difficult to eliminate noise using editing alone. This is the case for noises that are constantly audible within a specific frequency range, such as power-line hum (50 Hz or 60 Hz depending on the region) or excessive hiss from a guitar amp.

In other cases, the noise appears in the short silences between notes of a performance; editing it out in these situations is tedious or even impossible. At this prep stage, it's too early to intervene. It will be easier, during the mix, to decide whether corrective processing is necessary and, if so, to choose the most appropriate tool to reduce the background noise.

Bleed on Drum Tracks

Bleed is the sound of nearby sources leaking into the microphone of the main source. Although bleed can show up in recordings of any instrument, it can be particularly problematic on acoustic drum tracks. Since drums are a percussive instrument, it's practically impossible to completely isolate the sound of each component. On top of that, the various parts vibrate sympathetically with one another.

Aside from potential phase issues, bleed can reduce the clarity and precision of the performance. Paradoxically, in a good recording made in a suitable acoustic space, bleed can become an integral part of the instrument's sound. The strategy you choose will therefore depend on whether you feel the bleed contributes to or detracts from the drum sound.

This decision often hinges on the musical style. For instance, pop and heavy metal typically call for very clear separation between drum elements and therefore close control of bleed. Conversely, styles such as jazz, blues, or folk generally benefit from a more natural drum sound where the instrument is treated not as a collection of separate components but as a single entity—bleed included.

Tom Tracks

Tom tracks require particular attention. Toms are usually played only occasionally within a song. When they're not being hit, their mics pick up not only the tom's sympathetic resonance, but also the sound of the rest of the kit.

How you handle bleed depends on whether it improves the drum sound.

To deal with this bleed, gates are sometimes inserted on tom tracks during recording. However, dialing in the gate's parameters can be tricky. Snare and kick drum hits tend to trigger it unintentionally, and gates have an unfortunate tendency to cut off the toms' natural decay. In short, if a gate was used on the toms—or any drum in the kit—you'll simply have to live with the results, whatever they are!

A better way to control bleed is to duplicate each tom track and manually edit the copies so only the sections where the toms are actually played are kept. In the mix, using these edited tracks yields a more precise drum sound overall. For a more natural result, you can use the edited and original tom tracks in parallel, allowing you to dial in the amount of audible bleed. The same approach can also be applied to snare tracks, as long as the performance isn't too intricate.

Live or "Live in Studio" Recordings

When several sources are recorded simultaneously in the same room, as in live concerts or "live in studio" sessions, it's inevitable that bleed will end up on every mic track. This can be a challenge, especially if you're not used to this type of project.

Even though your first instinct might be to tame as much bleed as possible, that's rarely the best idea. Bleed is actually a big part of what gives these recordings their character. You have to work with it.

Completely eliminating bleed from a live recording is rarely a good idea.

The first step is to evaluate whether the bleed on each track sounds acceptable. "Acceptable" is admittedly vague, but bleed can be considered acceptable if it does not alter the sound of the instruments picked up by the mic.

It's generally easier to make this evaluation by listening simultaneously to the instrument that's "receiving" the bleed and the direct mic of the bleeding instrument. Suppose you want to assess the impact of drum bleed in the piano mics. First, listen to the drum tracks in solo to get their sound in your ear. Then add in the piano tracks and listen to how they change the drum sound. This comparison will help you gauge the quality of the bleed and how much of it you should keep. It will also inform many decisions about processing the piano track, particularly in terms of EQ.

Placing an edited copy alongside the original track facilitates instrument processing and allows for more precise effects assignment.

Along the same lines, bleed greatly influences how you treat individual tracks. EQing a track affects the sound of the bleed as well. Using a compressor will likely bring the bleed further forward.

Bleed can also complicate effects management. For example, you'll generally want to avoid a delay on the lead vocal repeating the snare drum as well.

To regain some precision, you can create an identical copy of the lead vocal track and place it on another channel. Insert a gate or edit this copy to remove bleed while leaving the original track intact. The edited track is then dedicated specifically to effects sends. It can remain inaudible by using its sends in pre-fader mode.

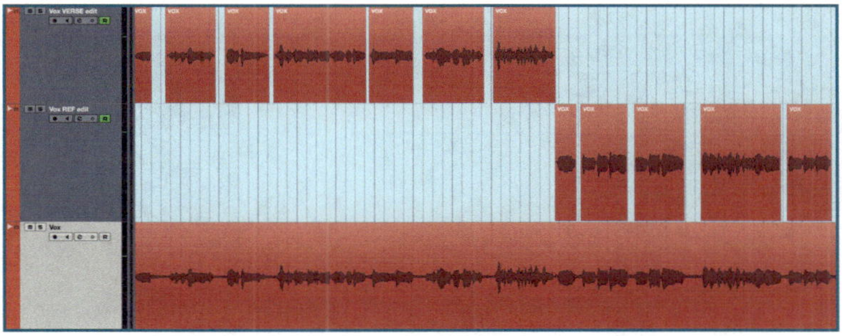

Here, the original vocal track (bottom) is used alongside an edited copy. Notice that the copy has been split into two tracks in order to process the verses and choruses differently.

At this stage of the work, you'll often already be able to spot one or more tracks that would benefit from this strategy. You can plan for this early in the prep phase.

5.5 Fixing Phase Problems

Sound Waves in Brief

At its core, a sound wave is a cyclical oscillation. In each cycle, the wave moves from positive amplitude to negative amplitude. The number of times this cycle repeats per second, measured in hertz, determines the pitch of the sound. The higher the number of repetitions, the higher the pitch.

Phase refers to the way the cycles of multiple waves heard simultaneously align with one another.

For example, the A above middle C on a piano oscillates at a frequency of 440 cycles per second. The A one octave below oscillates 220 times per second.

Phase

When two identical waves are heard simultaneously, the alignment of their respective cycles can vary. Even though, in real life, the harmonic content of sounds produces waves with irregular shapes, it's easier to understand the concept of phase by using a perfectly regular sine wave as an example—perfectly regular and perfectly boring!

Two waves are said to be "in phase" when their positive and negative amplitudes coincide in time. In that case, the amplitudes add together and the level increases.

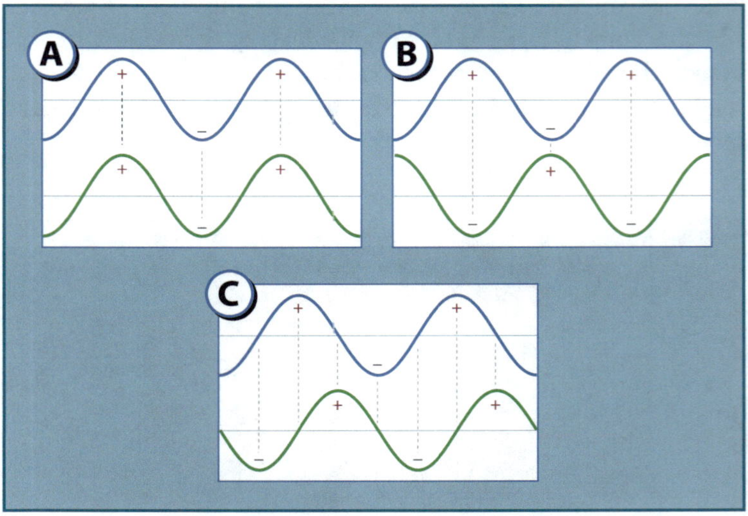

In A: Two waves in phase (0°), the levels add together.

In B: Two waves out of phase (180°), the levels cancel out.

In C: Two waves 90° out of phase, partial level increase.

Two waves are said to be "out of phase" when the positive amplitude of one wave lines up exactly with the negative amplitude of the other. In that case, the amplitudes cancel each other out and the two signals become inaudible.

Obviously, there are intermediate positions. The difference in the positions of the cycles, known as phase shift, is expressed in degrees; perfect alignment is 0°, and perfect opposition is 180°. The amount of addition or cancellation depends on the degree of phase shift.

Phase issues don't just cause level changes. In the presence of phase shift, some frequencies are boosted while others are attenuated. Changing the amount of phase shift also changes which frequencies are affected.

As a rule, the more low-frequency content there is when two signals are combined, the more likely it is that their phases will be coherent.

THREE SYMPTOMS OF A PHASE PROBLEM:

- ***The level decreases when switching from stereo to mono playback***
- ***Certain frequencies seem to be missing while others are overrepresented***
- ***The sound is difficult to localize in space and the stereo image is unstable; the signal seems to shift with the performance***

Mono Compatibility

Phase shift also causes problems when you switch from stereo listening to mono. Elements that are out of phase drop significantly in level in mono playback. Depending on the degree of phase shift, they may even disappear completely.

But who listens to music in mono anyway? To some extent, just about everyone! When you're walking through a shopping mall, listening to a song on a tablet or laptop, or driving in a car, the stereo image is restricted to the point where it's almost mono. If elements vanish in mono, your whole mix is compromised. That's why it's important to address phase issues before starting the mix.

POLARITY OR PHASE?

Put simply, polarity is an electrical term that refers to voltage. It can take only two values: positive or negative.

Reversing the polarity of an electrical signal turns its positive values into negative ones, and vice versa. A common example would be swapping the "+" and "–" on a battery or on any electrical cable.

Unlike phase — which results from the interaction of multiple overlapping waves — polarity concerns only a single signal.

Although purely electrical in nature, this concept has important implications in audio.

Like an electrical signal, a sound wave alternates between positive and negative amplitudes. Thus, when you reverse the polarity of a track from a console or within a DAW, you invert the values of its waveform.

Because polarity directly affects phase relationships, the two terms are often confused — a confusion reinforced by the incorrect labeling of some polarity switches as "phase" on certain devices.

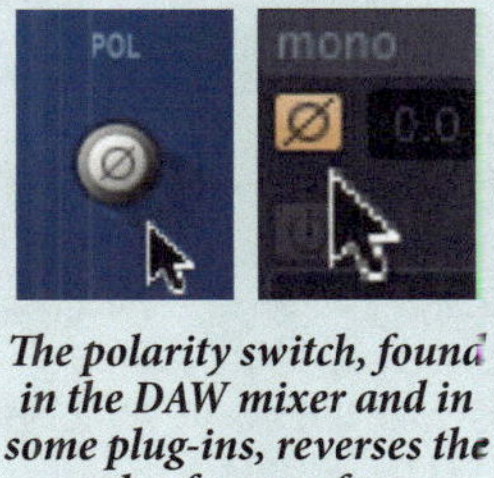

The polarity switch, found in the DAW mixer and in some plug-ins, reverses the cycle of a waveform.

5.5.1 POSSIBLE CAUSES OF PHASE PROBLEMS

Most phase problems stem from using multiple microphones to capture the same source during recording. If the sound from the source doesn't reach all the microphones at the same time, there will inevitably be phase shift between the signals. The same applies to instruments recorded both with microphones and with a direct box (DI).

When it comes to phase, it is wiser to verify than to assume.

Accidentally nudging a track during editing, parallel processing (such as compression), using (or overusing) plug-ins, or even a single cable with reversed soldering can all affect phase. For all these reasons, you should never assume that the delivered tracks are phase-coherent—no matter the reputation of the studio or engineer who recorded them. Nobody is immune to mistakes. When it comes to phase, it's always safer to check than to assume.

5.5.2 ACOUSTIC DRUMS

The drum kit—typically recorded with a whole bunch of microphones—is obviously the first instrument that comes to mind as a likely source of phase issues. Depending on the recording method, a drum session can easily contain more than a dozen tracks. Trying to get all those tracks perfectly in phase with one another is unrealistic. Instead, aim to make them as phase-coherent as possible. To do that, you need a methodical approach. Start with tracks that use two microphones on the same drum.

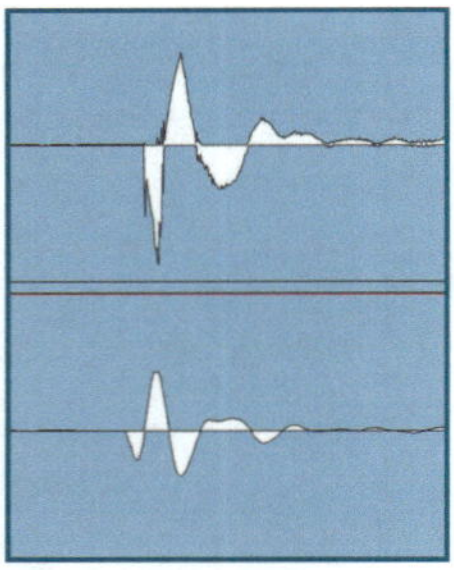

Here, the inside and outside bass drum microphones are out of phase.

Snare and Kick Drum

The snare is often captured with one mic on top and one on the bottom. Since the two mics are facing each other, their phases are reversed.

Check their coherence by listening to both snare tracks in solo. Use the polarity switch (typically labeled "Ø") in the DAW mixer or on a plug-in to flip the polarity of one of the tracks. Compare the normal and inverted polarity and choose the position that gives you the most low end.

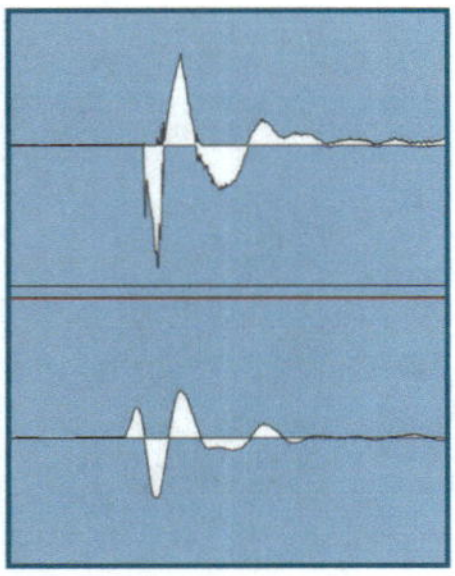

Coherence is restored by reversing the polarity of the outside microphone.

Do the same for the kick drum, which is often recorded with one mic inside and another outside. Again, use the polarity switch to find the setting that gives the most low-frequency content.

Overheads

Overheads are usually two mono tracks. Check their coherence as well. Locate a snare hit in the overhead tracks. By zooming in, you can see whether the waveforms of that snare hit line up on both tracks. If not, nudge one of the tracks to align them.

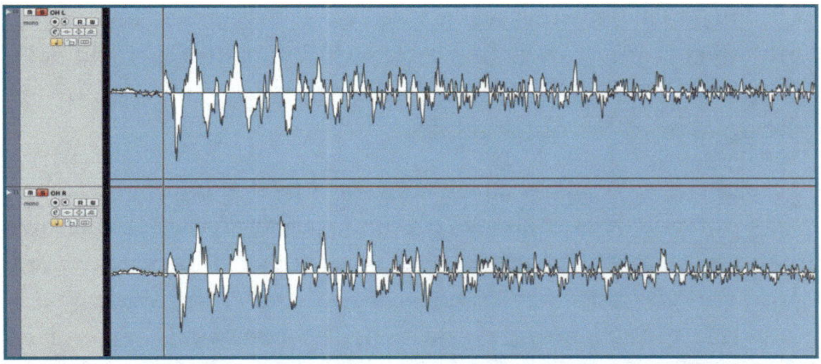

In these overhead tracks, the snare drum is slightly late in the left channel (bottom).

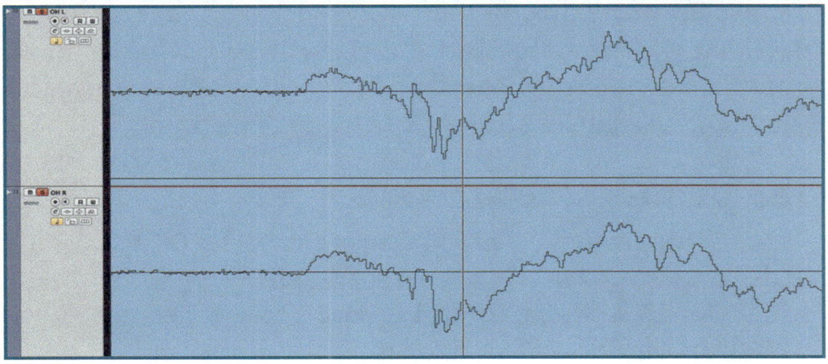

The two waveforms were aligned by advancing the left channel in the editor.

While you're at it, also check the stereo image of the overheads. Pan one track hard right and the other hard left. Then, by ear or using a stereo image analyzer, make sure the snare sits in the center of the stereo field. If necessary, adjust the level of one of the tracks to recenter the snare.

Once these adjustments are made, it's a good idea to export the overheads as a stereo track. Mute the original mono tracks and move them into your "Unused" folder.

Room Mics

Apply the same treatment to the room mics. Once they're properly in phase and centered, export them as one or more stereo tracks.

Comparing Each Track to the Overheads

You still need to make sure all of the drum mics are as phase-coherent as possible. The overheads will serve as the reference. To make phase issues more obvious, do the comparison in mono. You can use a dedicated plug-in for this or simply center the pan knobs on both sides of the master bus.

Start by soloing the overheads. Then add one other drum track. Using that track's polarity switch, choose the setting that gives the most level and the most low end. Repeat the process for each drum track, one by one, against the overheads.

Of course, if two mics were used on the snare or kick, their mutual coherence must be preserved. For example, if you have to invert the polarity of the inside kick mic, you'll also invert the polarity of the outside mic.

This exercise is not as straightforward as it might seem. Flipping polarity doesn't always produce a clear change in the low-frequency range. In some cases, one or two tracks may even produce contradictory results—for example, the snare and a tom might each be in phase with the overheads but out of phase with each other. In such cases, stick with the configuration that least compromises the element you consider most important to the song. Needless to say, you don't sacrifice the sound of the snare or kick to benefit one of the toms.

METHODS FOR REDUCING PHASE MISALIGNMENT:

- ***Move one of the tracks in time***
- ***Align the waveforms in the editor***
- ***Reverse polarity***
- ***Use only one of the tracks or channels***
- ***Use a phase-alignment plug-in such as Auto-Align, PHA-979, or IBP Phase Alignment Tool.***

5.5.3 MULTI-MIC RECORDINGS

Beyond drums, many other instruments can be recorded with multiple mics: guitars, choirs, horn sections, string sections, and so on. For all of these, try to improve phase coherence either with the polarity switch or by aligning waveforms.

Using different types of microphones on the same source—as is often done for guitar or bass—adds another layer of difficulty. Each mic captures sound in its own way, so their waveforms can look quite different, making visual alignment tricky.

In these situations, it's wise to rely more on your ears than your eyes. You can nudge one of the tracks very slightly and judge whether the adjustment improves the sound. Be careful, though: shifting by just a few milliseconds can completely change how the instrument comes across.

Recordings that use multiple microphones to capture the same source are likely to present phase issues.

5.5.4 RECORDINGS COMBINING MIC AND DI

In the same vein, bass, guitar, and keyboards are often recorded with one or more microphones combined with a DI. Since the DI is plugged directly into an audio input, its signal will inevitably arrive earlier than the mic signal, causing phase shift. In this case, the polarity switch is often no help. Instead, try to nudge the mic track to align its waveform with that of the DI.

Although you can align based on the first waveform at the start of the tracks, it's often more effective to use a distinct peak as a reference point. Scan through the tracks to find a clearly defined waveform to make alignment easier.

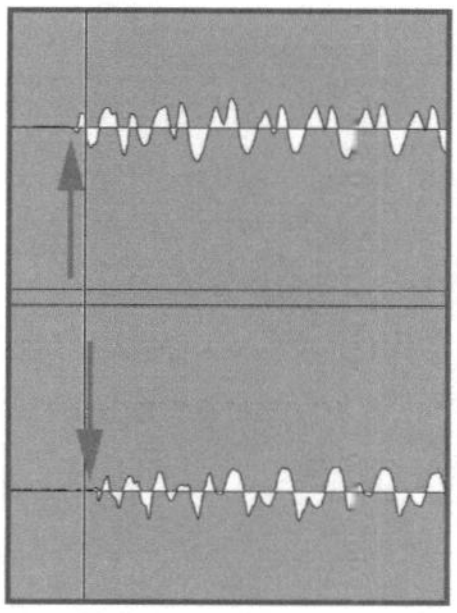

Here, the bass track recorded with a direct box (DI) precedes the track from the microphone placed on the bass amplifier.

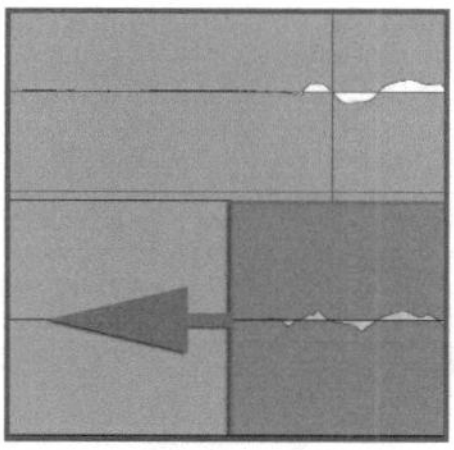

Moving the amplifier track allows the two waveforms to be aligned and phase coherence to be restored.

5.5.5 SPECIAL CASES

Too Many Mics on the Same Source

Let's be honest: sometimes the recording engineer, carried away in the heat of the moment, will put an absurd number of mics on a single source. Likewise, the producer may have been unable to choose the best combination of mics for the sound they wanted. Today's computers make it easy to keep everything that's recorded. This capacity, combined with indecision during tracking, often leaves the mixer with an excessive number of tracks for a single element.

Electric guitars are frequent victims of this kind of excess. There's no point in spending a long time juggling mic combinations or trying to align the waveforms of six or seven tracks of the same performance.

As Joe Barresi (Queens of the Stone Age, Sheryl Crow, Soundgarden, etc.) puts it: "Two mics on the same speaker is one mic too many." And that is often true. Choose one or a few tracks and move the extras into your "Unused" folder.

Stereo Tracks

If, unfortunately, mono tracks from different mics on the same source have been combined into a single stereo track, phase problems become harder to control. You can try splitting the left and right channels into two mono tracks and then adjusting phase by nudging one of them. However, this only works if the original mono tracks were panned hard left and right when the stereo track was created.

Sometimes you can salvage the situation with specialized phase-rotation plug-ins (like Voxengo PHA-979 or Little Labs IBP Phase Alignment Tool), automatic alignment tools (like

Auto-Align from Sound Radix), or stereo image processors (like Waves Stereo Imager or Center).

There are very few remedies when a stereo track presents phase problems.

If a stereo track really can't be fixed, you might consider hiding the phase problems by adding… even more phase problems! Using a chorus, flanger, or phaser can give character to an otherwise unusable track. The phase shift stops being perceived as a problem and becomes an effect.

Synth Sounds

Similarly, some synth tracks consist of one dry signal and another with delay and modulation. This technique creates an oversized stereo image that makes the sound more impressive. However, these kinds of sounds don't always translate well to mono.

It can be a good idea to use only one channel of the stereo track or to rebalance the two sides with a stereo-imaging plug-in.

You'll also often come across stereo synth tracks that are actually mono. A stereo-field analyzer will help you confirm this hunch. In large projects, it's often useful to convert such tracks to mono to reduce CPU load.

Samples

Despite the best efforts of software developers, drum-replacement plug-ins can also cause phase problems. In this case, the fix is usually straightforward: nudge the sample track forward in the editor. Avoid moving the original drum track so you don't compromise its phase relationship with the rest of the kit.

Parallel Processing

Sometimes a track is accompanied by a parallel-processing track, such as compression or distortion. Make sure the alignment between the two hasn't been altered by the processing.

Similarly, during the mix, stay alert to phase problems that can arise from using multiple parallel plug-ins. Plug-in latency can cause timing offsets between the original and processed tracks, especially when the computer's CPU is heavily loaded by a large project or high sample-rate / bit-depth settings.

5.6 Fixing Recording-Related Problems

5.6.1 CLICKS

Sometimes the signal on a track is cut very briefly. This abrupt interruption produces an unpleasant sound known as a click.

Clicks can be caused by the monitoring setup during playback or be part of the audio files themselves. First, identify the source of the problem.

Clicks Caused During Playback

If the click is intermittent and doesn't always occur in the same place, the problem isn't in the recording but in the monitoring setup. A quick look at the DAW's CPU usage meter will tell you whether your computer's processor is overloaded. If so, you'll need to reduce the number of plug-ins in the project or increase the buffer size.

When mixing, it is preferable to set the buffer size to its maximum value in order to avoid overloading the computer and audio interface.

Some studio setups include multiple digital devices connected together. In these systems, if a click occurs at regular intervals, there's a good chance the anomaly is caused by incorrect synchronization due to a word clock issue.

Clicks Embedded in the Tracks

Clicks can also occur during recording, in which case they become part of the audio on one or more tracks.

When you hear a click, first locate the offending track. Regions with hard cuts or crossfades are the first places to check, as they can easily cause clicks.

If the problem persists, scan the section where the click is heard and solo each track in turn to find which one contains it. Then zoom in on its waveform. The interruption causing the click generates a sudden jump in the waveform. Often a sharp spike will be visible in the editor.

Fixing Clicks

Unfortunately, there are very few ways to fix a click. Restoration plug-ins do exist, but they're often of limited use for this particular problem. Depending on the DAW, you may be able to manually redraw the waveform, but results are far from guaranteed.

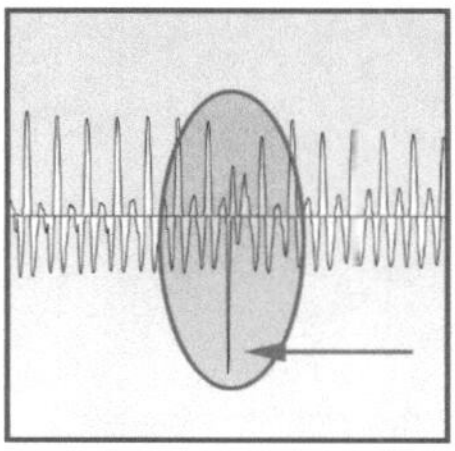

A click as it appears in the edit window.

Often, the best solution is to replace the problematic section. Find an identical passage elsewhere on the track and replace the damaged section with a clean one. A simple copy-and-paste with crossfades usually solves the issue—assuming you have a clean section to work with!

As a last resort, you can try to mask the click using volume automation. Find its exact location and place automation points so that only the click itself is affected. Obviously, a full cut to

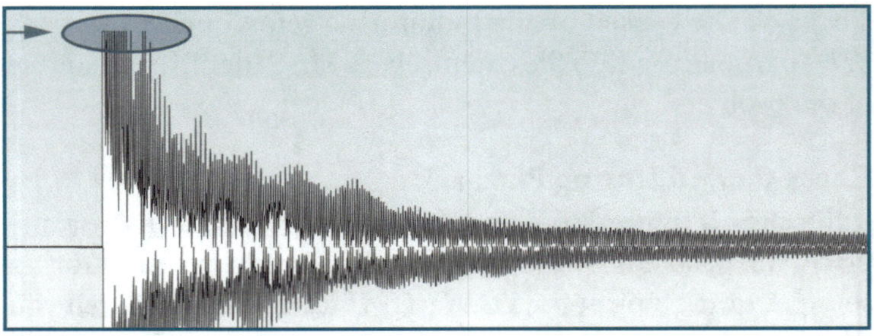

The upper portion of this waveform has been truncated due to clipping.

silence will be audible. Use your ears to determine how much gain reduction is needed to hide the click as best as possible.

5.6.2 CLIPPING

During recording, it's possible that the signal level exceeded digital zero. When that happens, the part of the waveform that goes over the limit is chopped off, producing an unpleasant sound known as clipping.

Clipping is one of the most difficult problems to fix. You can't edit it out, use a plug-in to remove it, or even effectively hide it; you simply have to live with it.

If you're lucky and the clipped track plays only a secondary role in the arrangement, it may be best simply to remove it from the mix. If, however, the track is essential, there are two possible strategies. The first is to use the same copy-and-paste method described for clicks. If there are no clean sections available, only one option remains. You may not be able to improve the quality of the track, but you can certainly make it worse! Inserting a saturation or distortion plug-in, or using a lo-fi type treatment, may save the day by giving the track a particular flavor. In that case, the degraded sound is no longer perceived as an error but as an effect. In desperate situations, it's an option worth exploring.

5.7 Fixing Performance-Related Problems

Capturing a performance in time on a recording is no small feat, no matter which side of the microphone you're on. The level of focus and preparation needed is hard to sustain over long stretches—for engineers and producers as well as for artists.

It's perfectly normal to find flaws in a musical performance here and there. It's up to us to decide whether these flaws undermine the musical content and, if so, to choose the best way to correct them.

5.7.1 THE BLESSINGS AND CURSES OF PERFECTION

Over time, opinions on what counts as an acceptable performance have changed dramatically. It's safe to say that the editing possibilities offered by computers have had a huge impact on this evolution. Just compare an album from the 1970s with a recent one and the differences are enormous.

As a general rule, if a performance issue is significant enough to draw the listener's attention, it must be corrected.

Still, the idea of a "perfect" performance is highly volatile and varies greatly depending on the musical style. Improvised music such as jazz or blues generally has more flexible standards. By contrast, it's unthinkable for a pop diva's performance not to be ruthlessly in tune. In EDM, the rhythm is usually locked tightly to the grid. Heavy metal, with its hyper-defined drums and almost inhuman rhythmic precision, has its own demanding standards as well.

We could spend hours debating how much this "perfection" really contributes musically. The concept is arguably nowhere as subjective as in the arts. But the fact remains that today's listeners expect the music they hear to be relatively in line with current standards. As mixers, we have to take these expectations into account.

As a rule, we can assume that any performance issue big enough to draw the listener's attention to itself needs to be corrected. That said, we must proceed with discernment. As Steve Churchyard (Céline Dion, The Pretenders, Duran Duran, etc.) notes: "Something that's perfectly in time and perfectly in tune can become perfectly boring." Corrections should therefore be applied sparingly and as transparently as possible.

The growing use of artificial intelligence should actually encourage us to correct only what's truly distracting. We simply can't compete with machine-level precision, and AI can't compete with the nuance and beauty of a human performance!

5.7.2 TIMING PROBLEMS

Since electronic music is usually programmed to fall exactly on the grid, we'll focus instead on performances played by real human beings… in flesh and blood!

Choosing a Reference Point

At first glance, it might seem logical to align performances to the grid displayed in the editor. However, while the grid can provide useful clues about the precise location of beats, it does not reflect the nuances that make rhythm the engine of a song.

Drummers spend countless hours learning how to play with the beat to create grooves that feel good. A quick look at the editor reveals that very few notes land exactly on the grid; they're always a bit ahead of or behind absolute tempo. That's part of what makes a well-played drum performance so compelling. Consequently, timing decisions should always be made with your ears, not your eyes.

In most cases, the drums serve as the reference for the other instruments. If there are no drums, identify which instrument most strongly carries the tempo of the song and use it as the base for evaluating the timing of other tracks.

The Drum Track

Since it will be the timing reference, the first step is obviously to ensure there are no serious timing problems on the drum track itself.

Tempo should always be adjusted using your ears rather than your eyes.

In track-by-track productions, this is rarely an issue. When working this way, drums often provide the foundation onto which the other instruments are overdubbed. The drum performance must therefore be tight enough from the start to support overdubs. By the time you reach the mix, it generally needs little or no timing correction.

However, in live ensemble recordings where musicians play together, timing flaws are more likely to creep into the drum performance.

It's much easier to evaluate the tightness of a drum performance in context rather than in solo, especially if you're not familiar with the song. It helps to add the other elements that support the rhythm—for example, in a rock song, the bass and main guitars. Timing problems and the tracks causing them will be easier to spot.

Technically speaking, you have to be careful when editing drums. As we pointed out earlier, bleed is omnipresent in drum recordings. Moving only one drum track will inevitably cause serious problems. Corrections must therefore be applied to all drum tracks, not just the one that's clearly late or early.

For example, if a snare hit falls off the beat, cut all the drum tracks just before that snare attack. Close the segment by placing a second cut just before the next on-time element—usually the hi-hat. Once the whole block is defined across all drum tracks, move it as a unit to the right place, using the snare as your reference. Finally, add crossfades to each track to complete the edit.

Pay special attention to cymbals when editing drums. You want to avoid ending up with leftover bits of a cymbal's decay before the edit point. You also don't want to chop off a cymbal's decay or have it change suddenly into a different cymbal as a result of the edit.

A FEW RECOMMENDATIONS:

- ***Make sure from the outset that the drum track has no tempo issues***
- ***Synchronize doubled instrument tracks and treat them as a group rather than individually***
- ***Start playback at least two full measures before the section being edited to fully internalize the groove***
- ***Cut tracks as close as possible to the attack***

The Bass

Once the drums are locked in, compare them with the other instruments one by one, starting with those that are most important rhythmically. The first candidate is usually the bass.

In most musical styles, the bass and kick drum work together. Once again, rely on your ears, not your eyes, to spot timing issues. The attack of a bass note is slower than that of a kick drum, so the bass actually benefits from leading the kick slightly to keep the two distinct.

Bass editing poses another challenge. Bass notes often run into one another without leaving silence between them. Editing continuous notes requires special care. A good method is to nudge the problematic region slightly so its waveform lines up better with that of an in-time region (see the illustration "Editing Sustained Notes"). You then make the edit transparent with crossfades. This technique works for any instrument whose notes connect without gaps.

Other Instruments

With drums and bass now sitting solidly in time, you can evaluate the timing of the other instruments. Solo the drums and bass along with each of the other instruments in turn, starting with those that contribute most to the rhythm. In rock or folk, that might be guitars; in pop or jazz, perhaps piano.

Add one instrument after another until all timing corrections have been made across all tracks. You'll likely notice that the further you get from the instruments forming the rhythmic foundation (drums, bass, percussion, etc.), the fewer corrections are needed. This is why it's often easier to finish the process with the lead vocal, which usually plays a more lyrical than rhythmic role—unless your project leans toward hip-hop, in which case you probably treated the vocal earlier in the process.

EDITING SUSTAINED NOTES

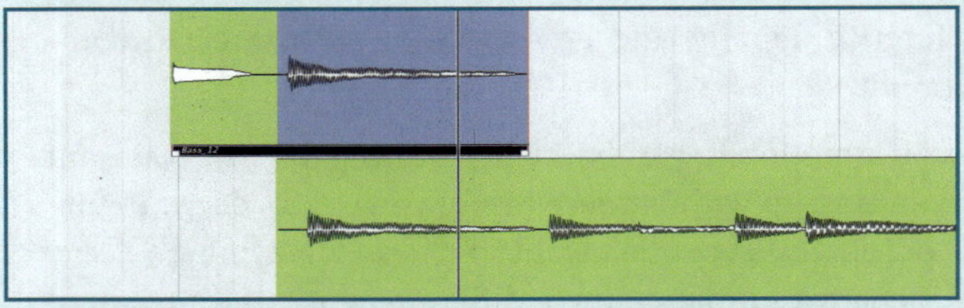

Here, the goal is to lengthen the bass note that is too short (top) and use the second bass performance (bottom) for the remainder of the song.

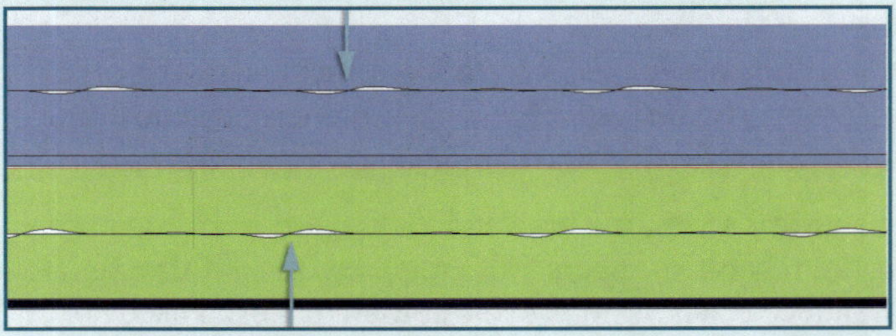

By zooming in within the editor, we can see that the waveforms are not aligned.

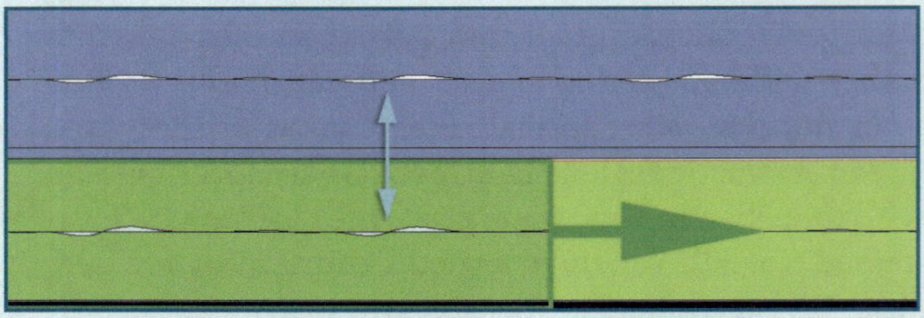

The lower track is moved to align the waveforms.

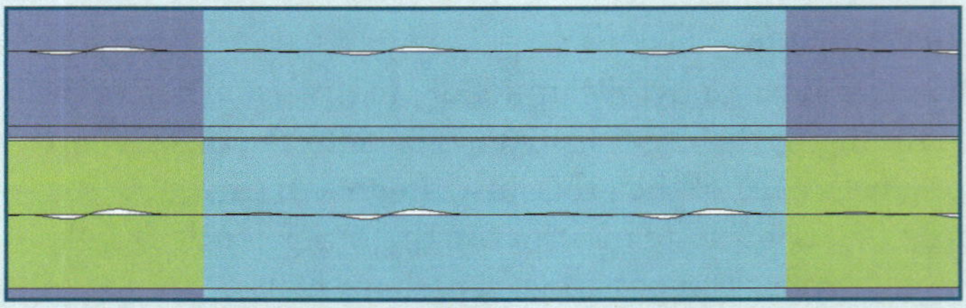

Once alignment is achieved, the fade area is selected.

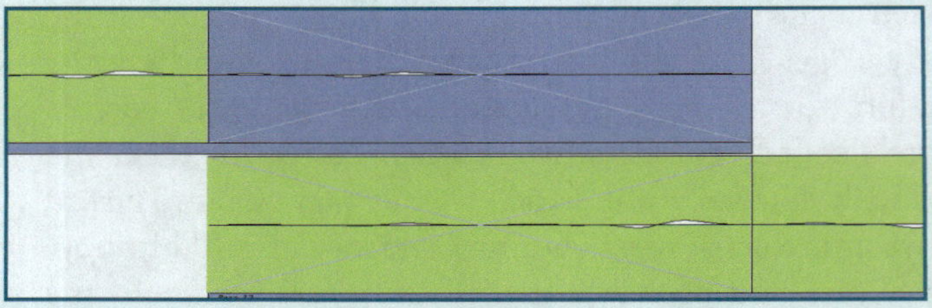

The crossfade is applied.

5.7.3 SPECIAL CASES

Double-Tracked Parts

Whenever a part is doubled, you obviously have to make sure the two performances are in sync. If not, determine which take is tighter and use it as your reference for adjusting its doubles. Then group the doubled tracks so they can be edited together relative to the rest of the song.

Time-Stretching

When adjusting the timing of an instrument, some notes may become too short to reach the next beat, leaving a gap between regions.

Copy-and-paste is generally more effective than time-stretching.

All DAWs include a time-stretching function that lengthens or shortens notes directly in the editor. For now, most of these functions still produce less-than-perfect results, often causing timbral changes or artifacts. In such cases, it may be better to find another note of suitable length elsewhere in the part and replace the problematic one with a copy-and-paste.

Automatic Alignment Functions

Many DAWs offer functions that automatically snap note attacks to a tempo grid (Snap to Grid in Pro Tools, Quantize Hitpoints in Cubase, to name just two).

Unless you're working on electronic music, this approach is far too heavy-handed to produce musically satisfying results. Not only are attack detections often imprecise, but the automatic movement of regions tends to create more problems than it solves.

As in many areas of mixing, your ears are often better than any algorithm. Use automatic alignment with caution.

Too Many Corrections

Sometimes you may be overwhelmed by the sheer number of corrections needed. This is common with projects recorded by musicians with little studio experience or where preproduction was neglected.

Faced with an excessive amount of editing, it may be necessary to ask for a re-recording of certain sections before continuing. If that's not possible, there's no choice but to carry out a painstaking series of copy-and-paste edits. With courage and patience, you should be able to reach an acceptable result.

Let me repeat this warning: it's crucial not to correct everything systematically just because you can, or because "it doesn't look right" on screen. Only fix what risks pulling the listener's attention away from the song.

5.7.4 PITCH PROBLEMS

Computers make it possible to get any singer perfectly in tune, regardless of how talented they are—or at least that's what people like to believe, especially when they're trying to explain the success of a singer they don't like!

Plug-ins such as Melodyne or Auto-Tune (to name just a couple) have at times had a bad reputation. For some, correcting a singer's pitch is like cheating at cards. In reality, the issue is much more nuanced. It's not the ability to correct that's the problem, but the misuse of that ability.

As we've already mentioned, listeners expect a certain standard of quality, and that includes pitch accuracy. Using pitch-correction tools is therefore common practice—so much so that most DAWs now include a pitch-correction module in their standard toolset. As with most mixing tools, the key lies in how you use it.

Automatic Correction

The first trap to avoid when using pitch-correction if you want transparent results is relying on automatic mode. In this mode, the corrector works on every single note from attack to release, completely removing the nuances of the performance. Notes become aggressively in tune, natural vibrato is erased, and attacks turn mechanical. In extreme cases, the singer ends up sounding like some sort of crooning droid.

Unless you intentionally want to create an obvious effect, the automatic function should be avoided.

Graphic mode makes it possible to fine-tune the treatment and achieve a more natural result. You can then correct only the notes that truly need it and control how much each note is adjusted.

Unless you're going for an obvious effect—like the one commonly heard in rap and pop—it's simply not an option to rely on automatic mode. Even when you do want that effect, you still need to tweak the automatic-correction settings to dial it in, and then clean up any awkward moves in graphic mode if necessary.

Correcting in Context

Another trap is correcting the performance in solo. Although A-440 is the standard tuning today, some recordings deviate from it. Some musicians (for reasons that remain obscure) prefer another reference pitch, and in other cases instruments are simply tuned to each other, using one of them as the reference.

Pitch-correction tools are calibrated by default to A-440. If you correct the vocal in solo, you have no way of knowing whether that tuning matches the rest of the song.

Listening in context reduces the number of corrections and yields a more natural performance than listening in solo.

Imagine your reaction when you take the vocal out of solo and realize it's now in a different key than the rest of the track! To avoid this nightmare, always correct pitch with at least a minimal harmonic backing.

Moderation

Once you're in the graphic editor, it's hard to resist the temptation to fix every little pitch wobble. Not only does this take a huge amount of time, but the result will end up similar to what you'd get with automatic mode.

A better practice is to correct as few notes as possible. As with timing corrections, the strategy is to treat only the flaws that are likely to attract the listener's attention. Listening in context makes them easier to identify.

Unless you deliberately want to create an effect, always aim to correct as few notes as possible.

Moderation is also important in terms of how far you move the note. Sure, you can drop it exactly on the center of the pitch with a single mouse-click. But you'll get a more natural result by leaving it a few cents below or above the perfect pitch.

Once again, your ears are far better than your eyes at determining how much correction is needed.

5.7.5 SPECIAL CASES

Vocal Harmonies

Vocal harmonies, often used in the background, don't draw as much attention as the lead vocal. They can therefore tolerate more aggressive pitch correction. In fact, the more harmony parts there are at the same time, the harder it is to perceive the individual corrections on each track.

Background vocal harmonies tolerate pitch correction better than the lead vocal.

Correcting Instruments Other Than Vocals

Pitch-correction tools can also be used on instruments. The quality of the result depends on how accurately the algorithm can identify the notes based on the instrument's range and timbre.

Although polyphonic pitch-correction tools exist (Melodyne, for example), most correctors are designed for vocals and can only handle one note at a time. Polyphonic parts therefore produce unexpected results. In addition, pitch-correction tools don't handle distorted sounds very well and often struggle to detect notes outside the vocal range.

A FEW RECOMMENDATIONS FOR A NATURAL RESULT:

- **Always use the pitch corrector in graphic mode**
- **Do not correct the vocal in solo**
- **Aim to correct as few notes as possible**
- **Do not tune exactly to pitch**
- **Trust your ears rather than your eyes**
- **Listen to the entire track to ensure that your corrections are transparent**

Too Many Corrections

Some vocal performances may require a large number of corrections. If re-recording is impossible, try salvaging the performance by copy-and-pasting sections that have fewer pitch problems. When the track can't be fixed, you can still minimize pitch issues with modulation. With the right settings, a chorus or doubler can help smooth out the flaws.

Similarly, adding subtle modulation to delay effects can sometimes make slightly off-pitch performances more acceptable.

Doubling naturally helps mask pitch issues by making the tuning more diffuse. So if certain parts are repeated within the song, you might consider doubling the vocal—provided it contributes positively to the song's impact.

In the end, only your ears can tell you whether any of these remedies suit the project at hand.

5.8 Creating Subgroups

The Many Joys of Subgroups!

Using subgroups is an extremely powerful way to streamline the mixing process and speed it up. It consists in routing the signals from several individual tracks to a single destination so they can be processed as a single group.

Using subgroups is an extremely powerful technique for simplifying and accelerating the mixing process.

Take drum recording as an example. By routing all of the individual drum tracks to a subgroup, you can control the overall drum level with a single fader: the subgroup's output level. You can also apply processing (such as compression) that acts on the drums as a whole.

Beyond making level management easier and allowing you to process grouped tracks in one place, subgroups tend to reduce the total number of plug-ins used in a project, easing CPU load.

Finally, subgroups also reduce the size of the mixer you have to manage. You can hide the individual tracks and show only the subgroups to which they're assigned.

The 56 tracks in this project (top) were grouped into 13 subgroups (bottom).

The Procedure

At the prep stage, the mix is rarely advanced enough to make decisions about the level or stereo placement of individual elements. But you can still group them into subgroups.

The procedure is simple. First, create a subgroup (or aux bus, depending on the DAW) in the mixer. Then assign the outputs of the tracks you want to group to that bus using their output routing menus.

Grouping Tracks

For now, the goal is simply to group tracks that can be considered parts of a single instrument or ensemble. Create subgroups for drums, backing vocals, brass, strings, and so on.

Any multi-mic recording can also be routed to a subgroup. For example, three guitar tracks recorded with three different mics can be sent to a single guitar subgroup.

Grouping Subgroups

The subgroup concept can be applied to the subgroups themselves.

Consider a project with orchestral arrangements. First, create subgroups for each orchestral section: one for strings, one for woodwinds, one for brass, and another for percussion. Then route these four subgroups to a master orchestra subgroup. You'll then be able to control both the individual sections and the orchestra as a whole.

5.9 The Benefits of Templates

Over time and with experience, mixers develop a working method that largely dictates how they prepare their projects. The order in which they arrange the tracks, the routing strategies they use, and their preferred tools are more or less the same from mix to mix. As a result, certain preparatory tasks recur from one project to another.

To reduce prep time, many mixers use what's known as a template. A template is a "stock" project in which most recurring organizational tasks—such as track layout, basic routing, and common processing chains—are already set up. The audio files for the new mix are then imported into this framework.

The template defines the starting point for your projects and, in that sense, embodies your preferences and way of working. The way it's designed has a major impact on the fluidity and efficiency of your workflow. Building a template is a delicate task that we'll discuss in detail in a later chapter.

6
VOLUME TOOLS

MIXING WORK relies largely on volume management. It is, in fact, the most decisive point of intervention we have to establish a mix balance and thus define its character. In this respect, the fader is, of course, our primary ally. But other tools exist to help us govern this important aspect of mixing. That is what we will discuss in this chapter.

6.1 Track Grouping

In large projects, one of the first tasks is to reduce the number of tracks and faders to manage by creating groupings. By simplifying the mixing console in this way, we speed up and facilitate the mixing process. Let's review the options available to us.

When our goal is to blend several elements into a coherent ensemble, creating a subgroup is the best way to proceed.

6.1.1 SUBGROUPS

As we have seen previously, a subgroup allows us to adjust the volume of a set of tracks from a single fader. That is, of course, one of its advantages. But a subgroup also makes it possible to process all the tracks assigned to it in one place. This avoids having to repeat processing one by one on the individual tracks.

More importantly, by focusing our intervention on the set of tracks rather than on each of them, we give them a unity that reinforces their role as an ensemble in the mix. Thus, in addition to simplifying volume management and speeding up the mixing process, the subgroup is the best way to shape the overall tone of tracks that share a common role—drum tracks, orchestral sections, brass sections, or vocal harmonies, for example.

6.1.2 LINKED TRACKS

Most DAWs allow tracks to be linked together, via a function generally named "Link", to apply the attributes of one track to the other tracks included in the link. Very often, the list of shareable parameters is presented in a menu.

This function is mainly used to save time by avoiding the need to set, one by one, the parameters that are common to each track. It can, for example, assign the same routing destination to linked tracks, or arm their record function simultaneously. You can also choose to link inserts in order to quickly apply the same processing to each track in the link. Thus, by inserting and adjusting a plug-in on any track in the group, it is automatically replicated in the insert slots of the other tracks.

The same can, of course, apply to input gain. For instance, you can reduce, in one move, the gain of tracks that were delivered too hot.

Generally, as soon as you apply the link function to a group of tracks, the faders for those tracks become automatically linked. From that point on, moving the fader of any track in the group proportionally modifies the other linked elements. Suppose two elements: a vocal track whose fader is currently at −3 dB, and a parallel compression track of that same vocal set to −5 dB. Once those tracks are linked, moving either fader will affect the volume of both tracks.

During mixing, however, the fact that certain track parameters are linked complicates the individual adjustment of the group members. It is true that you can change an individual setting without applying that change to the other tracks, but doing so requires an additional keyboard command. If, by accident, you forget that command, you modify all linked tracks! Nothing is more frustrating.

Linked tracks are most useful as a temporary tool during mix prep.

The situation becomes even more complicated when some linked tracks are hidden in the mixer. Your memory is put to the test: are there tracks linked to this one, and which parameters are shared? Needless to say, the risk of unintended changes increases dangerously.

Another drawback: in some DAWs, the automation of one element in the group is applied to all linked tracks, which is obviously not always desirable.

For all these reasons, it is often preferable to reserve linked tracks for the preparation stage and to use this function temporarily. You link the tracks, apply the shared settings, and once the operation is done, you disable the link to restore each track's independence. In fact, some DAWs feature a clearly visible button that temporarily links the tracks you select.

6.1.3 VCA FADERS

Inspired by large analog consoles, the VCA (Voltage Control Amplifier) is a fader that lets you simultaneously adjust the volume of each track assigned to it. It is the audio equivalent of the One Ring in The Lord of the Rings trilogy: one fader to rule them all!

How you create a VCA fader varies by DAW. Some require that you first add the VCA fader to the console and then assign tracks for it to manage; others let you select the tracks and assign them a VCA fader from a menu.

A VCA lets you group the output levels of any type of track. You can, for example, create a VCA to manage the level of a mix's subgroups, or group reverb effects so you can adjust a mix's overall ambience in one move.

VCAs are particularly useful for managing the internal balance of subgroups made up of large sections—orchestras, brass, choirs, percussion, and so on. Suppose, for example, a vocal harmony subgroup receiving eight tracks: three soprano voices, three tenor voices, and two bass voices. By creating one VCA fader per section, you could simply raise the soprano VCA to increase the level of the soprano tracks simultaneously and uniformly.

The Differences Between the VCA, Linked Tracks, and Subgroups

Since the VCA fader shares many characteristics with linked tracks and subgroups, it is often confused with them. It is important to clarify the scope of its use.

Unlike the linked-tracks method, a VCA offers the freedom to retouch the individual level of a track without changing the levels of the other tracks it governs. When writing automation, it is therefore possible to program the individual level of each track in addition to that of the VCA itself.

Another difference is that you can adjust a VCA even if its tracks are hidden in the mixer. It therefore becomes possible to declutter the mixer by hiding, as needed, the tracks controlled by VCA. Each VCA fader can also be named and color-coded to make it easier to locate on the mixing console.

VCA faders also have two characteristics that differentiate them from subgroups. First, they can govern the level of tracks that have different routing destinations. Thus, even if the kick drum is routed to a drum subgroup and two bass tracks are routed to a bass subgroup, you can still use a VCA to adjust the level of those three tracks simultaneously.

Another important property is that a VCA preserves the proportion of post-fader sends used on the tracks it controls, which is not the case with subgroups. For example, suppose we have assigned a reverb to a snare drum via one of its sends. This snare is routed to a drum subgroup and is also under the control of a VCA fader that manages the level of all tracks in that same drum kit. If I lower the VCA fader, unsurprisingly, the snare's output level decreases. Since its send to the reverb is post-fader, lowering the output level also reduces the amount of signal sent to the reverb. The proportion between the snare and its reverb therefore remains unchanged.

Now, if I lower the level of the drum subgroup, the snare sound decreases accordingly. However, the amount of snare signal reaching the reverb remains unchanged. Thus, although the

This example illustrates managing the internal balance of a subgroup using a VCA.

A VCA governs each section of this small choir. It therefore becomes possible to adjust the sections' levels without having to manipulate each individual track fader.

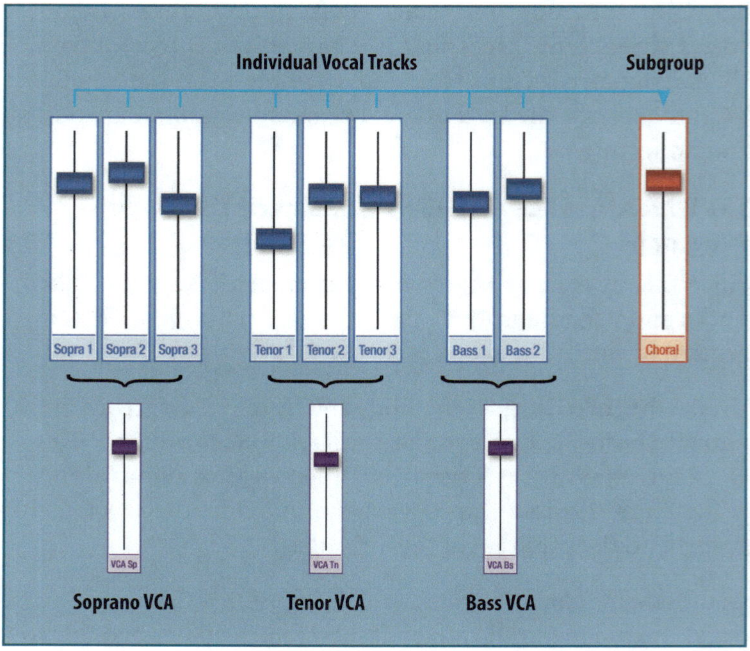

original signal decreases in what we hear, that decrease has no effect on post-fader sends. What we hear, then, is snare reverb... without the snare! Let's admit that is rarely what we want.

Thus, since it affects no parameter other than the faders of the tracks it governs, the VCA should be seen for what it is: a specialized tool that facilitates volume management.

6.2 Automation

For many years, finalizing a mix on an analog console meant that all maneuvers—especially fader moves—had to be performed in real time. When a mix required several simultaneous moves, the engineer would ask studio staff or band members for help—just to get a few extra hands on the desk. Tasks were then assigned to each participant:

— Mike, you pan guitar 1 to the left before each chorus, then bring it back to the center after. Also raise guitar 3 by 2 dB in the solo.

— Jeff, on the words "my love," raise the vocal harmony bus by 1 dB. Same for the "yeah, yeah" right before the end ad libs. And while you're at it, drop the synth by 3 dB in the solo—its fader is on your side of the console anyway.

Once everyone's roles were assigned, you'd hit play and everyone would jostle elbows around the console to perform their

SUBGROUPS, LINKED TRACKS OR VCA FADERS?

Here are a few possible applications depending on the type of grouping used.

	SUBGROUPS	LINKED TRACKS	VCA FADERS
Apply processing (EQ, compression, etc.) to a set of tracks	X		
Apply a global effect (reverb, delay, etc.) to a set of tracks	X		
Manage the level of a subgroup's subdivisions			X
Manage the level of an entire mix's subdivisions	X		X
Quickly set individual parameters across a set of tracks		X	
Speed up multitrack recording		X	
Simultaneously control the level of multiple tracks whose balance is established	X	X	X
Simultaneously control the level of multiple tracks with different routing destinations		X	X
Visually declutter the console	X		X
Automate the individual level of tracks within a group	X		X
Preserve the proportion of a group's individual sends			X

part of the choreography! If someone missed their move, you started over from the beginning.

When the first song was done, you would pull out the next song's setting notes (scrupulously recorded on what were called Recall Sheets) and spend several minutes setting the console and outboard processing as close as possible to the noted values. Then you'd work out a new choreography and start dancing around the console again!

Needless to say, this way of working was, to say the least, tedious. Not to mention the dreaded possibility that someone from the label might strongly suggest raising the vocal level on all mixes, for example. You'd have to start the whole circus from scratch!

In the early 1970s, several analog console manufacturers—including API, Neve, and SSL—tried to simplify the process by integrating a revolutionary concept: automation. Improvements began with the integration of motorized faders and, a little later, the development and addition of VCA faders. For many years now, major manufacturers have offered console models where all parameters are automated. This is what is known as Total Recall. Of course, you still have to note the settings of external processing devices, but let's admit the task is far simpler today than it was back then.

6.2.1 AUTOMATION IN A DAW

In a DAW, all of this is taken for granted. Routing, the plug-ins used and their settings, as well as the mix console settings, are saved within the project file itself. In short, you always find your project exactly where you left it.

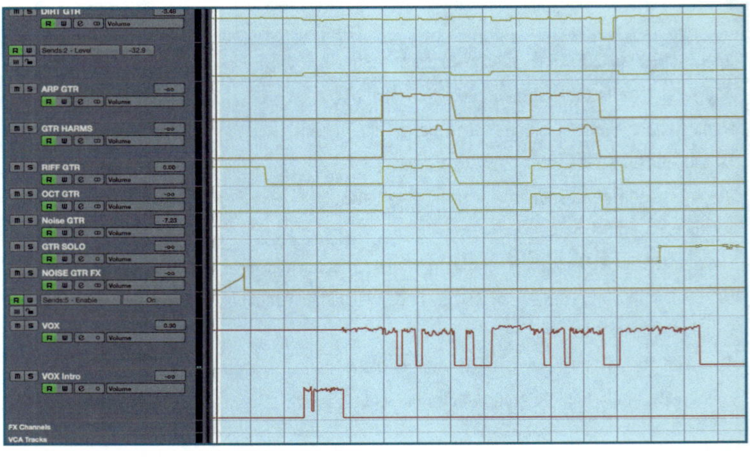

Automation often appears this way in the main project window of DAWs.

DAWs also make it possible to record, using a digital console, an external control surface, or the computer mouse, real-time manipulations of any parameter. Faders, plug-ins, virtual instruments—in short, everything can be automated. Naturally, automation can also be created and edited directly on screen.

Automation write modes

Automation is recorded by enabling the appropriate function, whose name and location vary by DAW. Several operating options are offered, the most common being Write, Touch, and Latch.

In Write mode, the manipulations you perform are recorded and replace existing automation.

Touch mode lets you retouch existing automation. The previous writing is replaced as soon as you touch a parameter, and it remains replaced for as long as the control is touched.

Latch mode works almost the same way as Touch. However, once you stop manipulating a parameter, that parameter's last value replaces the existing automation.

Control surfaces can be useful for automation, especially for those who feel more comfortable manipulating real knobs than a mouse.

Of course, automation can also be edited directly on screen. In most DAWs, automation lanes are accessible in the main project window under each automated track. It is therefore possible to precisely locate where a parameter is modified relative to the track's waveform.

Real-time writing has the advantage of being fast and intuitive. This makes it very effective for reproducing broad mixer moves. However, it is less precise than on-screen editing, where you can accurately set the value and the timing of each manipulation.

Note as well that real-time writing is often visually more chaotic, since all intermediate values are recorded. In practice, it's often better to capture the essentials in real time, then clean it up on screen to simplify the moves.

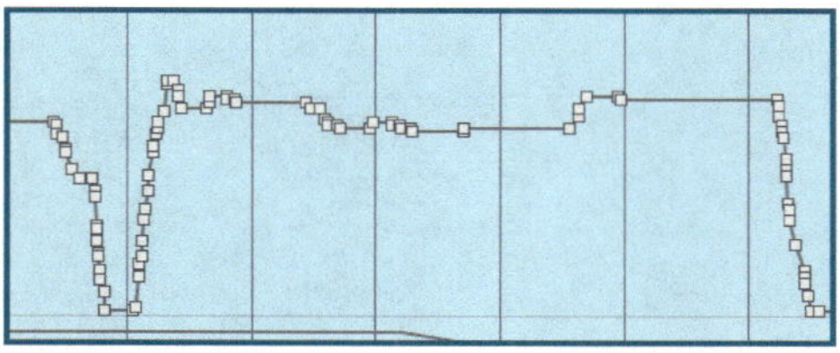

An automation pass written in real time.

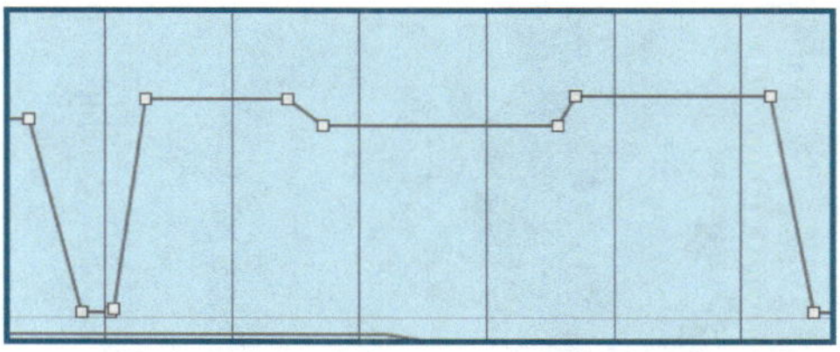

The same pass once manually revised on screen.

6.2.2 OBJECTIVES OF VOLUME AUTOMATION

Automation allows you to change the setting of any parameter over the course of a mix. Its main advantage is that it lets us apply contrast strategies to break a piece's linearity and hold the listener's interest. We will discuss these strategies in more detail in a subsequent chapter. For now, let's focus on the valuable services automation can provide when used to manipulate volume.

Objective 1: Improve the effectiveness of the vocal track

No plug-in, no matter what it is, has any musical sensitivity.

In nearly all mixes, a compressor is inserted on the vocal track to level the volume. However, its only capability is to apply processing when the signal exceeds a given threshold. It accounts neither for the meaning of the lyrics nor, even less, for their intelligibility. Thus, even if a compressor contributes to the rendering of a vocal performance, it often needs a helping hand to compensate for its blatant lack of musical sensitivity!

Volume automation on the vocal track aims to make each word of the performance intelligible and to highlight the emotion it contains. Since the arrangement density varies throughout a song, this automation must be performed manually while listening to the piece. That is the only way to ensure that each syllable has the level needed to be clearly heard.

Automation can also increase the emotional effectiveness of a vocal performance. For example, you can highlight key words simply by raising their level. Breaths—often very emotionally expressive—can be dosed according to the needs of the lyric and the song. Raising the level on strong beats or at the beginnings of phrases can also help enhance the rhythmic aspect of the performance.

As you can see, vocal automation work requires attentive listening and great precision. Seasoned mixers often point to this

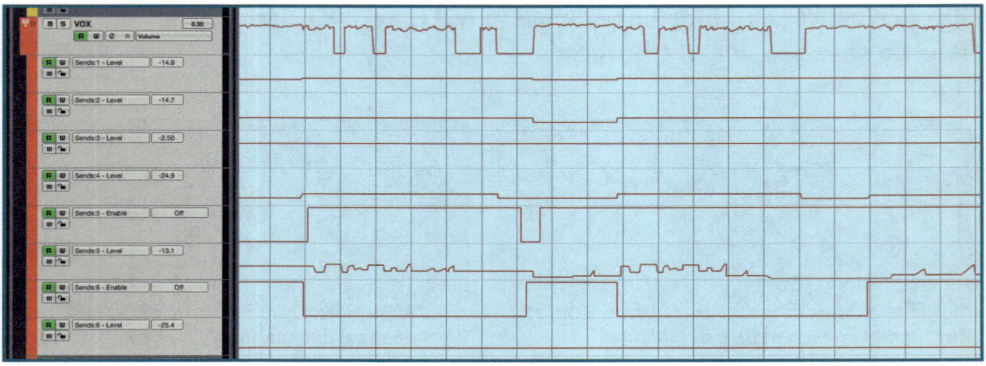

A screenshot of the lead vocal's automation. At the top, you can see the very slight level fluctuations used to enhance the effectiveness of the vocal performance. The other automation lanes control the sends, adjusting the balance of the different effects on the vocal as the song requires.

aspect as one of the elements that most clearly differentiates amateur mixes from professional ones. The succession of these very slight volume fluctuations has a very strong influence on the effectiveness of the vocal performance. It is therefore worth spending as much time on it as necessary.

Objective 2: Reduce disparities in an instrument's volume
In an ideal world, an instrument's dynamics would remain stable regardless of the note played. We know, however, that this is rarely the case. Sometimes the instrument does not project its register uniformly. Other times, the performer unintentionally attacks certain notes more vigorously than others. Processing applied to the track—equalization and modulation effects in particular—can also change the level of certain parts of the register. All these circumstances lead us to consider automation in order to correct these fluctuations in dynamics.

Since it often serves as the foundation of the entire mix, the bass is, among all instruments, the one that most often benefits from this kind of adjustment. Its level can therefore be automated to reduce disparities between notes and smooth out attacks. Naturally, this work is done by ear, taking the arrangement and the song's needs into account.

Let's emphasize once again that you should not assume that inserting a compressor will automatically fix such level variations. It is sometimes necessary to automate a track's gain to reduce occasional peaks that overload the compressor's input level. In other cases, the compressor itself can create level disparities. Then it will be the track fader that needs automation. Only careful listening allows you to judge where to intervene and by how much.

Objective 3: Use a repetitive pattern to create motion
Using repetitive automation is a method that adds character to mix elements that lack sparkle. The idea is to program a series of fluctuations to obtain a basic rhythmic pattern, which you then repeat.

Applied to panning, this technique makes it possible to add motion to a track or an effect you consider too static.

You can also apply an automation sequence to a track's volume—for example, a pattern that increases level on beats one and three, to reinforce the piece's rhythm.

Of course, there are many specialized plug-ins that do similar work. Automation, however, gives you the freedom to set the

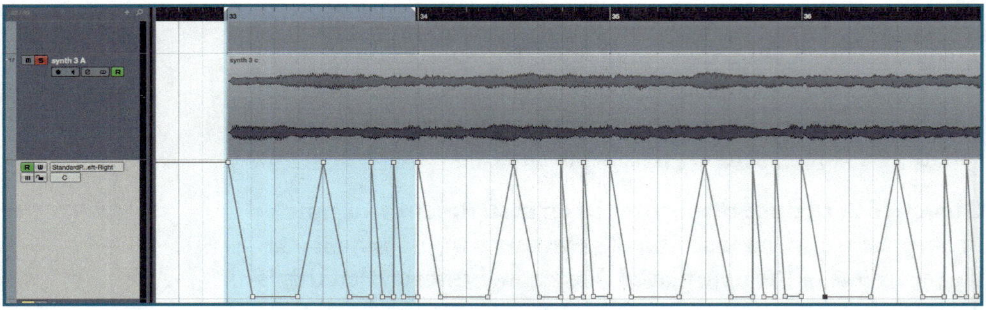

In this example, the panning of this synth track is automated using a repetitive pattern in order to move it within the stereo image in time with the song's rhythm.

amplitude of each movement and allows the programming of complex or irregular fluctuations. Thus, although the pattern is repetitive, its values remain malleable—something plug-ins do not offer.

6.2.3 RECOMMENDATIONS

Avoid automating plug-ins

As mentioned, everything can be automated, including the parameters of any plug-in used in the mix. Even if the concept is very attractive at first glance, automating plug-in settings complicates their manipulation during mixing.

Suppose you put a compressor on a vocal track. You find a plug-in that works perfectly and you set it for the first verse. Once you reach the chorus, you notice that the intensity of the vocal performance is restricted by your current setting. You decide to automate an increase of the threshold value.

Then comes the second verse. The performance becomes more intimate and, as a result, its level is no longer sufficient to be properly compressed. So you program a new threshold move.

Next you add an equalizer. Unfortunately, since the singer was closer to the microphone during the verses than during the choruses, the low frequencies demand your attention. No problem! You automate two bands on your equalizer and the job is done!

You can probably see where I'm going with this, can't you? If automation is used without restraint, you quickly end up facing an incredible number of automation lanes. Since mixing is rarely a linear process, there is a strong likelihood that settings will need to be revised along the way. In the previous example, if you want to revise the EQ, you necessarily have to modify the automation. It would have been far simpler to create two distinct vocal tracks: one for the verses and one for the choruses. Not only would you have avoided having to adjust the compressor and equalizer through automation, but you would also have had the option of using a processing chain better suited to the work required in the choruses.

Another important point: not all plug-ins respond to automation in the same way. With parametric EQs, for example, changing the gain of a band often generates three automation lanes: one for the band gain, one for the affected frequency, and one for its Q. Worse still, some will create automation for each plug-in parameter even if you modify only one. The placement of these automation data can also be relatively arbitrary, which complicates both locating and editing it. Not to mention that, in some cases, the value displayed in the automation lane uses a different scale than the parameter you touched. You then have to keep the plug-in window open to establish the relationship between the two values yourself.

Plug-in automation should be used only in exceptional cases.

Another drawback is that plug-in automation, unlike faders, sends, or panning, is not visible in the mixer. It becomes very difficult to know exactly where the changes you hear are coming from, unless you keep automated plug-ins on screen.

For all these reasons, plug-in automation should be reserved for exceptional cases, when it is the only option available.

Do automation at the end of the mix

It is generally counterproductive to begin automation as long as the role and settings of the mix elements are not clearly established. Indeed, It's much simpler to adjust parameters freely than to keep revisiting and rewriting automation that was done too early.

That is why automation is generally one of the last stages of mixing. You need a sufficiently clear overview to assess whether it makes sense to add motion to mix elements, to stabilize an instrument's level, or to clarify the song's overall structure. It is only at the end that you have the necessary distance to get the most out of what automation has to offer.

6.3 Meters

Whether on mixing consoles, DAWs, processing tools, plug-ins, or audio interfaces, there is always at least one component used to visually assess signal level.

Meters come in various forms. Their display, their calibration, and especially their response time determine how they measure level and, consequently, define the kind of help they can provide in mixing.

6.3.1 THE UNITS USED

Before looking at this more closely, it is important to understand that we do not measure level in the same way in digital audio as in analog audio.

In digital audio, the level scale covers the available range before clipping. The unit used is dBFS (dB full scale). Thus, a reading of 0 dBFS represents the maximum level you can reach without compromising signal integrity.

In analog audio, meters evaluate a signal's level based on the voltage it generates. In that case, the unit used is dBu. Although the correspondence between dBu and dBFS depends on the device's calibration and response time, a reading of 0 dBu on an analog meter generally corresponds to −18 dBFS.

6.3.2 THE RMS METER

The RMS (Root Mean Scale) meter determines a signal's level by measuring its voltage. It generally uses a response time around 300 ms. This relatively slow speed prevents it from reproducing in real time the level fluctuations produced by fast attacks and transients. That is, in fact, its main quality. Its analysis over an extended time window makes it possible to evaluate the level of a track or a mix more generally. The RMS meter therefore provides valuable indications about perceived loudness and dynamic range.

The RMS meter provides clues about a mix's perceived loudness.

Most RMS meters are calibrated so that a reading of 0 dB corresponds to the point where you achieve the best signal-to-noise ratio while keeping enough headroom to avoid saturation. A snare hit, for example, can easily reach −5 dBFS on a peak meter while still showing 0 dB on the RMS meter.

We also know that, in an analog context, a signal's rendering varies with how hard the devices are being driven. The RMS zero therefore indicates the approximate level where saturation begins to color the signal. The excess portion (in red) makes it possible, in a sense, to visualize the amount of saturation being applied. That is why it is not unusual to intentionally exceed zero to take advantage of analog saturation.

6.3.3 THE PEAK OR PPM METER

Unlike analog audio, a digital signal's characteristics do not vary with level. The rendering of the same signal does not change, whether its peak level is −3 dB or −20 dB. The uniform response of digital therefore reduces the relevance of RMS meters, at least as far as signal-to-noise ratio is concerned.

Moreover, as we mentioned in a previous chapter, digital audio is constrained by an absolute ceiling, beyond which the signal clips. What matters most, then, is whether the level exceeds that critical point. Needless to say, the average level displayed by an RMS meter is of no use in that respect.

The peak meter informs us about a signal's maximum level.

That is why DAWs use PPM (Peak Program Meter) displays, more commonly called peak meters.

The very fast reaction time of a peak meter lets it display a signal's maximum level. The traditional needle of an RMS meter is often replaced by a more or less extended series of colored LEDs: green at the bottom of the scale, yellow in the middle zone, orange just before zero, and red beyond it. In addition, one or two extra LEDs at the top of the scale light up as soon as the level exceeds the absolute ceiling. To ensure the user has acknowledged the warning, manual intervention is required to turn them off.

The highest value reached by the signal is often displayed at the bottom of the meter. That number remains unchanged until a higher peak replaces it. You can manually reset this value to identify the loudest peak in a section of the piece.

Many peak meters offer a function called Hold. When activated, the LED representing the maximum value remains lit momentarily.

6.3.4 RECOMMENDATIONS

Consider RMS meters as a validation tool

As you have seen, a meter's reading is not only a matter of level, but also a matter of time and calibration. For example, a reading of −15 dB RMS at 300 ms can become −10 dB RMS at 150 ms. Likewise, if the meter's zero is calibrated to −20 dB instead of −18 dB, all readings will be 2 dB lower.

Many plug-ins—especially those emulating physical devices—include analog-style RMS meters used to assess either input or output level. In general, you can assume they behave like traditional analog meters. However, it is often difficult to know their exact calibration, which undermines their reliability when it comes to interpreting level.

Note that most level meters—whether RMS or peak—use a scale that often mirrors the fader markings.

Knowing this, it becomes clear that it is preferable to adopt a single RMS meter for level measurements. Strictly speaking, its exact calibration matters less, as long as it remains consistent. With time, you will learn to relate what it displays to what you hear. The RMS meter then becomes an excellent validation tool.

Experiment with an RMS meter on the digital output bus

Peak meters, although very practical for ensuring we do not exceed digital zero, tell us very little about perceived loudness and a mix's dynamic range. That is why an RMS meter is a much more interesting indicator for evaluating level on the output bus. By keeping a needle dancing around zero on the meter (a value often calibrated to −18 dBFS), you ensure you are not crushing the mix's dynamic range. You preserve maximum impact and greatly facilitate the work of the mastering engineer who will finalize the project.

6.3.5 OTHER LOUDNESS MEASUREMENT TOOLS

Over the years, other measurement devices have been added alongside RMS and peak meters. Most of these tools were created to better meet the technical specifications of various distribution and broadcast media. Even if mastering is not the subject of this book, it is still appropriate to briefly review these tools and to have an idea of how they work and what they are used for.

True Peak Meter

As mentioned, the peak meter warns us when level exceeds 0 dBFS. Even if its very fast reaction time (generally around 50 ms) usually allows it to do this job successfully, it can occasionally happen that particularly fast peaks escape its attention. These overs can compromise audio playback and distribution.

The True Peak Meter was created precisely to ensure that the signal never exceeds digital zero. Its response time, generally around 5 ms, allows it to identify every occurrence of an over, even when it happens between two samples.

The LUFS unit

First, a bit of history. As early as the mid-1980s, key players in the music industry assumed that the louder a musical piece was, the more it would stand out from competitors and thus capture the listener's attention. Of course, they expected this added attention to automatically translate into dollars.

The idea spread like wildfire. Very quickly, the loudness of audio material—across all media—became higher and higher. The most sought-after mastering engineers were the ones who could squeeze the most decibels out of an audio file. Even musicians and producers joined in, shuddering in horror when their song sounded lower in level than the one next door.

In the early 2000s, the industry reached the peak of what is called the loudness war. Thanks to new compression technologies, loudness was pushed to the maximum on all distribution platforms. That was the era when advertisers seemed ready to tear your TV speakers apart just to be sure they were heard!

Any medium, analog or digital, has limits. Pursuing maximum loudness at all costs therefore comes at the expense of dynamic range and sonic integrity. Not to mention that constantly high loudness is exhausting for the listener's ear.

Around the same time, the International Telecommunication Union (ITU) addressed this noisy reality in order to find an effective way to measure the average loudness of an audio production and to suggest guidelines for optimal broadcast loudness.

It was in this atmosphere that the LUFS (Loudness Unit Full Scale) unit was created.

In the early 2010s, major broadcasting organizations adopted the standards proposed by the ITU. However, the music industry, not being directly targeted by these recommendations, was much slower to follow suit. In fact, it was only around 2015 that the main streaming platforms (YouTube, Spotify, Apple, and others) established standards for the loudness of the audio material they distribute. Based on LUFS measurement, the standards primarily aim to guarantee the listener a uniform average loudness even when moving from one piece to another. Thus, when a track's level exceeds the prescribed LUFS value, its loudness is automatically reduced. In the opposite case, it is increased until it reaches the standard. Although the LUFS standard varies from one platform to another, it generally sits around −14 LUFS.

There is no point in pushing a mix's final loudness excessively, since it will lose impact during playback.

The establishment of these standards has an increasingly audible impact on the loudness of music productions and, consequently, on mastering techniques. It is now pointless to push the final product's loudness excessively, since it will eventually be reduced during playback—and the dynamic range sacrificed in favor of a higher level will, for its part, be lost. In the end, excessive overshooting of the prescribed standards is, in a way, penalized by a piece that clearly lacks impact.

A simple way to understand the new unit is to see it as an RMS reading whose analysis time extends over the entire duration of the audio program (a narration, a video, a song, or even an entire album). To simplify interpretation, you can also think of LUFS as, roughly, the equivalent of dBFS. For example, a song that reads −11 LUFS has an average loudness of −11 dBFS. Note also that LKFS (Loudness, K-weighted to Full Scale) has exactly the same value as LUFS.

The different readings displayed by a LUFS meter.

LUFS meters often provide several types of readings. The long-term measure (called Long Term Loudness or Integrated Loudness) represents the overall average loudness of the analyzed piece. This is the most interesting reading, since it tells you whether the audio material meets the broadcast medium's standards.

There are also measurements over shorter periods. Momentary Loudness has a response time comparable to a classic RMS meter. Short Term Loudness responds more slowly and provides a loudness interpretation that sits somewhere between long-term and momentary readings. Range represents the difference between the softest passage and the loudest passage in the analyzed material. Most LUFS meters also include a True Peak Meter, discussed above.

Unlike RMS readings, LUFS measurement applies filters to the material before analysis in order to model the ear's non-linear frequency response. The LUFS meter therefore offers the most faithful representation of perceived loudness. That is why this way of measuring audio power is increasingly common in the world of audio production.

7

FREQUENCY PROCESSING TOOLS

We have all, at one time or another, adjusted the proportion of lows or highs by turning the bass or treble knobs on a hi-fi system. The basic principle of a frequency equalizer is therefore no secret to anyone: it allows you to increase or decrease the level of one or more frequencies within a signal.

Using an equalizer is one of the core skills to master in order to succeed in mixing.

Often, the simplest concepts are also the most powerful. The frequency equalizer is a prime example. Behind the disarming simplicity of how it works lies an essential tool for sculpting the frequency spectrum of a mix. No wonder using an equalizer is one of the core skills to master in order to succeed in mixing.

7.1 Frequency Spectrum Characteristics

Before going deeper into how equalizers (EQs, for short) works and into equalization techniques, we should define its domain of action: the frequency spectrum.

7.1.1 ITS RANGE

As we noted in Chapter 5, the human ear theoretically perceives frequencies from 20 to 20,000 Hz. This range is where equalizers operate. In fact, most of them offer no controls that exceed the limits of the audible spectrum.

7.1.2 ITS DIRECT LINK TO PITCH

Those of you who are musicians already know about "A 440," the standard pitch used to tune acoustic instruments. The "440" in question is actually a frequency value. By generating a waveform oscillating at 440 Hz, we obtain the note A.

Frequencies are more than mere numbers; they have a direct link to pitch.

Frequencies are therefore much more than mere numbers; they have a direct link to pitch. Each note of the scale corresponds to a frequency value across the ten octaves covered by the audible spectrum.

This makes it easy to locate the range of fundamental frequencies covered by any instrument's register. A standard bass guitar, for instance, can produce all notes between E1 and D#3. We therefore know that all bass fundamentals fall between 41 and 156 Hz.

Even without getting into harmonic theory, a bass note, of course, contains other frequencies that shape its timbre. However, it is possible to establish an instrument's lower frequency limit and to convert any of its notes into hertz—two pieces of information that, as we will see later, can help when equalizing.

NOTE-TO-FREQUENCY CONVERSION TABLE

Notes	Octaves 0	1	2	3	4
C	16	33	65	131	262
D♭	17	35	69	139	277
D	18	37	73	147	294
E♭	19	39	78	156	311
E	21	41	82	165	330
F	22	44	87	175	349
G♭	23	46	92	185	370
G	24	49	98	196	392
A♭	26	52	104	208	415
A	28	55	110	220	440
B♭	29	58	117	233	466
B	31	62	123	247	494

Frequency values, expressed in hertz, are rounded to the nearest whole number.

Standard Piano Keyboard

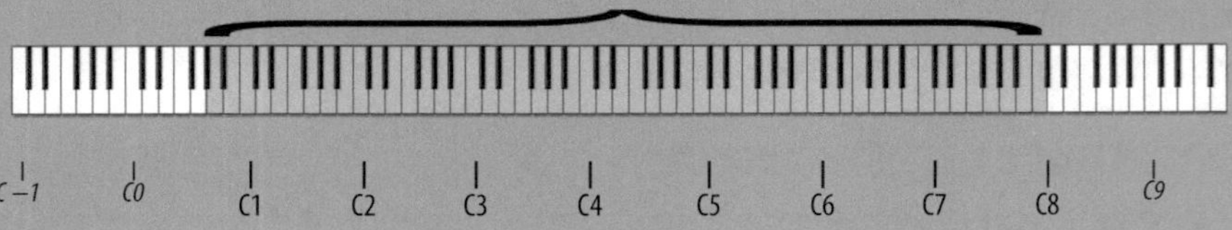

7.1.3 ITS NON-LINEARITY

By looking at a note-to-frequency conversion chart, we can see that doubling a given frequency yields the octave above that note. To return to the A 440 example, generating 880 Hz gives an A one octave higher. We can of course continue this sequence upward (1,760 Hz, 3,520 Hz, 7,040 Hz…) as well as downward (220 Hz, 110 Hz, 55 Hz, etc.).

The distribution of the frequency spectrum is therefore not linear. As a result, boosting a 300 Hz-wide band has proportionally far more impact in the low frequencies than in the highs, since it affects a greater number of fundamentals. Consequently, the frequency chosen during equalization—and the width of its action—affects a signal's pitch more directly in the lows than in the highs.

7.1.4 ITS SUBJECTIVE DIVISIONS

Musicians and audio engineers use countless qualifiers to describe sound: "the mix is muddy," "the guitars are powerful," "the piano is nasal," and so on. While it is always difficult to explain sound with words, these qualifiers are not arbitrary. Certain parts of the frequency spectrum are intuitively associated with emotions and qualities.

Much like pitch, the frequency region associated with a given attribute shifts from one instrument to another. For example, if we want to add presence to a bass, we will likely focus around 1,500 Hz. In the case of an electric guitar, we would instead target around 5 kHz. Each instrument type therefore has a set of sensitive regions, and knowing them is a major asset when equalizing.

The chart titled "Sensitive Zones by Instrument" can serve as a guide for qualifying the frequency regions of several instruments. This makes it possible to approach equalization not only in technical terms, but also in terms of the sonic and emotional character of an instrument's frequency signature.

Any change we make to one part of the frequency spectrum will have the opposite effect on its opposing part.

7.1.5 ITS RECIPROCITY

A signal's frequency spectrum works somewhat like a balance: raising one side lowers the other. Thus, increasing a signal's overall low frequencies yields a listening result similar to decreasing its overall highs. In short, any change we make to one part of the frequency spectrum will have the opposite effect on its opposing part.

This principle applies both to the spectrum as a whole and to its different regions. For example, it is just as possible to make a signal clearer by reducing 300 Hz as it is by boosting 5 kHz.

Although this reciprocity is not exact, given how an equalizer actually works, it remains a key concept in equalization.

7.2 Filter Types

Essentially, an equalizer increases or decreases a frequency re-

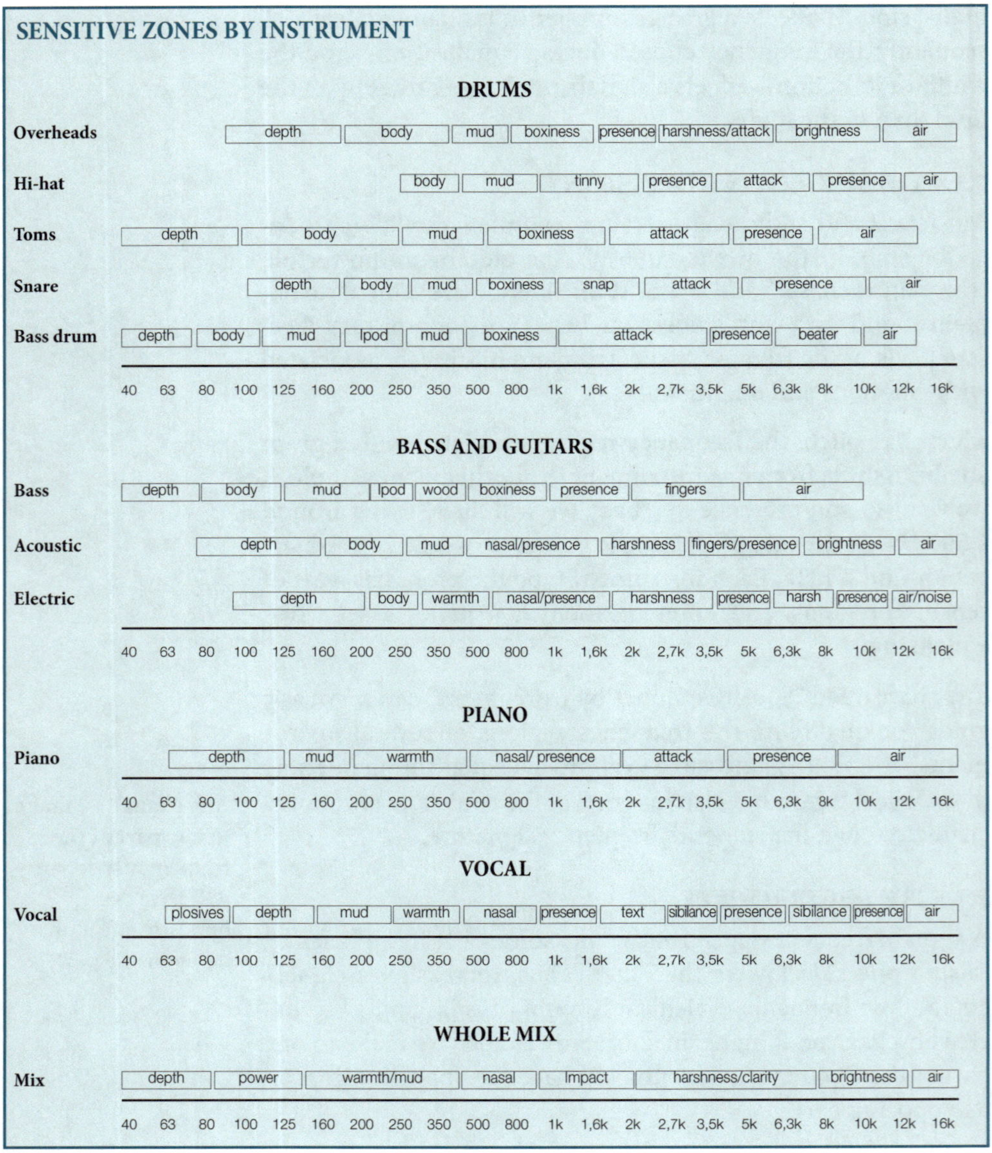

gion by applying a filter. The type of filter determines how the equalizer will act on the signal.

Filter types can be grouped into three major families: cut filters (high-cut/low-pass and low-cut/high-pass), shelf filters, and bell filters.

Filter Types and Their Common Symbols

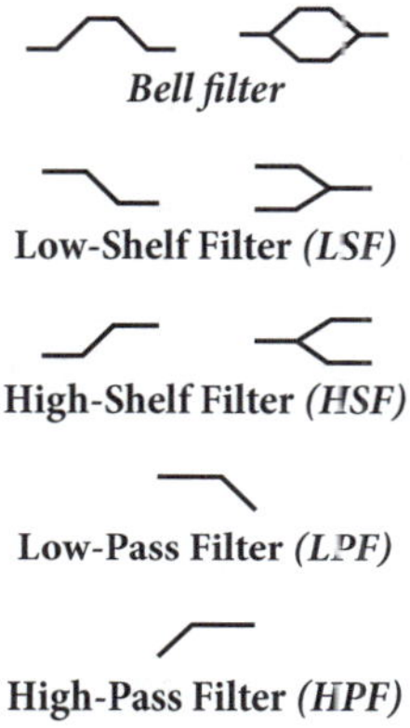

7.2.1 CUT FILTERS (HPF/LPF)

Cut filters are applied at the extremes of the spectrum in order to reduce the level of an entire section of the signal starting at a given frequency, known as the corner frequency.

Depending on the device, this type of filter may have different names. When it affects low frequencies, it is called a High-Pass Filter (HPF) or Low-Cut Filter (LCF). Regardless of what we call it, this filter modifies all frequencies below the chosen corner frequency.

When it affects high frequencies, it is called a Low-Pass Filter (LPF) or High-Cut Filter (HCF). It cuts frequencies above the selected frequency.

Slope

To make their action less abrupt, cut filters progressively reduce the chosen frequency region through a curve called the slope. This slope is defined in decibels per octave. For example, with an HPF set to a 12 dB-per-octave slope, the amplitude will progressively decrease from the corner frequency, reaching 12 dB less one octave lower, 24 dB less two octaves lower, and so on.

Obviously, the higher the slope value in dB, the faster the frequencies are affected.

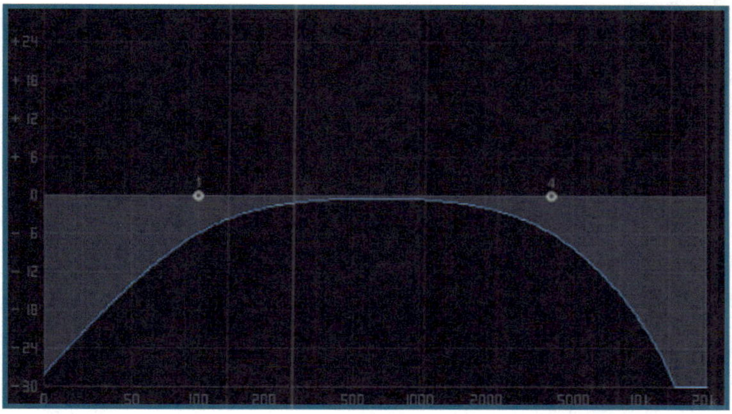

Cut filters are found at the ends of the frequency spectrum.

Using a High-Pass Filter (HPF)

This filter is primarily used to remove low frequencies that are not useful to the mix (microphone handling noise, air-conditioning rumble, electrical hum, and so on). It also makes it possible to define the lower limit of a signal's frequency spectrum. We will return to this in detail a bit later.

Notes on Cut and Shelf Filters

On most equalizers, the affected frequency region starts slightly before the selected frequency. For a cut filter, for example, the displayed frequency is usually where the signal is attenuated by 3 dB, which implies that the reduction begins before that frequency. This offset is also present on shelf filters.

Using a Low-Pass Filter (LPF)

The LPF performs the same cleanup work as the HPF, but in the upper part of the spectrum. It is useful for reducing hiss generated by analog devices (tape machine, amplifier, outboard processing module, and so on). It also helps reduce masking. For example, the high frequencies of a hand percussion track can interfere with those of a hi-hat. We can therefore remove some high frequencies from one or the other to resolve the conflict. The same is true for reverb and echo effects, whose high frequencies can mask the original signal.

The LPF is also useful for adding warmth to an instrument. This approach is particularly effective for attenuating the high frequencies of distorted instruments such as electric guitar. You can thus reduce the harsh frequencies associated with that type of signal and give the instrument more body.

7.2.2 SHELF FILTERS (HSF/LSF)

Unlike cut filters, which only allow attenuation, shelf filters let you boost or cut a region and set the amount of change. They apply at the extremes of the spectrum.

With a low-shelf filter, all frequencies below the chosen frequency are modified. With a high-shelf filter, it is the frequencies above the selected frequency.

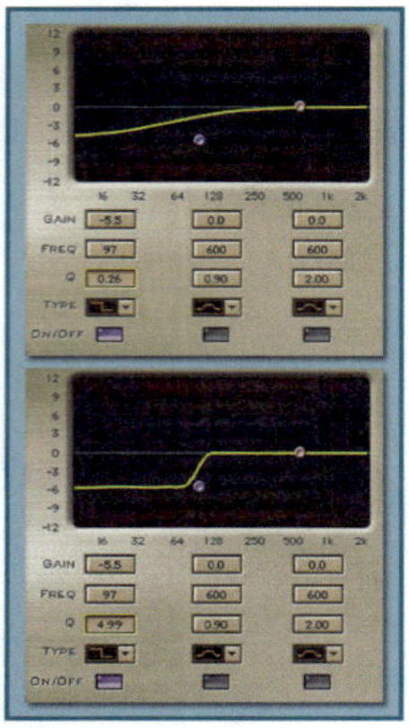

Some equalizers allow you to adjust the slope of shelf and cut filters using the Q parameter.

Slope

Shelf filters also use a slope to ensure the transition between the selected frequency and the modified region. Because slope is closely tied to the amplitude of the modified region, it is rarely expressed per octave. When slope is adjustable, its control is displayed as a percentage or a related scale (though some EQ models use rather esoteric scales!).

Using Shelf Filters

Since shelf filters are very common on consumer audio devices, most of us already know how they work. Instinctively, we can anticipate their effect. Their wide range of action allows quick corrections to a signal's frequency distribution. In addition, their progressive action makes them more transparent than other filter types.

Shelf filters are therefore the ideal tool for sketching broad-strokes EQ moves at the beginning of a mix. Their predictability helps you move quickly, without getting bogged down in unnecessary details. Do not be fooled by their apparent lack of precision: this type of equalization is often all that many tracks in a project will need.

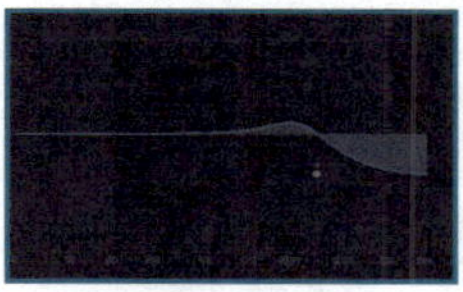

Resonant Filters

Rather than modifying the frequency progressively, resonance is introduced following the selected frequency. This type of filter often produces more musical results than standard filters.

When applying a shelf filter, as with a cut filter, pay attention to what happens when you move the corner frequency. Also listen to how the slope changes the sound. The two go hand in hand, even more so when using a resonant filter. It is often easier to set the corner frequency first, then choose the slope that best suits what you are trying to achieve.

7.2.3 BELL FILTERS

Unlike the previous filters, which only apply at the extremes, the bell filter lets you modify frequencies anywhere in the spectrum. You can adjust the amplitude at a center frequency as well as the spread of its action on either side of it.

Controls

The frequency parameter determines the center frequency to be modified. How you set that frequency depends on the device. Some offer a stepped switch that lets you choose from a range of predetermined frequencies, typically associated with analog devices. Digital EQs, for their part, allow you to sweep the spectrum and select the center frequency precisely.

The bell filter's high precision makes it an excellent corrective tool.

The Q parameter defines the width of the frequency region affected by the equalization. Visually, it widens or narrows the

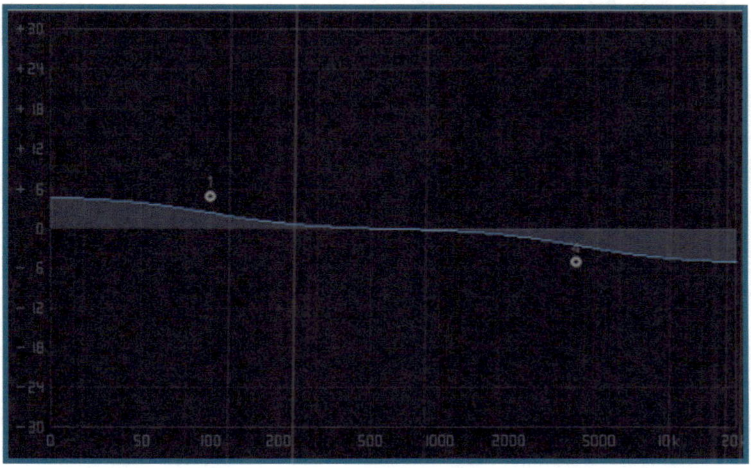

At the beginning of a mix, the shelf filter is the ideal tool for sketching broad-strokes EQ moves.

bell's shape on either side of the center frequency. It therefore provides the flexibility needed to modify a wide band or to apply more targeted corrections.

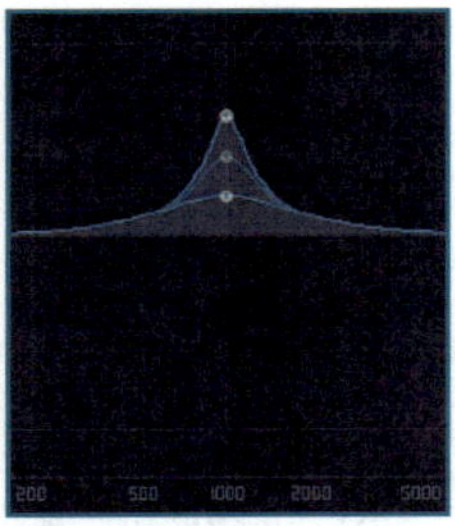

On some equalizers, the width of the affected frequency band (Q) decreases as you increase gain. This characteristic, called proportional Q, allows the equalizer to be precise for major corrections and transparent for more aesthetic changes.

Using Bell Filters

The bell filter's high precision gives it the ability to modify a narrow region of the spectrum without altering the rest of the signal, making it an excellent corrective tool. It can also counter masking by focusing only on competing frequencies while preserving the instruments' sonic signatures.

A bell filter can also significantly reshape a signal's frequency spectrum. It is therefore useful for creating many effects that require drastic modification of the original signal.

7.3 Equalizer Families

Frequency equalizers come in various forms. Their controls and how they affect the sound vary depending on the application they were designed for. It is through the organization of their filters that the four major families of equalizers are distinguished.

7.3.1 GRAPHIC EQUALIZER

Graphic equalizers divide the frequency spectrum into several sections called bands. Each band lets you increase or decrease the level of the corresponding frequency region.

Its name comes from the bands' horizontal layout on the device, which displays the applied corrections as a graph.

Graphic EQ is typically used in live sound to deal with a venue's acoustic characteristics. It is particularly useful for quickly identifying and correcting feedback.

The most common professional models divide the spectrum into third-octave bands, making it possible to adjust 30 or 31 bands.

Graphic EQs are rarely used in mixing, as engineers often prefer models with more flexible controls. They remain an excellent learning tool for becoming familiar with the effect of equalization and for developing your ability to translate a signal's spectral characteristics into technical terms. A common exercise is to boost or cut a band and then, blindly, try to identify which frequency was changed.

7.3.2 PARAMETRIC EQUALIZER

The parametric equalizer is based on bell filters. For each band, you can select a center frequency, define the width of the band being processed (Q), and set the amount of correction. Many also offer different filter options.

The parametric equalizer lets you choose a center frequency, define the processed band's width (Q), and set the amount of correction (gain).

They also include cut and shelf filters to handle the extremes of the spectrum. Digital versions of these EQs often allow you to visualize the location, amplitude, and width of the modification. Some even display a frequency analyzer in the background.

The precision and flexibility of the parametric equalizer make it the most common tool for shaping the frequency spectrum in mixing.

7.3.3 SEMIPARAMETRIC EQUALIZER

A semiparametric equalizer is essentially a simplified version of a parametric EQ. As a rule, the Q of bell filters and the slope of shelf and cut filters are preset on the device and cannot be adjusted.

This type of equalizer is very common in both consumer and professional audio. The EQ on a hi-fi system (its bass and treble knobs) is a familiar example. The same is true of tone controls on most guitar amplifiers, microphone preamps, and many analog live-sound consoles.

The semiparametric equalizer often adds a particular color to the sound.

Although they do not offer the precision of a parametric EQ, these devices are very useful in mixing for quickly applying corrections to a signal.

Another major strength of this type of device is the particular color it brings to the sound. Analog devices from different brands—and their plug-in emulations—have filtering characteristics and electrical components of their own. As a result, the same treatment on two different EQ models will not sound identical, even if their settings match. In fact, few experienced engineers fail to develop, over the years, an affinity between certain EQ models and specific tasks.

7.3.4 DYNAMIC EQUALIZER

A dynamic equalizer is laid out like a parametric EQ. However, instead of using a fixed boost or cut, the amplitude of its action varies according to the signal's dynamics.

A good way to think about dynamic EQ is as a de-esser you can place anywhere in the spectrum. Since its operating principle is based on dynamics, we will discuss this tool in the chapter devoted to dynamic processing tools.

7.4 Equalization Objectives

Now that the frequency spectrum has revealed several of its secrets, and now that we know the filter types and EQ families, let's look at the six main objectives that justify using equalization.

Objective 1: Reduce noise floor

Equalization can very often reduce—or even eliminate—noise floor, especially when it sits at the extremes of the spectrum.

In the highs, an LPF can easily reduce the hiss of a tape machine or analog device, the whine of a guitar amp, or electrical crackle. In the lows, an HPF will quickly deal with ambient noises that creep into that part of the spectrum.

Objective 2: Reduce resonances

Solo can help you identify suspicious frequencies. The mix is where you can best judge whether they really need attention, and by how much.

Whether it is the piercing frequencies of an electric guitar, the muddiness of a bass, or the nasal quality of a vocal recording, it is very common to detect one or more unpleasant frequencies in a signal that are not useful to the mix. While these resonances may come from the microphone used or the room's acoustics, they often originate directly from the source.

Instruments of the same type generally present resonances in similar places. The sensitive-zones chart by instrument can serve as a guide for locating regions likely to cause problems.

An effective method for reducing resonances is to use a bell filter with a very narrow Q. Apply a strong gain and slowly sweep the area until the resonance becomes clearly audible. Typically, it will be a frequency that seems constantly present in the

PASSIVE EQ OR ACTIVE EQ

Technically, the difference between passive and active EQs is mainly in how the signal is processed.

The filtering circuits of passive EQs contain no amplifier. They can therefore only subtract elements from the signal. The amplifier is instead placed after the filtering section and boosts the overall output level afterward. Thus, when you "boost" a frequency on a passive EQ, you are actually reducing how much that frequency is being subtracted from the overall signal.

Active EQs, on the other hand, use amplified filtering circuits Introducing an amplification loop makes it possible to boost selected frequencies.

Many consider passive EQs more musical and natural because they only amplify at the output, thereby eliminating potential phase issues often blamed on lower-quality active designs.

sound, regardless of the note being played. Then reduce the gain until the problematic frequency is attenuated. If needed, widen the affected area by increasing the Q value.

Note that this approach has limits. When you sweep the spectrum by aggressively boosting a narrow band, all frequencies become unpleasant—especially if you do this with the solo button engaged. Without discernment, you can quickly punch holes in the signal and turn it into Swiss cheese. Solo can help you spot suspicious frequencies. But it's easier to decide whether to act, and how much, in the context of the mix.

Objective 3: Counter masking

As soon as several instruments are heard simultaneously, their frequencies overlap. Sometimes they will complement one another; other times, they will interfere.

For example, if guitars have a lot of energy around 5 kHz, it is very likely that the lead vocal will seem weak in that region. Similarly, a hand percussion with a lot of 10 kHz can make a hi-hat sound dull and distant. This overlap is called masking, and it is undoubtedly one of mixing's main challenges.

Fortunately, a frequency equalizer makes it possible to sculpt the spectra of competing signals in order to distinguish instruments more clearly. Managing masking issues is an exercise in compromise. When two elements compete, you must determine which frequency regions of one signal can be sacrificed to make the other audible—and vice versa.

Managing masking is undoubtedly one of mixing's main challenges.

A common mistake is to boost the "missing" region of the masked signal. Returning to the hand percussion masking a hi-hat: assuming both elements are equally important in the song, our first reflex is to boost 10 kHz on the hi-hat track. The hi-hat will indeed become clearer, but the percussion will lose definition. Moreover, that boost will likely affect more important instruments (such as the vocal or an acoustic guitar). We will then be tempted to boost the same region on those instruments too.

You do not have to be a prophet to see the vicious circle that follows: we will hop from track to track boosting high frequencies without actually solving the problem. To avoid this escalation, mirror equalization is often called for. Apply a slight boost in a region on one instrument while cutting that same region on the competing instrument.

A soloed track's sound ultimately does not matter if it blends with the rest of the mix.

In a dense mix, managing masking may sometimes require outright removing wide frequency bands in order to create a slot for each instrument. Of course, in this kind of procedure, the instrument may sound deficient when listened to in solo—but remember that a mix is much more than the sum of its parts. A soloed track's sound ultimately does not matter if it blends with the rest of the mix.

Objective 4: Clean up low frequencies

Low frequencies have the particularity of occupying a large portion of a mix's dynamic headroom. It is therefore common practice to remove excess low frequency from each track with an HPF.

This will of course target superfluous noises: an HPF will remove ventilation rumble or hum caused by a faulty electrical installation (typically around 50 Hz in Europe and 60 Hz in North America). It will also counter the excess low end created by the proximity effect when recording at very close range.

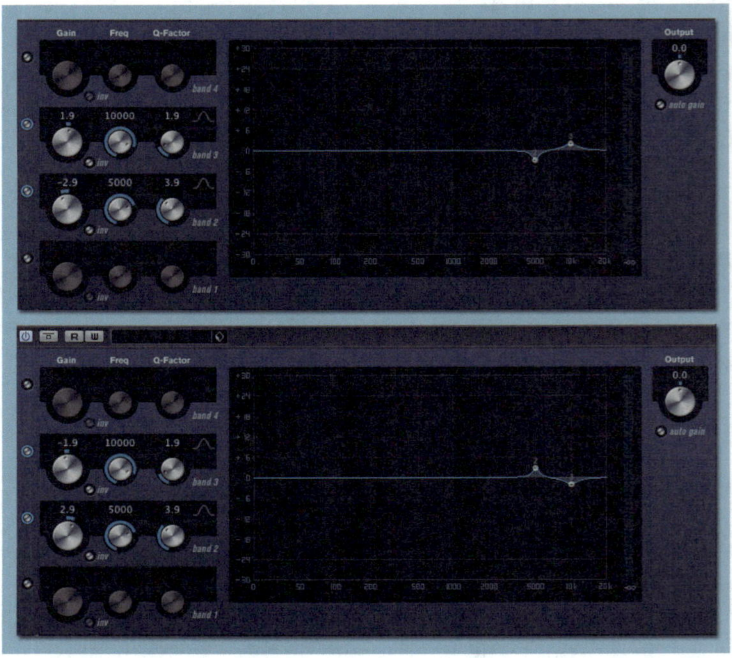

An example of mirror equalization. Here, the 5 kHz region is reduced on one track and boosted on the other. The same mirror treatment is applied to these tracks around 10 kHz.

On vocal tracks, the HPF is useful for reducing plosives (the burst of air the microphone captures when a singer pronounces certain consonants—"p" and "b," for example) or noises from handling the microphone. Of course, if these noises overlap the instrument's useful frequencies, it can be preferable to use a shelf filter to attenuate them without changing the instrument's timbre too much.

Beyond cleanup, the HPF has the advantage of adding clarity in the low frequencies. The buildup of unnecessary low frequencies produces a result similar to masking. It is therefore appropriate to reserve low frequencies for instruments that play an important role there by placing an HPF on all tracks whose contribution in the lows is not essential to the mix.

In our discussion of the spectrum's characteristics, we established that it is possible to express an instrument's lower limit in terms of frequency, based on its register. That lower limit is often a good starting point for setting the HPF frequency. The final adjustment is made by listening to the full mix. The method consists of raising the cutoff frequency until the instrument's timbre is affected, then lowering it slightly.

The HPF has an almost magical effect on a mix's low-frequency clarity.

The HPF has an almost magical effect on a mix's low-frequency clarity. By removing excess low end from all tracks, it creates space for the instruments associated with that region (typically bass and kick drum). It also frees dynamic headroom from useless frequencies, giving the mix more power.

It is often said that applying an HPF to an instrument that plays a predominant role in the low frequencies—such as bass or kick drum—is sacrilege. However, there are no absolutes in mixing. This filter can very well be used on those instruments to counter masking and to define the space each one occupies. Moreover, these tracks are just as likely as any other to contain excess low frequencies. Rules that rigid should never override your judgment and your ear.

Objective 5: Move an element closer to or farther from the listener

In everyday life, the frequencies present in a signal give the brain clues about its position in the environment. For example, a train passing half a mile away will not sound the same as it does nearby. The way air filters frequencies helps our brain interpret distance.

A source will feel closer to the listener if its low and high frequencies are well defined.

Obviously, in stereo playback, the loudspeakers are always the same distance from the listener. Depth and ambience are illusions created during recording and mixing. The brain's ability to locate a source based on its frequency signature can help us create that sense of depth.

In principle, a source will feel closer to the listener if its low and high-frequency content is well defined. By shaping the extremes of the spectrum, we can therefore suggest a source's relative position. Boosting the extremes creates an illusion of proximity; cutting them creates an illusion of distance.

Shelf filters are very effective for shaping this illusion. For example, it is common to boost the extremes of a lead vocal track to bring it closer to the listener. Reducing the extremes on vocal harmonies can help push them farther back.

TABLE OF LOWER LIMITS BY INSTRUMENT

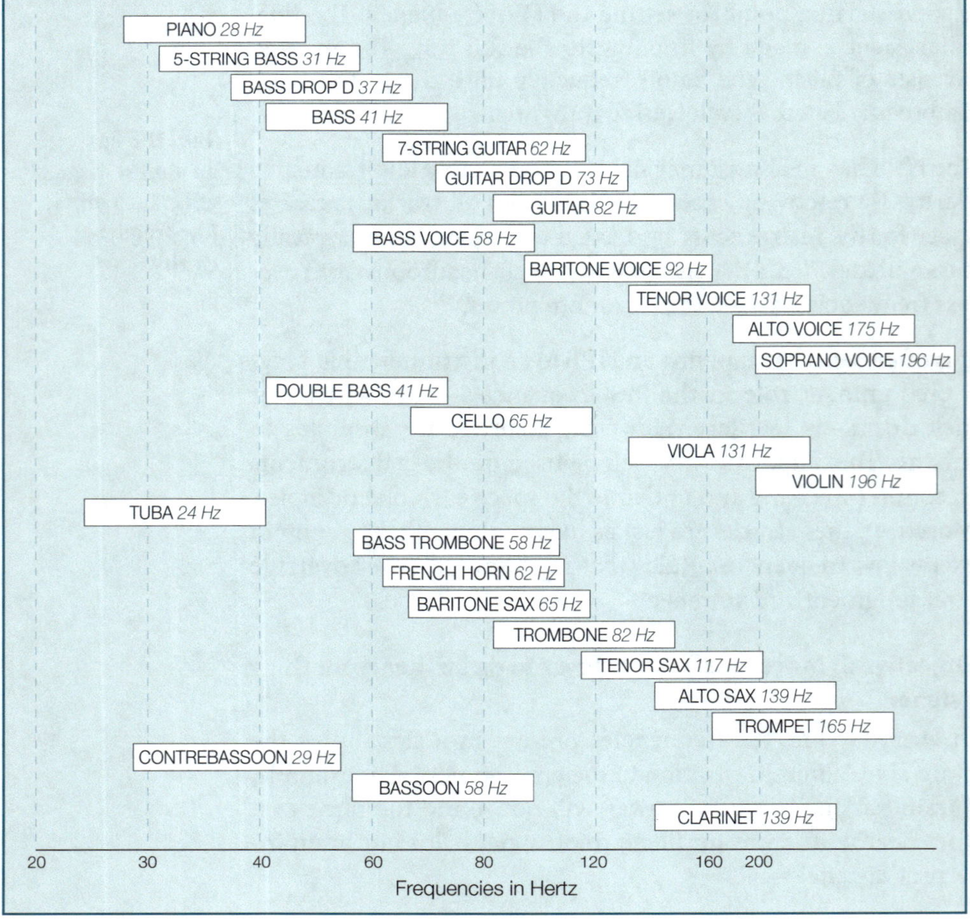

Cut filters can also be useful for moving a source farther away. They also have the advantage of restricting the range of audible frequencies in a signal and, by extension, reducing masking. For example, an ambient synthesizer (a pad) generally does not need to sit close to the listener. We can of course assign reverb to push it back. However, by applying cut filters to the extremes of its spectrum, we can push it back while also reducing the amount of frequencies likely to cause masking.

For the same reasons, reverb and echo returns, as well as room mics (such as those used on drums), often benefit from reduced frequencies at the extremes.

Objective 6: Create an effect

Of course, equalization is powerful enough to shape an instrument's timbre as we please, and can therefore be used to create effects. The classic "telephone voice" is an example: the equalizer exaggerates midrange frequencies.

This type of processing is also common on effect returns (such as echo) in order to distinguish their timbre from the original signal.

7.5 Equalization Strategies

Subtract to correct; boost to color

We previously established that the frequency spectrum works somewhat like a balance. In theory, boosting the low frequencies is equivalent to cutting the highs (and vice versa).

However, the way equalizer components actually work means boosts and cuts are not handled the same way. Generally speaking, equalizers are more transparent when subtracting frequencies than when boosting them. We can use this to our advantage.

Generally speaking, equalizers are more transparent when subtracting than when boosting.

Thus, to correct a sound, it is beneficial to favor attenuation. Not only will the correction be more natural, but we will also avoid the escalation problem mentioned earlier.

If, on the contrary, we want to change the timbre of a track or instrument, boosting lets us take advantage of the saturation generated by some equalizers. Indeed, many equalizers—especially analog versions or their digital emulations—are often described as musical because they impart their own color. Using them for boosts often yields a more interesting result than more neutral models.

Subtract narrow; boost wide

An equalizer's effect on frequencies depends on both the gain applied and the width of the band being processed. Gain and Q therefore work together.

When the equalization is corrective, it is recommended to subtract while affecting only a narrow band of the signal. Using a narrow Q value lets us precisely target the frequencies we want to correct without changing those we want to keep. Even with surgical precision, the correction remains fully transparent.

That same narrow setting will generally produce much more colored results when boosting, and that coloration will be proportional to the gain. Thus, when a transparent boost is needed, we will use a lower Q value to affect a wider band. This makes it possible to obtain a more uniform change.

Process tracks in order of importance

One of the best ways to counter masking is to process tracks by priority. Tracks are introduced one by one according to their importance in the song and remain audible throughout the EQ process. The goal is to ensure that introducing a new element—and equalizing it—does not harm what is already in place. This approach simplifies the compromise management inherent to reducing masking.

Equalize in mono

Mono listening is probably one of the best ways to approach equalization.

Mono listening is probably one of the best ways to approach equalization. Mono ignores placement in the stereo image. Thus, even if two competing elements are panned opposite one another (one left, the other right), that separation is of no help in mono. The effects of masking are therefore immediately revealed.

In addition, since we do not know the listener's playback context, this method ensures the mix stays well balanced even

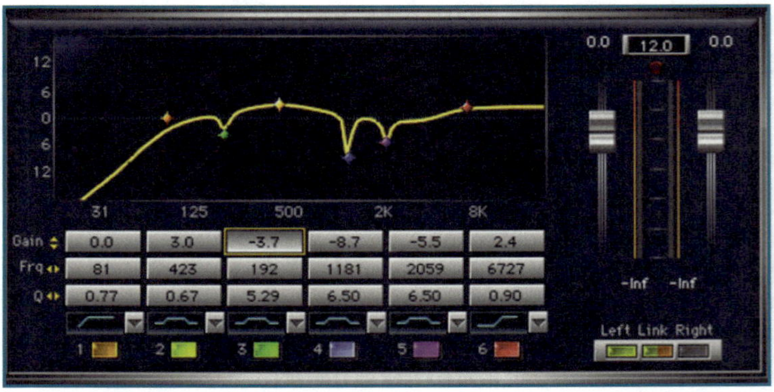

To keep corrections transparent, affect a narrow band when subtracting and a wider band when boosting.

when stereo is compromised (in a car, on a laptop, from a system in another room, and so on).

Adjust a track's EQ while listening to its impact on another track

To prevent secondary tracks from masking more important ones, it is often useful to listen to the effect of our equalization not on the treated track, but on the more important tracks.

Suppose reverb is used on the lead vocal. That reverb may interfere with essential vocal frequencies. Thus, even though the equalizer is affecting the reverb, it is the lead vocal that will guide our decisions. For example, cutting high frequencies on the reverb may suddenly make the lead vocal more intelligible.

This strategy is very effective when processing effects and other supporting elements whose sound can be compromised in favor of more important tracks. Pad synths and ambience recordings are examples.

This technique is generally easier to apply when you isolate the two conflicting elements in solo. The impact of the equalization becomes more audible, making the adjustment easier.

Adjust output level

Frequency moves inevitably cause level changes. If the equalizer has an output control, it is preferable to set it so that the post-EQ level is similar to the track's level without processing. This way, a level difference won't influence your decisions.

Avoid the solo button

One common EQ trap is to spend long minutes refining a track's sound in solo, only to realize it no longer fits with the whole once placed back in context.

In all but rare cases, an equalizer should be adjusted in context.

After reading the previous strategies, it should now be obvious that EQ in solo is often futile and counterproductive. Aside from correcting resonances or noise floor, frequency EQ adjustments should always be made in context to ensure the mix works as a whole.

Eliminate contradictory modifications

As we noted earlier, mixing is rarely a linear process. Some decisions will need to be revisited as you incorporate new sonics into the mix. It is therefore entirely possible to end up with contradictory EQ settings, especially toward the end of a mix.

For example, you cut 300 Hz on a keyboard early in the mix. Near the end, you feel the mix lacks a bit of warmth. You then use a second equalizer to boost the very region you previously cut.

Similarly, you may have boosted or cut the same frequency region more than once. You must then assess whether it is possible to achieve that equalization in one place, so as to reduce the number of processes applied to the signal.

This double equalization—whether contradictory or additive—must also be monitored when using subgroups. For example, if the highs of each track in a subgroup have been boosted, it is often possible to apply that boost only on the subgroup instead.

It is necessary to identify these situations and eliminate them whenever possible. You will reduce the amount of processing applied to the signal while simplifying EQ settings.

7.6 Equalization Limits

Equalization is a powerful tool, but it also has limits.

Obviously, an equalizer cannot modify a frequency that is absent from the signal. Even if this seems self-evident, you can spend long minutes trying to boost a frequency that simply does not exist on the track. When in doubt, a frequency analyzer will allow you to verify whether your fight is hopeless.

If you are facing arrangement problems, equalization will not help much. If an element won't sit in the mix without extensive processing, consider muting that track.The whole must always take precedence over its individual elements.

Equalization is also not a good remedy for phase problems. The amount of EQ required to integrate a well-recorded element into a mix is rarely very large. Thus, if you struggle to obtain a convincing result even after doing a lot of EQ work, it is often appropriate to check whether you are dealing with a phase issue.

Always keep in mind: the more you process a signal, the greater the risk of degrading it.

An equalizer itself can generate phase problems, especially when overused. These effects are even more present when boosting—another argument for favoring correction through attenuation. In digital, excessive equalization can also contribute to degrading very high frequencies, which may make certain mastering steps more difficult. Eliminating contradictory or additive EQ is a good way to reduce processing and therefore preserve the signal from these potential anomalies.

Always keep in mind: the more you process a signal, the greater the risk of degrading it. Equalization is no exception. It is therefore better to approach EQ by aiming for optimal results with a minimal number of interventions.

7.7 The Filter Effect

The sweep effect originates from filter controls found on most analog synthesizers. At its core, it consists of sweeping a track—or an entire mix—with a filter in order to progressively reveal the content of its frequency spectrum. Other effects control the filter's motion using an oscillator or characteristics of the processed signal.

7.7.1 FILTER PLUG-INS AND THEIR CONTROLS

While it is entirely possible to create a filter effect using an equalizer and automation, many plug-ins specialize in producing this type of effect and allow you to shape its details through a more or less extensive set of parameters.

Among these is a selector that lets you choose the filter type used to sweep the spectrum. The most common options are high-pass, band-pass, and low-pass—the latter being by far the most frequently used. Filters for this type of effect are always resonant. You can therefore set how much the region adjacent to the chosen frequency is emphasized using a control called resonance.

Most filter plug-ins include a resonance control that sets how much the frequency region just before the cutoff frequency is boosted.

Very often, you can set how the sweep is performed. You can control it with an LFO offering various waveforms (sine, triangle, random, and so on). It can of course be synced to the track's tempo through a switch.

It is also possible to drive the filter's movement from the envelope of the processed signal. This creates an effect similar to a wah-wah or auto-filter guitar pedal. In that case, the filter's response is shaped by its threshold, attack, and release settings.

As for how the sweep will move across the spectrum, you can of course write automation on one or more plug-in parameters.

7.7.2 OBJECTIVES

Objective 1: Create anticipation and emphasize a drop

By slowly revealing a signal's content, a sweep effect creates a feeling of anticipation. This is why it is often used on an element of the mix to mark the transition into a new section of a song, or to emphasize its impact.

This trick is characteristic of what is commonly called a drop—in other words, the moment in a piece that marks a sudden rhythmic change, or the return of the groove later in the arrangement. Originally associated with techno, the drop is now an integral part of pop and rap.

The effect is achieved by moving a low-pass filter across the signal of one or more mix elements using automation. The sweep often lasts several bars and, although its motion is largely uniform, it often accelerates near the end. It is also common to leave a short silence after the sweep to heighten the impact of the drop that follows.

If you want to apply a sweep effect to a large portion of the mix, it is preferable to create a bus to group those elements before they reach the master. You can then route the tracks to be processed to that bus and apply the filter effect there.

Objective 2: Temporarily change a track's atmosphere

A sweep can also radically change the atmosphere of a section. The goal is to mark a transition and add variety.

In this sense, it is often applied after a chorus to mark the return of a verse. It can give that verse a different flavor from the previous ones.

For this type of effect, the sweep is typically applied to the whole mix except the lead vocal. A low-pass sweep usually removes high frequencies quickly, then gradually brings them back over one or more bars.

As with the previous objective, it is clearly simpler to create a bus that receives the mix elements to be processed, and to control the movement there through automation.

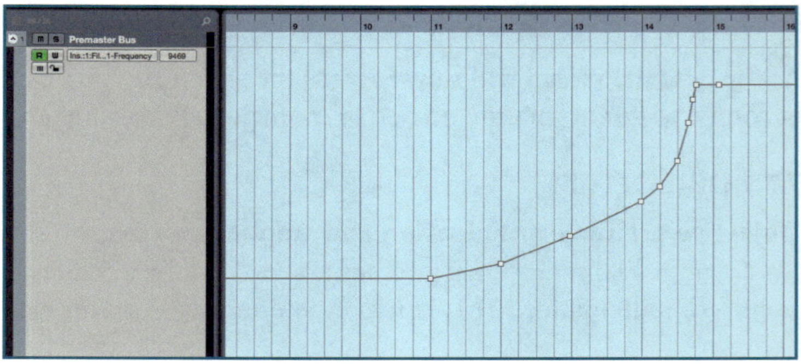

Here, sweep automation spanning four bars. Note the acceleration of the movement in the last bar, and the stop on its fourth beat in order to leave space between the sweep and the drop that follows.

Filter effects are also effective for creating contrast between a song's intro and the section that follows. For example, you can limit the range of audible frequencies by placing filters at the extremes of the spectrum, or progressively reveal the whole signal with a sweep.

Objective 3: Draw attention to a mix element

Because a sweep effect is anything but subtle, it inevitably attracts the listener's attention. It can therefore be useful for temporarily forcing the listener to focus on a specific mix element. A sweep can, for example, mark the introduction of a new element and ensure its presence does not go unnoticed.

A sweep inevitably attracts the listener's attention.

Objective 4: Create motion

So far, we have focused on sweep effects. However, other filter effects offer several interesting ways to shape a signal.

Filters driven by an oscillator add motion to a static element by varying its frequency distribution in time with the track. The processed track thus contributes to the song's rhythmic feel.

As mentioned in our discussion of automation in Chapter 6, it is also possible to achieve a similar effect by creating repetitive automation patterns to drive the filter's motion. This preserves the ability to change the pattern at different moments in the song, without having to open the filter plug-in to readjust its parameters.

Envelope-driven filters are very characterful and can therefore become fatiguing for the listener. However, when used with moderation, they can help shape an element's sonic signature and add a bit more character. For example, a subtle filter effect that varies with the attack of a rhythm guitar or bass can sometimes make the instrument more interesting.

8
STEREO IMAGING PROCESSING TOOLS

THE PROCESSING TOOLS we discussed in previous chapters are used primarily to manage the level and frequency distribution of the elements in a mix. We must also define how those elements will unfold within the stereo image, both horizontally (from left to right) and in depth (from background to foreground). In this chapter, we will explore the main methods available to us for shaping the spatial presentation of our mix.

8.1 The Panning

The panning control has a very simple function: it governs an element's position along the left/right axis of the stereo image. Turn the knob fully to the left and the sound will come out of the left speaker. Turn it to the right and there it is in the right speaker. Disarmingly simple! Which in no way lessens the need to use it judiciously.

8.1.1 PANNING OPTIONS

In the case of a monophonic track, the pan control is a simple rotary knob or horizontal strip that reproduces the left/right axis. Generally, the center position has a value of 0, while the extremes are marked down to −100 on the left and up to 100 on the right. The sound's position in the image will follow that of the knob or slider. So much for mono.

What about a stereophonic track? In a DAW, the panning control offers several operating modes depending on the software

The Phantom Center

Stereo playback obviously assumes the use of two speakers: one on the left and one on the right. Since there is no center speaker, how is it that we can localize sound in the center just as clearly as at the sides? A signal reproduced at the same level and in the same phase through both loudspeakers will be perceived as coming from the center. The phantom center is therefore the result of signals that are identical in both speakers.

Toms

Hi-hat

Overheads

Here, the tom track's panning control features two position selectors separated by a shaded area. This made it possible to narrow its stereo spread uniformly.

The hi-hat is monophonic and therefore has only a single position selector. It is shifted slightly to the left in order to match the hi-hat's position in the overheads.

The overhead track is stereophonic, but since we do not want to alter either its position or its internal stereo spread, the single-selector panning mode is used.

being used. These variants will generally appear in a drop-down menu when you click on the pan control. Among these options, two main modes stand out, with completely different effects.

The first looks similar to the mono version. We therefore recognize this operating mode by the presence of a single position selector. What matters here is understanding that, in this mode (often called balanced panning), the control changes the signal's position by altering the proportion between the left and right channels within the track itself. Thus, as the slider is moved to the left, the volume of the left channel in the stereo track increases while that of the right channel decreases.

This mode of operation has obvious consequences. Take the example of a stereo drum overhead track. If the panning slider is moved to the right, the volume of the right microphone is increased and that of the left microphone is decreased. We should therefore not be surprised to hear the hi-hat become louder and the snare shift toward the right. This mode is therefore rarely useful for stereo tracks. We will see later that there are in fact much more effective tools for reworking the internal balance of a stereo track.

The second option is much more practical. Depending on the software being used, this operating mode will go by various names. It is nevertheless easy to recognize by the presence of a shaded area between the two position selectors.

Unlike the first method, which affected the left/right ratio of the stereo track, this control instead allows us to place the track within the stereo image without altering its internal proportion. This method also allows us to reduce the width a track occupies in the stereo image. This can be especially useful when placing an instrument or effect within a limited space, whether to define its position more precisely or to reduce masking.

8.1.2 THE OBJECTIVES

Objective 1: Expand the stereo image

The primary goal of panning is, of course, to expand the stereo image by distributing the elements of the mix along the left/right axis. But what exactly should be placed where? Here are a few general guidelines.

An unwritten rule holds that the lead vocal, kick drum, bass, and snare drum should be placed in the center position. This is indeed the most common approach.

Generally, drum overheads are used in stereo and naturally spread out on either side of the horizontal axis. The width they occupy often depends on the density of the mix. It can sometimes be useful to reduce it in order to leave room for other instruments located at the extremes of the stereo image.

When there is only one vocal harmony, it will generally be placed in the center. If there are several, they will be distributed evenly on either side of the lead vocal.

Double-tracked parts, typically electric and acoustic guitar tracks, are commonly placed at the extremes of the stereo image: one 100% left and the other 100% right. As with overheads, it may be appropriate to bring them closer to the center in denser mixes.

It should be emphasized that the more low frequencies a track contains, the more advantageous it is to place it near the center position. Since low frequencies are not directional, it is difficult to clearly detect their point of origin, which limits placement options.

The *Pan Law*

As we mentioned in our discussion of phase, identical in-phase signals add in level. The same principle applies in stereo. When the two speakers reproduce an identical signal, its level increases by 6 dB.

This brings us to the concept of pan law. This rule compensates for that increase so that a signal is perceived at the same volume regardless of its position along the horizontal axis.

Fortunately, pan law is preset in DAWs; you will generally not need to change this parameter in your preferences.

Objective 2: Reduce masking

To make it easier to place the other tracks in the mix, it is worth keeping in mind that panning helps reduce masking. Obviously, the denser the arrangement, the more precisely tracks must be placed to ensure the mix remains clear.

When two instruments are competing for the same frequency range, it is generally better to oppose them within the stereo image. For example, if we need to place an acoustic guitar and a mandolin, we will improve the clarity of each instrument by putting the guitar on one side and the mandolin on the other. The same applies to percussion instruments. If we are dealing with a hand percussion instrument rich in high frequencies, it may compete with the hi-hat for space, for instance. It will therefore be advantageous to position that percussion instrument opposite the hi-hat.

An instrument's rhythm can also influence our placement choice, particularly when several percussion instruments are present in the mix. We will therefore oppose not only instruments that overlap in the same frequency range, but also those that share a similar rhythmic line. This enhances the intelligibility of each percussion part and its contribution to the song's rhythm.

Objective 3: Highlight important elements

A monophonic track is easier to localize by ear and therefore draws the listener's attention more quickly than a stereophonic track. This is often the case with important elements such as the lead vocal, solo instruments, or the snare drum, which tend to have a narrow stereo image. By contrast, ambient reverb or pad-type synthesized sounds, for example, will fulfill their supporting role better if they are pushed into the background because of their greater spread.

The horizontal space an element occupies goes a long way toward defining its role in the mix.

We therefore understand that the horizontal space occupied by an element goes a long way toward defining its role within the mix. In general, wide tracks tend to play a secondary role, while those with a narrower dimension tend to function more in the foreground. Setting wide tracks against monophonic or narrow-stereo tracks thus allows us to direct the listener toward the important elements in the mix. This contrast also enhances the sense of depth and contributes to the overall clarity of the mix.

Objective 4: Momentarily destabilize the listener

Of course, all rules are made to be broken! Panning can therefore be used to create occasional effects intended to hold the listener's attention. We may, for example, unbalance the stereo image by placing a single element on one side (a solo passage, for instance), or temporarily narrow the width of the mix and then suddenly expand it again. These techniques are also classic treatments for song intros and bridges.

We may also choose to arrange instruments temporarily in an unusual way. For example, we send the entire drum signal to the left side and the lead vocal and bass to the right. The idea is to create a strong enough imbalance to renew the listener's interest. The style of song must obviously justify such a shock, but when it does, this technique is worth exploring.

The LCR Method

Most early stereo consoles did not have a rotary pan control, but rather a three-position switch: L (left), C or M (center or middle), and R (right).

The LCR method, inherited from those early consoles, places mix elements only in the center or at the far left and right. Many mix engineers still use this technique, and it is certainly worth trying because of its simplicity. It is clear, however, that the inability to use intermediate positions can make it difficult to mix songs with dense arrangements.

Objective 5: Mark the transition from one song section to another

Panning can also be used to clarify a song's structure by altering the position of its elements, more or less subtly, from one section to another.

A classic technique consists of reducing the overall width of the mix in the verses and then suddenly making it more stereophonic in the choruses. Even though the arrangements generally do a good part of this work, they may still need this small boost, particularly when dealing with a song built on sparse, linear instrumentation.

8.1.3 RECOMMENDATIONS

Maintain a balanced stereo image

The stereo image of a mix should ideally always remain balanced. We therefore aim for equivalent proportions of level and frequency on each side of the spectrum. The output bus meter and a stereo image analyzer will help you visually assess the balance of your panning.

As a general rule, a mix's stereo image should always remain balanced, unless the goal is to momentarily destabilize the listener.

Check your mix in mono

A very wide stereo image has many virtues, but it can also create a major problem: it can make the mix ineffective in mono. Indeed, when an element in the mix has an excessively wide stereo image, its level will be considerably reduced in mono playback. It is therefore strongly recommended that you periodically check the result of your work by listening to it in mono. That way, you can make the necessary adjustments to ensure that the essential elements of your mix remain clearly audible in any listening situation.

8.2 Reverb

You probably know that certain animals, bats for example, use sound waves to assess their distance from objects. They can thus catch insects while skimming low over a lake or, more entertainingly, send people into a panic by brushing past their heads without ever touching them! Although we do not possess such a faculty, we use a similar process to perceive our surroundings: reverb.

Reverb does indeed inform our brain about the space around us. Even blindfolded, simple listening is enough to tell whether you are in an elevator shaft or a cathedral. Likewise, if someone coughs behind you in a movie theater, you can roughly estimate how many seats away that person is. In an underground parking garage, you can tell whether a car is approaching or moving away. Reverb therefore allows us not only to infer the size of the immediate environment, but also to locate the objects or people within it, whether stationary or moving.

The importance of reverb in the flat world of stereophony is therefore easy to grasp. After all, how can we create the impression of space and depth for someone listening to a song through two loudspeakers or headphones if not by playing with their perception?

8.2.1 WHAT IS REVERB?

In our brief discussion of acoustics, we defined early reflections as sound waves that bounce off a wall and reach the listener a few milliseconds after the direct sound.

Of course, not all of those waves will be reflected directly toward the listener. Most will continue on their path toward a second wall, then a third, and so on. As the wave travels through the room, encountering obstacles along the way, it progressively loses amplitude until it dies out and becomes inaudible. A wave's decay will vary according to several factors, including the distance traveled and the composition of the walls and objects it encounters.

Reverb helps us form a mental image of the space around us.

The listener therefore receives these waves echoing from all around the room. The delay separating these reflections is so short that the brain interprets them as forming a whole. That phenomenon is what we call reverb.

It is partly thanks to the accumulation of these waves reflected by the walls and objects in a room or space that we form our auditory image of the immediate environment. That image is shaped by a multitude of variables, including clarity, density, duration, and the delay between the reverb and the original sound.

8.2.2 REVERB FAMILIES AND THEIR ORIGINS

Over the years, engineers have shown great ingenuity in trying to control reverb and integrate it into audio production. Four major reverb families emerge from this fascinating history.

The first is natural reverb, the kind we hear in everyday life. Its sound and duration are therefore directly linked to the acoustic characteristics of the physical space in which the sound propagates.

Natural reverb was the first type of reverb used in audio production, more or less consciously. For many years, recordings were made using a single microphone around which the instruments were arranged. When listening back, the instruments placed farther from the microphone were not only quieter, but also perceived as being more distant. Thus, even though the placement of the instruments was based on their level, the room's reverb worked its way into the recording and gave it depth.

At the very end of the 1940s, an engineer named Bill Putnam had the brilliant idea of artificially adding reverb to a recording.

He modified the bathroom at Universal Recording Studio in Chicago in order to use it to produce reverb. The method is as simple as it is effective. A recording is played into a room through loudspeakers and, by placing microphones farther away in that same room, that playback is recorded in order to capture the room's ambience. The balance between the ambience thus captured and the original recording makes it possible to adjust the degree of depth added to the recording. Brilliant, isn't it?

The use of natural reverb through re-recording is a commonly used method.

At least, that is what many engineers thought. Putnam was in fact hired by several renowned studios to build similar rooms. Recordings from the 1950s would therefore be largely colored by the sound of these spaces known as echo chambers. This method is still used today because it remains effective overall.

One of the main disadvantages of natural reverb is that it depends directly on the room's acoustics. This leaves only two options: either move in order to find a studio or location whose acoustics suit us, or modify the room's characteristics. That is why many studios use acoustic treatments that can be adapted as needed in order to shape the reverb during recording. Movable absorptive panels or diffusers, temporary partitions, curtains on tracks, and, of course, echo chambers are among the many means studios use to capture that precious reverb. Beyond the obvious space requirements, the whole process inevitably becomes very costly.

By the end of the 1950s, engineers therefore set about creating a reverb that would not require one or more rooms to be specially fitted out for that purpose. This brings us to the family of mechanical reverb.

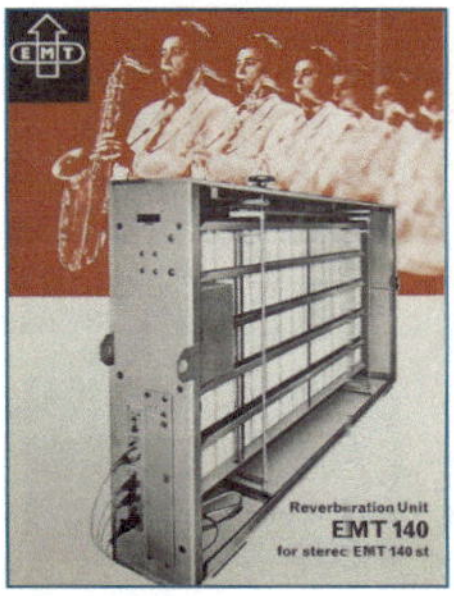

The cover page of the EMT 140 user manual.

The first functional device was designed by a German company called Elektro-Mess-Technik, better known as EMT. The first plate reverb was born. A loudspeaker, whose cone is replaced by a large thin metal plate suspended on springs, plays the audio material. Two pickups, functioning somewhat like those found on an electric guitar, are placed at either end of the metal sheet to capture its vibrations. An adjustable damper touches the plate in order to make it possible to reduce its vibration and thus shorten the reverb time.

This device, the EMT 140, therefore became a studio staple of the era. The unit is enormous: 2.5 m wide by 1.4 m high by 0.6 m deep (about 8 ft 2 in by 4 ft 7 in by 2 ft), and once assembled it weighs 168 kilograms (about 370 lb)! Even though its size requires studios to devote an entire room to it, the possibilities offered by the 140 made it an economical alternative to building an echo chamber.

Plate reverb was used very frequently. Its lack of naturalism is more than compensated for by a density that adds a great deal of size to the source. For obvious reasons, plate reverbs are now often replaced by digital emulations.

At about the same time, another type of mechanical reverb appeared: spring reverb. Operating in a manner similar to plate reverb, spring reverb uses a series of short springs to generate the vibrations that will produce the reverb. First popularized by the Hammond organ company, spring reverbs were quickly adopted by amplifier manufacturers because of their compact format.

In the 1990s, it was common to see Lexicon's little white reverb box in studios. Here, the controller of a Lexicon 480L sits on an SSL console.

As with plate reverb, spring reverb is not used to obtain a natural sound. Its instantly recognizable metallic timbre brings to mind the era of California surf rock, jukeboxes, and cars of endless proportions!

The early 1980s saw the birth of the third reverb family: digital reverb. These devices attempted to reproduce various kinds of reverb and, above all, made it possible to shape them. With the advent of computer-based music production came reverb plug-ins in addition to physical units. These tools are varied and accessible, and they make it possible to reproduce other reverb processes—more or less faithfully—as well as to create realistic or fictional spaces.

The world of reverb experienced another turning point in the early 2000s with the emergence of the last family: convolution reverb.

Essentially, the process aims to recreate the reverb characteristics of acoustic spaces using complex mathematical models.

To gather the basic data, a short, intense sound (a starter pistol, for example) is produced in the space to be emulated. One or more microphones are placed there to capture the room's reaction to that sonic impulse. Analysis of that recording yields an algorithm that recreates the reverb characteristics of the sampled space. This is the impulse response method.

This type of reverb provides virtual access to a vast range of real spaces, often beyond the reach of ordinary mortals. Want your track to sound as though you were seated in Row F at the Sydney Opera House? Done. A French cathedral, a cave, Wembley

Convolution reverb makes it possible to recreate the ambience of places as inaccessible as the Sydney Opera House concert hall.

Stadium, Studio B at Westlake Studio, or the trunk of a van? No problem! In short, name a place, and there is a good chance an algorithm exists to reproduce its ambience.

Convolution reverb also allows the user, through a procedure that is more or less complex depending on the device chosen, to sample spaces to which they themselves have access. It is therefore possible to build one's own catalogue of ambiences and use them at will.

In its early days, this type of reverb required tremendous computing power. Nowadays, the power of computers allows us to add convolution reverbs to our arsenal without too much trouble.

There is, however, one drawback inherent in this way of recreating a space. Convolution reverbs are not very willing to be modified without losing a large part of their naturalism. In that sense, the effectiveness of a convolution reverb will depend directly on how well the emulated space matches the needs of the mix. Put simply: if a preset fits the mix, great; if not, too bad!

8.2.3 TYPES OF REVERB

In the digital world, reverbs are grouped into various types, each with its own properties. The tasks each of these types can accomplish in mixing will vary according to those properties. Let us briefly examine each of them.

Hall reverbs reproduce the characteristics of large spaces such as concert halls, stadiums, opera houses, and the like. Reverbs called church or cathedral are exaggerated versions of the hall type and, as their names suggest, attempt to reproduce the vast ambience of a church or cathedral.

Hall reverbs usually offer a highly reflective, long-lasting reverb (more than 1.5 seconds) with a natural sound. They are especially effective for slow-tempo songs with sparse orchestration. The reverb thus fills the empty space with its presence. It can be used to add a natural, enveloping atmosphere to the mix as a whole or directly to the vocal or individual instruments. It is also suitable for placing large ensembles, such as an orchestral section or a choir, in a realistic space.

Room reverbs likewise specialize in reproducing rooms, but smaller ones: a recording studio, a bathroom, a living room, a closet, and so on.

The properties of each type of reverb determine how well it can fulfill certain mixing tasks.

Their reverb time is normally under 1.5 seconds. Their natural timbre ranges from dry to highly reflective depending on the acoustic characteristics of the space being evoked.

This kind of reverb makes it possible to add depth to instruments without drawing too much attention to its presence. It is useful for creating a general ambience in a moderate- or fast-tempo piece, or for placing an instrument in a space of its own. In that respect, it works wonderfully on electric guitar tracks and percussion.

Chamber reverbs attempt to reproduce the ambience of echo chambers. They therefore also have a natural timbre, though with more character than the two previous types. Their duration is generally comparable to that of room reverbs.

This type of reverb can work on many kinds of sources, but seems particularly well suited to drum tracks and synthesized instruments. Chamber reverb is of course useful for tinting an entire mix with the retro ambience of the 1950s.

Convolution reverbs, derived from the mathematical modeling of existing spaces, are effective when one wants to place an instrument or an entire mix in a specific kind of location. Their duration and tone will vary according to the characteristics of the modeled space. As we noted earlier, they are difficult to modify. The match between the preset and the needs of the mix will therefore determine how effective they are.

The four types of reverb we have just listed are all based on the reproduction of real spaces and therefore have natural sonic characteristics. The ones that follow are more colored and, as such, more distinctive and better suited to processing individual instruments.

Plate reverbs have the property of increasing in density more quickly than natural reverbs. We therefore feel the effect of the reverb sooner and more strongly. When used alongside a natural ambience, plates make it possible to bring one or more elements of the mix forward by placing them in a space of their own. They are therefore highly effective for processing vocals, snare drum, or any instrument featuring solo parts.

Spring reverbs have a distinctive metallic sound that automatically evokes a retro quality. As such, spring reverbs are perfect for coloring guitars, organs, electric pianos, and other instruments that might be described as vintage. Another very interesting characteristic of this kind of reverb is that it seems to reduce intelligibility less than other types of reverb. That is surely one of the reasons spring reverbs are making a strong comeback in vocal processing.

Non-linear reverbs do not aim to recreate the reverb of an existing space or that of a mechanical process. Instead, they introduce anomalies into the usual characteristics of reverb, whether by abruptly cutting off the tail (gate reverb) or by completely reversing the reverb curve (reverse reverb).

Non-linear reverbs are highly malleable, which makes them easy to shape to the needs of the mix. By setting the reverb length according to the tempo of the song, we reduce masking while creating an ambience that fits the song's rhythm.

Despite their irreverence toward natural acoustics, non-linear reverbs contain enough information to give the listener an impression of depth and dimension. They are therefore practical for bringing out an element in the mix and, of course, for creating occasional effects.

8.2.4 THE COMPONENTS OF REVERB

The vast majority of reverb units and plug-ins divide the effect into two main components: early reflections and the reverb tail. This distinction is, however, criticized by acousticians, who consider early reflections inseparable from reverb. But since units offer separate controls for each of these components, a brief description is in order.

As we saw earlier, early reflections are made up of the sound reflected directly toward the listener by the walls of a space.

They give the brain clues about the room's size, its composition, and the position of the source and the listener. The frequency distribution of the reflections also gives us clues about the kind of room we are dealing with. A highly reflective surface, such as concrete, for example, implies strong early reflections in the high frequencies, whereas a room full of acoustic treatment, such as a recording studio, will have a more even distribution across the spectrum.

The reverb tail is made up of the accumulation of waves reflected within a space. Its duration gives us clues about the size of the room. Its density—the speed at which the reverb develops—tells us about the composition of the environment. Our concrete room, for example, will have a reverb that builds in density more quickly than a room with wooden walls.

Early reflections seem to give width to the source, whereas reverb contributes more to its depth.

Based on my observations, early reflections seem to affect the source's width more, whereas the reverb tail contributes more to its depth.

8.2.5 THE MAIN SETTINGS

Despite the often extensive number of controls found on many reverb units, the essence of their action is governed by four main parameters.

A reverb type selector allows us to choose among the kinds of reverb mentioned earlier (hall, room, plate, etc.).

A length control sets the reverb time in seconds.

One or more controls determine the proportion of reverb. At a minimum, we will therefore find a knob called dry/wet or mix to set the ratio between the original source and the reverb effect. On many units, each component (source, early reflections, and reverb) has its own level control.

A pre-delay control inserts a delay between the source sound and its reverb. Its length greatly changes the effect of the reverb.

Let us take a moment to clarify the action of this last parameter. Pre-delay is probably the control whose significance is most often overlooked by aspiring mix engineers. As we have just mentioned, pre-delay introduces a gap that separates the source from its reverb. The source will therefore be audible without effect for a brief moment, which prevents it from being masked by its own reverb. In addition, introducing a delay gives the impression of bringing the source closer to the listener without compromising the illusion of depth created by the reverb. The best of both worlds!

8.2.6 ADDITIONAL SETTINGS

A reverb's controls often reflect both the complexity of the phenomenon and the way the manufacturer chose to handle it. They can therefore be numerous and, of course, will be named differently from one unit or plug-in to another. Do not worry: although you may occasionally encounter esoteric terms, most controls generally have names clear enough to suggest their functions.

We regularly find a control called size that determines, more or less precisely, the dimensions of the room.

A density control is often provided to define how quickly the reverb develops. On some units, we also encounter a parameter called diffusion, which refers to the way sound disperses within the room. These two controls are often confusing because their actions are very similar. Above all, remember that they do not directly alter the duration of the reverb, but rather the way it develops.

Another control, often called decay, may also be present to manage the way the reverb dies away. It makes it possible to have a linear reverb curve or to truncate it more abruptly, as if placing a gate after the reverb.

Finally, we often find frequency equalizers whose effect will vary depending on their position in the reverb chain. Some affect the source before it is sent to the reverb (pre-EQ); others are used to modify the signal after the reverb (reverb EQ or post-EQ). It is also possible for an EQ to be dedicated exclusively to processing early reflections (early reflections EQ).

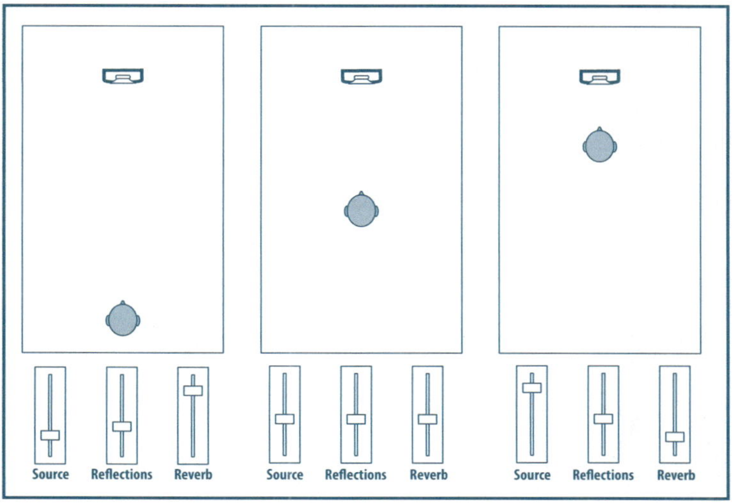

The impression of distance created by the reverb settings.

Although these equalizers may at first seem like useful additions, they are mainly helpful when a reverb is inserted directly on a track. In send/return mode, it is often simpler to insert an equalizer before or after the reverb effect when needed. That also gives us the advantage of choosing one or more equalizers that we are more familiar with.

8.2.7 THE OBJECTIVES

Objective 1: Add depth

We saw earlier that the pan knob is used to place instruments along the left/right horizontal axis. In much the same spirit, reverb can often be thought of as a front/back control.

Like panning, which sets position along the left/right axis, reverb can in a sense be thought of as a front/back control.

Reverb is highly effective at adding depth to a mix. Indeed, an instrument to which we add reverb is necessarily pushed farther back in the mix.

Although reverb can itself cause masking, the depth it adds can help manage conflicting instruments. Let us suppose, for example, an acoustic guitar and a piano are fighting for the same place in the mix. We can add reverb to the piano in order to place it behind the guitar. By moving the piano onto a different front/back plane from the guitar, we reduce masking between these two elements while also adding depth to the mix.

Objective 2: Widen the stereo image

It often happens that an important monophonic track in the mix could benefit from occupying more space in the stereo image, as is often the case with the lead vocal or a solo instrument.

To widen a track's stereo image, we can assign it a very short room reverb. Often, a duration of about 50 milliseconds will suffice. A long pre-delay, set in tempo, will prevent the reverb from pushing the element too far back in the mix. The goal is for the sound to gain width without the reverb itself becoming identifiable.

Objective 3: Place tracks in a shared space

Adding a single reverb across all tracks helps glue them together.

ADJUSTING PRE-DELAY

Since we all have a range of delay plug-ins at our disposal, it is easy to use one of them to determine, in milliseconds, the duration of a tempo subdivision (quarter note, eighth note, sixteenth note, etc.) according to the song's tempo.

The method is simple. Just insert a delay plug-in on any track, activate its tempo-sync function, and choose the desired subdivision. For reverb, the sixteenth note (1/16) is generally a good starting point.

Once that selection has been made, deactivate the sync function. The vast majority of delay plug-ins will then display the duration of the chosen subdivision in milliseconds. That value can then be entered into the pre-delay section of the reverb.

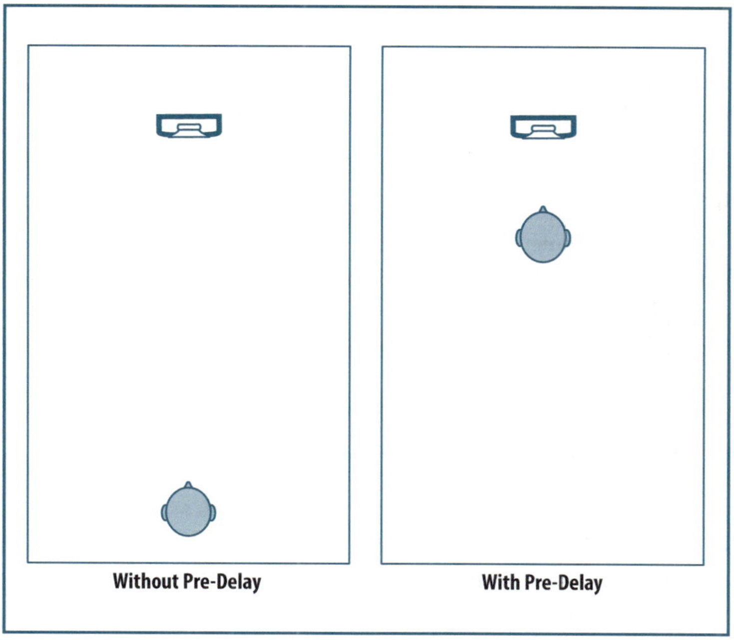

Adding pre-delay reduces masking of the source and brings it closer to the listener.

This technique is particularly appropriate when the song has been built from individual recordings (overdubs). Adding a general reverb thus helps create the illusion that everything was recorded simultaneously in the same space. Reverbs that reproduce natural ambiences (hall, room, chamber, convolution) are best suited to this kind of work.

Even though it is entirely possible to insert a reverb for this purpose on the output bus, it is far more advantageous to create an effects channel (bus or aux) and work in send/return mode. This preserves the ability to place tracks more precisely within the space through their respective sends. For example, if we want to place the guitars in the background of our virtual space, all we need to do is increase their send level.

Since we are trying to give the impression that everything was recorded simultaneously in the same space, the reverb should be felt more than heard. It is therefore generally useful to insert an equalizer to reduce the extremes of the frequency spectrum. A low shelf around 150 Hz and a high shelf around 2 kHz will make the reverb more discreet without harming the sense of depth it provides.

All that remains is to set the overall level of the reverb channel. A good starting point is to listen to the whole mix and lower the reverb level until it is barely perceptible. We can then validate the setting by switching the reverb channel from audible to muted using its mute button. When we feel the mix become more unified and larger without being able to clearly identify the reverb, the effect level is generally optimal.

Objective 4: Add size to a percussion instrument

We often want to give more space to percussion elements such as the snare drum, claps, or toms. In these cases, adding a non-linear reverb will make it possible to enlarge those tracks. Care should be taken to set the reverb length so that it dies out before the instrument's next hit. To avoid disrupting the rhythmic figure, it is often preferable not to use pre-delay. The reverb level will be set according to whether we want an audible effect—in the style of the 1980s—or simply an increase in size.

Objective 5: Extend the duration of a sound

In some situations, we feel the need to fill the gap created by the overly abrupt end of a sound. This is often the case with acoustic drum tracks, especially toms and snare.

To extend a sound's duration, the reverb and the source must be placed in the same position within the stereo image.

In a previous chapter, we saw that it is common to clean tom bleed by editing manually or by using a gate. This operation can, however, make them feel as though they cut off a bit too abruptly. A reverb can be used to extend their duration and restore a more natural ending. To do this, we choose a non-linear or plate reverb and set its pre-delay fairly short (25 to 35 ms is a good starting point). We reduce the level of the early reflections so that the reverb blends more naturally with the original sound. The reverb time should be long enough to extend the resonance without drawing attention to itself. For this effect to work, it is essential that the reverb and the source be in the same place within the stereo image. The use of one or more mono reverbs should therefore be considered.

The case of the snare drum is somewhat different. Its playing, being more complex than that of the toms, makes it difficult to remove bleed without attenuating the nuances that contribute to the rhythm. Adding reverb to the entire track may sometimes make it blurry. It is still possible to extend the duration and add size to the snare by copying the performance onto another track and keeping only the strong beats. By assigning only that track to the reverb, we give size and duration to the strong beats without altering the softer hits.

In live recordings or live-in-the-studio recordings, we can also use a sample to generate the reverb. This method has the advantage of feeding the reverb a naturally sounding source free of any bleed, thus ensuring precise assignment of the effect. The use of a sample for this purpose is also highly effective when processing acoustic drum recordings that require a well-defined sound or that exhibit significant hi-hat bleed in the snare track.

The way this treatment is applied will vary according to the result we want to achieve. If the goal is to restore naturalism to snare endings that are too dry, reverb settings similar to those used for tom processing will do the job. We can also pull down the level of the strong-beat track or sample and use pre-fader mode so that only the reverb is heard. This yields an effect that integrates subtly into the overall drum sound.

In general, reverb should be felt rather than heard.

If we want a more colored effect, it is worth experimenting with the duration of the snare hit. By keeping only the initial part of the attack, we allow the reverb to generate the resonance. Using a non-linear reverb gives us all the flexibility we need to shape the duration and tone of that resonance to fit the song.

Objective 6: Color a track

Obviously, mechanical reverbs, particularly spring reverb, automatically color any track assigned to them with their distinctive character. That color can help give an element in the mix more personality.

The effect is often more successful when the reverb is placed in the same spot as the original sound within the stereo image. A narrowed stereo image or mono use will in fact help the listener associate the source with its reverb.

Objective 7: Create a distance effect

Of course, reverb can be used as an occasional effect to place an element far from the listener. A heavy dose of reverb will pro-

RE-AMPING A RECORDING YOURSELF

It is entirely possible to re-amp a recording yourself by turning a room into an echo chamber with loudspeakers and one or more microphones.

Re-amping also contributes to the realism of virtual instruments designed to reproduce the sound of existing instruments (piano, organ, brass, strings, etc.). The touch of naturalism it adds often makes it easier to integrate those tracks into an organically sounding mix.

If your goal is to unify the tracks in a mix, this method works especially well when you use the same room in which some of the original recordings were made.

It can also create striking occasional effects. A bathroom, a closet, a stairwell, or even the inside of a suitably sized object (an oven, a garbage can, a fireplace hearth, etc.) can place your instrument in an unusual space and color it in an unexpected way. Not to mention that the process is also a lot of fun.

duce that ethereal sound that seems to float at the back of the mix. To create this effect, we use a long hall or cathedral reverb with no pre-delay. In general, we strongly reduce the reverb's high frequencies to place it behind the other elements in the mix. We also reduce the frequencies likely to mask them.

It is often interesting to feed the sound to the reverb in pre-fader mode so that we can reduce or even mute the original source level in order to heighten the impact of the effect.

8.2.8 RECOMMENDATIONS

Use reverb in send/return mode

With a few exceptions, reverb should almost always be used in send/return mode. This keeps full control over its level and makes it possible to assign more than one track to it. The dry/wet control of a reverb used on an effects bus must be set to its maximum wet value in order to ensure that only reverb passes through. This prevents the levels of tracks sent to it from being increased when reverb is added. Needless to say, such a situation makes level management impossible.

Except on a few rare occasions, reverb should be used in send/return mode and post-fader.

Place the reverb send post-fader

Again, apart from a few rare exceptions, the send used to route the signal to the reverb should be post-fader. That way, the amount of effect will follow the level of the track in the mix. Not to mention that it prevents us from having a reverb that comes out of nowhere when a track's level is turned down.

Use a preset as a starting point

Reverbs come with a wide variety of presets, often grouped by reverb type. Someone has therefore already done a good part of the work for you! Chances are you will find a preset that comes close to the kind of effect you want to apply. Do not hesitate to dig through that library and use a preset as a starting point. Over time, you will develop preferences for certain units and certain presets depending on the task at hand.

Ensure a match between the space and the instruments

To achieve realistic reverb effects, the size of the reproduced space must match the kind of instruments being used. For example, placing an orchestral section in a room the size of a closet will inevitably produce an unnatural sound. We would instead expect that orchestra to be in a room large enough to hold a hundred musicians!

Set the reverb time according to the tempo and the density of the mix

A fast song or one with dense orchestration calls for the use of a short reverb. This reduces the risk of the reverb masking the instruments. Conversely, a ballad with simple arrangements may benefit from a longer reverb that fills the empty spaces.

Avoid using all reverbs at full width

With the exception of the reverb used to create a general ambience and those receiving more than one track, it is rarely advantageous to use reverbs at full width. This is even more true in dense arrangements where instruments are already fighting one another for space in the mix. By narrowing the stereo image of reverbs, we reduce the likelihood of masking and make it easier to localize instruments. In addition, the space freed up at the extremes of the stereo image will help us hear the instruments placed there.

Do not let the reverb mask your source

Without EQ, reverb inevitably becomes a source of masking that makes the mix sound distant and blurry. It is therefore good practice to use a low cut to filter the low frequencies from the reverbs in the mix. A high cut will also frequently be added to remove high frequencies so that they do not compromise the presence and intelligibility of the important elements in the mix.

The middle of the spectrum should also be examined. An effective technique for handling it consists of raising the reverb level until it is equal to that of the source. On the equalizer, we choose a narrow bell filter and apply a strong boost (around 10 dB). Here comes the interesting part: we slowly sweep the middle range with this filter while listening not to its effect on the reverb, but to its effect on the source's presence and intelligibility. As soon as a frequency conflicts with the source, we reduce it until the masking disappears.

To reduce masking, insert an EQ before or after the reverb and make your adjustments by listening to its effect on the source rather than on the reverb.

For vocal tracks, it is often preferable to eliminate potentially conflicting frequencies before they enter the reverb. A quick way to do this is to insert an equalizer before the reverb and work on the frequency extremes. We therefore use a low cut placed somewhere between 200 and 600 Hz and a high cut removing frequencies from 3 kHz or 5 kHz upward. This practice was so common at Abbey Road Studios that the technique now bears their name. Inserting a de-esser before the reverb can also be useful to prevent sibilance from carrying over into the reverb.

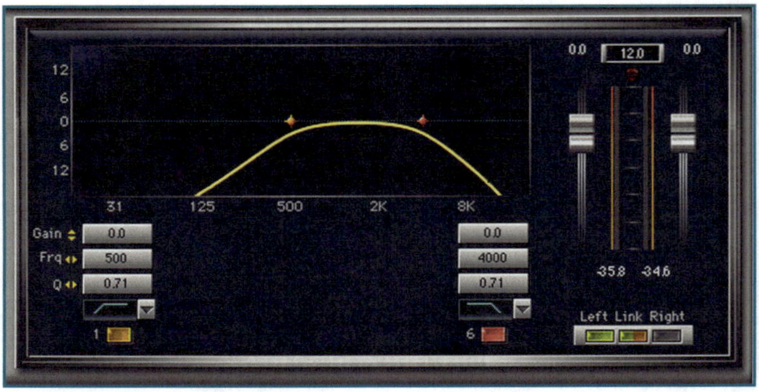

A typical Abbey Road-style EQ setting applied to the signal before it enters the reverb.

8.3 Delay

Delay (or echo) is fortunately much simpler to approach than reverb. The concept is familiar to us: an echo is the repetition, one or more times, of an original signal. That repetition is generally far enough removed from the source in time to be perceived as a separate element. Often less intrusive than reverb, delay is one of the effects at our disposal for shaping the sonic space of our mix.

8.3.1 TYPES OF DELAYS

Like reverb, delay effects are divided into various categories sharing common traits.

The first form of echo used in audio production is called slap delay or slapback delay. A signal is sent from the console to a tape machine. The physical distance between the record head and the playback head creates a short delay between the source and its playback on the tape machine. The speed at which the machine is run—7.5, 15, or 30 ips (inches per second)—determines the interval between the original sound and its repetition. Slap delay is therefore a single repeat whose delay time typically ranges from 60 to 120 ms.

This type of echo is highly characteristic of 1950s recordings, especially those of Elvis Presley. The effect is in fact very audible in "Heartbreak Hotel." Slap remains one of the most widely used techniques today for adding dimension to a vocal or guitar recording.

Single delay is a single echo repeated at regular intervals. Usually monophonic, it is regularly used on the lead vocal track to dress up the ends of phrases.

Double delay, as its name indicates, involves two echoes produced at different intervals. Normally, each echo is placed at one of the extremes of the stereo image: one on the left and the other on the right. It is therefore useful for adding a rhythmic element to the track or simply for giving the source more size.

Ping-pong delay works on the same principle as single delay, except that the repeats alternate from one speaker to the other. The effect is easy to spot, which somewhat limits its usefulness. It can nevertheless add movement to a track.

Rhythmic delay arranges the source's repeats according to a predefined rhythmic pattern. Normally, that pattern is organized into tempo subdivisions and synchronized with the song's rhythm. The number of subdivisions and the level of each repeat can be defined. This category of echo makes it possible to create a wide range of rhythmic patterns, whether to create an occasional effect or to add interest to a simple element by having it contribute to the song's rhythm.

Finally, reverse delay records the source for a certain amount of time and then plays it back starting from the end. Its highly stylized effect, which is reminiscent of the psychedelic era, often limits its usefulness to effect creation.

8.3.2 THE SETTINGS

As always, the controls and their names will vary depending on the unit or plug-in being used. Here, however, are the most common parameters.

First, one or more delay time controls set the interval between the source and its echo.

A synchronization switch, often called sync or tempo, links the delay time to the song's tempo. When selected, the delay time display changes from milliseconds to rhythmic subdivisions corresponding to the song's tempo.

A feedback control adjusts the number of repeats. In fact, the repeats are fed back to the delay input—hence the term feedback—which creates a loop and ultimately allows us to determine the number of repeats. It should be noted that the vast majority of delays are designed so that the repeats progressively decrease in level. The first repeat will be the loudest and the last barely audible. The feedback value may be presented as an exact number of repeats, as a percentage, or simply not be graduated at all.

Most delays are designed so that the repeats gradually decrease in level.

On stereo units and plug-ins, a pan control specifies the placement of the echoes along the left/right axis of the stereo image.

A blend control, called mix or dry/wet, determines the proportion between the level of the source and that of the echo at the unit's output.

It is also common to find equalizers for modifying the frequency spectrum of the repeats. The number of available bands and the complexity of these EQs will vary from one unit to another.

It is also common to encounter a saturation control, used to add character to the echo, and a modulation section that varies the pitch of the repeats.

The Roland Space Echo uses a tape loop to generate repeats. This unit, highly prized for its distinctive character, is in fact an integral part of the sound of reggae music. In live performance, it is common for one person to be specifically assigned to adjusting the unit's settings in real time.

Some units offer additional functions. One of the most common is tap tempo, which allows the song tempo to be set manually by tapping or clicking the selector in time with the music. This option can be useful when the song's tempo is unknown or fluctuates.

We also occasionally find a control called ducking, which reduces the echo's level when the original signal is audible. It therefore makes it possible to considerably reduce the masking of the main source by its echo. In a way, it also enhances the echo effect by making it more audible during pauses in the source.

8.3.3 THE OBJECTIVES

Objective 1: Add width

Using a stereo echo is a very effective way of giving more horizontal space to a monophonic or narrow-stereo track. This technique is commonly used to process the lead vocal and instruments with solo passages.

To do this, we use a double delay with very short delay times (between 60 and 120 ms) and a small number of repeats. In fact, a single repeat will very often do the job. Synchronization with the song tempo is optional, although it is entirely legitimate to choose a very short duration value that matches the song tempo (a 1/32 subdivision, for example). Each echo is placed at one of the extremes of the left/right axis.

The trick here is to vary the delay time of each echo very slightly. We might, for example, use a delay of 85 ms on the left and 80 ms on the right. That slight difference will be enough to enhance the perceived width. If the unit or plug-in has a modulation section, using it will also help increase the space occupied by the track. A modulation of around 6 to 9 cents will generally produce the desired effect.

This technique is more effective when the echo is kept discreet and difficult to identify as such. Its effect is very similar to that of a doubler, which we will discuss in more detail a little later.

Objective 2: Add depth

As we have said, echo can often give depth to an element in a less intrusive way than reverb. Because it is separated from the source in time, echo tends to cause less masking than reverb. In general, it also keeps the sound closer to the listener than reverb does.

A small number of repeats adds width, whereas a larger number adds depth.

We will choose either a single echo (single delay or slap) or a double delay depending on whether we want a monophonic, localized effect or a wide stereophonic one. Of course, it may be appropriate to modify one of the two delay times of a double delay slightly in order to enhance the sense of width. What matters is using a short delay time (a 1/16 or 1/32 note value, for example) synchronized to the song's tempo. We then increase the feedback setting to obtain enough repeats to reach a duration similar to that of a reverb. It is also good practice to insert an equalizer before or after the echo to cut the frequency extremes, just as we would with a reverb effect.

Objective 3: Fill empty spaces

Adding a single echo to the ends of lead vocal phrases is a common technique for filling the space left open by the end of the sung line. This technique, called a vocal throw, uses a single echo, generally placed in the same position as the lead vocal. The delay time is often synchronized with the song tempo and relatively long (1/4 or 1/2 note).

Since we usually want this kind of effect to be audible, we make sure to create a clear distinction between the vocal sound and its echo. It is therefore common to color the latter with saturation and to alter its timbre with an equalizer.

Vocal throws are more easily achieved in send/return mode and are almost always automated. We increase the send level only at the ends of phrases or on the words we want to send to the echo. It is also possible to automate the activation and deactivation of the send to define the moments when the echo will be present. This technique also works very well on instruments with solo passages.

Objective 4: Add movement

Echo makes it possible to heighten the interest of an element in the mix by adding movement. This effect is especially useful when processing synthesizers or monophonic tracks that would benefit from a bit more space and color.

Needless to say, ping-pong delay is well suited to this kind of treatment. Its distinctive back-and-forth motion adds dimension and movement even to the dullest instruments.

It may also happen that we want to enhance the rhythm of a song by adding to a track an echo synchronized to the song tempo (think of the guitar in "Another Brick in the Wall" by Pink Floyd). Generally, the level of this echo will be equal or very close to that of the source, and its number of repeats very small, so that it blends with the instrument's sound.

A rhythmic delay can also be used to create more complex rhythmic movement. It can be applied to a percussion instrument or to a track with a clear, well-defined attack in order to enhance its rhythmic contribution to the song. It may also serve as a temporary effect to make an element of the mix stand out. Whatever the goal, we generally want this kind of echo to be clearly audible.

Objective 5: Create an effect

Of course, echo can be used to create a multitude of effects, more or less pronounced, in order to hold the listener's attention or shape the emotional content of a song. We may, for example, evoke a sense of confusion by radically altering the repetition of a source through heavy modulation or by repeating it for several bars.

Sending part of the delay signal to the reverb pushes the delay farther back in the mix.

A reverse delay applied to a guitar solo, a vocal, or the drum track will act on the listener like a virtual psychotropic substance, making them ready to stick flowers into the barrel of any rifle that comes within reach!

In short, the range of possibilities is immense, provided of course that the song lends itself to that kind of exercise.

8.3.4 ADVANCED TECHNIQUES

Sending the echo to the reverb

In mixing, echo can sometimes prove too prominent, especially when it is being used to create width or contribute to the ambience. In such cases, it is possible to send all or part of the echo signal to a reverb effect through its send. The amount of echo sent to the reverb determines how clearly the repeats remain audible: the more send is applied, the more the echo blends into the reverb.

This method works particularly well for all kinds of vocal echoes. For example, by sending a small amount of reverb to a slap effect, we subtly increase the width of the vocal while making the echo itself less easily identifiable as such.

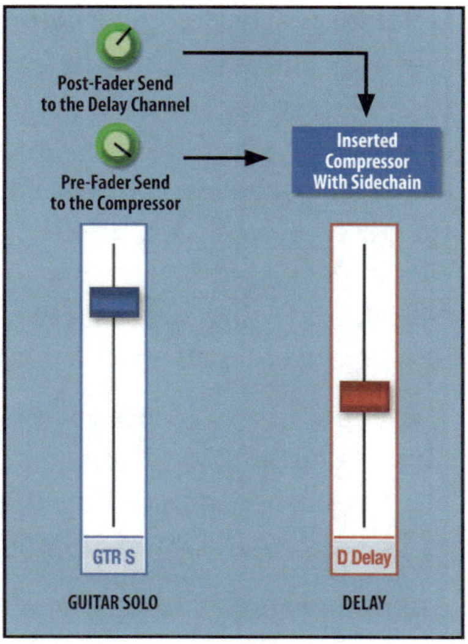

The routing used to create a dynamic delay applied to a guitar solo. A post-fader send routes the guitar to the effects channel. A pre-fader send sends that same signal to the sidechain of the compressor inserted after the delay.

Dynamic delay

Like the ducking control mentioned earlier, dynamic delay is a kind of intelligent echo whose repeats are attenuated when the source is heard and raised when it is silent. When the source is audible, this reduction in level not only reduces masking, but also has the effect of bringing it closer to the listener. When the source is silent, the echo returns to full level to fill the space.

If none of your delay units offers a ducking function, it is easy to create one yourself using the sidechain method. First, add an effects bus on which you insert a delay followed by a compressor with a sidechain function. On the track being processed, use two sends: the first to route the track signal to the effects bus, and the second, in pre-fader mode, assigned to the compressor's sidechain. The compressor's ratio and threshold settings will determine how much the delay is attenuated, while its release setting will determine how quickly the delay comes forward during pauses in the processed track.

This type of treatment works very well on elements featuring solo passages (a saxophone solo, for example). It may, however, sometimes lack precision for processing the lead vocal. In that case, automation is generally preferable.

8.3.5 RECOMMENDATIONS

Use echo in send mode and post-fader

As with reverb, echo is almost always inserted on an effects bus so that it can be used in send mode. This preserves the ability to change its level and assign more than one track to it. Post-fader mode is also preferable.

Determine whether your echo should be synchronized
The decision to synchronize or not synchronize the delay time to the song tempo should depend on the objective you want to achieve. As a general rule, the more the echo is synchronized to the song, the less it draws attention to itself. Thus, when the echo is specifically intended to increase the space a track occupies in the stereo image, it is generally appropriate to synchronize it. The same applies when we want to integrate the echo into the instrument so that it contributes to its rhythm.

There are, however, occasions when the absence of synchronization helps bring an element of the mix forward. For example, an unsynchronized slap effect placed on the lead vocal will add character and strengthen its foreground role.

Another example: lead guitarists regularly use fixed delay times regardless of the song tempo. It may be interesting to reproduce that effect by setting a double delay to values that do not correspond to the tempo. We might, for example, use one delay time of 250 ms and another of 500 ms.

Along the same lines, it can be interesting to use compound synchronization to obtain a similar effect. On a double delay, one parameter can be set to a note value and the second to the dotted or triplet version of that same value (1/8 and 1/8t, for example).

Be wary of tempo changes
Most delay plug-ins do not react very well to tempo changes. During the brief moment they need to adjust to the new speed, they modulate the pitch of the repeats in a way that is, let us say, aesthetically questionable! Thus, when we synchronize our echo's delay time, we must make sure that the tempo will remain the same throughout the entire section being processed. Needless to say, automating delay time is also a rather perilous adventure.

8.4 Stereo Enhancers

Stereo enhancers (sometimes called stereo imagers or stereo expanders) are designed to widen the internal stereo image of a track. This kind of plug-in or unit includes a highly variable number of parameters depending on the model being used. At the core of all these devices, however, is a width control that narrows or widens the stereo image. This control is very often graduated as a percentage, where 100% means the track is used at its original stereo width. Below 100%, its stereo width is reduced; above 100%, it is increased.

Let us keep in mind that stereo enhancers work on a track's stereo image by altering the level balance between the center and the sides. Thus, when we widen a track, we increase the level of the sides at the expense of the center. The element therefore becomes more ambient and, by the same token, moves farther away from the listener. Conversely, if we reduce its width, the center content is emphasized, making the element more precise and directional.

When a track is widened, the level of the sides is increased at the expense of the center.

8.4.2 THE OBJECTIVES

Objective 1: Modify the width of the stereo image

Stereo enhancers are obviously useful for processing elements that might benefit from a little more width in the mix. Since they work from the track's internal stereo image, it should be made clear that they naturally have no effect on a monophonic track.

Likewise, they can be used to reduce the space a track occupies along the left/right axis. This kind of processing is useful for narrowing the often exaggerated stereo image of sounds coming from virtual instruments. We can of course obtain a similar result using the pan control. It is nevertheless good to give an element of excessive width a more functional dimension at the very beginning of the mix and to reserve the pan control for setting its position within the mix.

Objective 2: Add space to a mix

A stereo enhancer can be used to add another placement zone on each side of the stereo image.

In very dense mixes, we sometimes wish we had a bit more space for placing additional elements. The stereo enhancer can then help by adding another placement zone on each side of the stereo image. This technique makes it possible to limit congestion at the extremes of the stereo image. This extra space helps prevent elements from piling up and reduces the risk of masking. We might, for example, add a stereo enhancer on a subgroup of vocal harmonies to prevent it from being masked by the other instruments.

We must of course avoid compromising mono playback by adding too much space. A stereo image analyzer can help us avoid going too far beyond the limits of the left/right axis. Obviously, we will also refrain from placing essential mix elements in the extra zones created by the stereo enhancer.

A stereo enhancer inserted on the output bus inevitably changes the mix balance.

Objective 3: Adjust the stereo image of an entire mix

Mastering engineers regularly use the stereo enhancer to fine-tune the width of a final mix. This tool can also be useful during mixing to refine our mix's stereo spread.

To do so, we insert a stereo enhancer on the output bus. Since this effect alters the balance between the center and the sides, it inevitably changes the mix balance. It is therefore better to make only subtle adjustments to the stereo image.

Objective 4: Modify the internal balance of a stereo track

In most cases, instruments recorded with two microphones are delivered to us as individual monophonic tracks. Sometimes, however, those tracks are already combined into a stereo track. When the stereo image of that track is flawed, it is very difficult to recover.

Some stereo enhancers make it possible to modify the internal balance of a stereo track by changing the level relationship between the left and right channels or by reversing the polarity of one side. Acoustic pianos, for example, are often recorded by dedicating one microphone to the low strings, typically placed on the left in the stereo image, and another to the high strings, placed on the right. With this type of enhancer, we can alter the level proportion of each microphone and thus rebalance the frequency distribution without resorting to an equalizer. It can also be used to recenter the image of unbalanced drum overheads.

In the extreme case where an instrument recorded with two microphones has been delivered to us in stereo and the microphones are clearly out of phase, this type of enhancer will allow us to invert the polarity of one side and see whether there is any improvement. We can also alter the proportion between the two sides in order to favor the sound of one microphone over the other.

Although these are exceptional cases, it is good to know which of the stereo enhancers at your disposal is capable of becoming your lifeline in such situations.

8.4.3 RECOMMENDATIONS

Check the effect of your settings in mono

A wide stereo image is very appealing. However, we must be aware that excessive width may unbalance the mix when heard in mono. It is therefore important to validate the effect of stereo enhancers by listening regularly to the mix in mono. That way, you will be able to verify whether important elements have been attenuated because of excessive stereo spread.

Be selective in your use

As mentioned at the beginning of the chapter, the more monophonic an element is, the more clearly the listener can localize it. The use of stereo enhancers should therefore be limited to tracks playing a supporting role or to slightly improving the stereo image of main elements.

8.5 Modulation Effects

There is a wide variety of effects that modify the signal by adding modulation. Here is an overview of the different families of this kind of effect.

The doubler is very similar to a stereo slap-type delay effect. It generally generates two short-delay echoes placed on either side of the stereo image. These repeats are then slightly modulated. Some doublers let you adjust the amount of modulation for each echo, usually in cents; others use fixed values instead. The doubler is generally easier to use in send/return mode.

The main advantage of the doubler is that it gives size to a monophonic signal without moving the element farther back in the mix. That is why it is very frequently used on the lead vocal and on monophonic instruments acting as soloists. When its level is set judiciously, its presence is almost imperceptible to the listener.

The doubler adds size to an element without pushing it farther back in the mix.

When pushed hard, the doubler produces a distinctive effect not unlike that of a chorus. It is also commonly used in this way in rap music to process the lead vocal. These less discreet settings can also be used to add size to an acoustic instrument (such as guitar, for example) or, more occasionally, to vocal harmonies.

Chorus adds slightly delayed (generally between 10 and 40 ms) and modulated copies of the original signal to that original signal. In doing so, it creates the impression that the same performance is being played simultaneously by several people.

Many chorus models have only two controls. Depth defines the amount of modulation applied. The higher the setting, the more the pitch of the copies added to the original signal is modulated. The rate control determines the speed of that modulation.

Other parameters are sometimes offered to refine the effect. We may thus find controls such as delay time (the length of the delay between the original signal and its copies), chorus size (the number of copies added), stereo width (the width occupied by the effect), and mix (the proportion between the effect and the original signal). The availability of a mix control will in fact guide our decision whether to use the chorus in send/return mode or to insert it directly on the track being processed.

Chorus has a warm sound and is very often used to add dimension and movement to a source, whether monophonic or not. It is of course a common effect for processing acoustic guitars, electric pianos (such as the Rhodes), and synthesizer sounds. Chorus can also be used to color vocal harmonies, especially in pop songs.

At times, chorus can also help us clear out the center of a mix somewhat. Suppose a passage where a mono acoustic guitar shares the stage with a vocal. By assigning a chorus to the guitar, the delay created by the effect will move the guitar slightly back and spread it out on either side of the vocal. Each element will live in its own space: the vocal up front and firmly in the center, and the guitar behind it, wrapping around it on both sides.

Chorus can sometimes help disguise pitch problems.

Bass can also benefit from a chorus effect in open mixes where it plays an important role. The modulation effect helps draw the listener's attention and, just like our guitar in the previous example, extends its presence on both sides of the center.

Finally, the modulations generated by chorus can prove useful for disguising pitch problems that cannot be corrected. An out-of-tune guitar, a wavering vocal, or vocal harmonies that have undergone heavy pitch correction can sometimes be saved with a pronounced chorus.

The flanger effect dates back to the era of tape machines. A track—or an entire mix—is played simultaneously on two machines. The engineer applies slight finger pressure to the top of the reel flange on one of the tape machines, slowing the tape speed. The superimposition of this slowed playback over the normal-speed playback creates a series of resonances that seem to sweep back and forth across the frequency spectrum.

Flanger has a limited number of controls. As with chorus, we find a rate to define the speed of modulation and a depth control (sometimes called intensity) to determine how pronounced the effect will be. The feedback knob reinserts the generated copy at the start of the loop. This control is in fact the one whose effect is most characteristic of flanger. Some models also provide parameters allowing us to define the range of frequencies affected by the effect, its width, and, of course, a mix knob.

Flanger has an extremely colored sound. For that reason, it is most often used to create an occasional effect, with all sails set! The drum subgroup, vocal harmonies, or the entire mix are classic candidates for this kind of treatment. In the same spirit, it is possible to insert it after a reverb or echo in order to color them and add movement. It is also occasionally useful for tinting electric guitars, both in rhythm parts and solos. However, too much flanger very quickly throws us into the realm of cliché.

The flanger has a highly colored sound that lends itself well to processing vocal harmonies or creating occasional effects.

Used more discreetly, flanger can also help us add width to a bass, much as chorus would, except that its unique timbre will give it more personality.

Unlike the previous modulation effects, the phaser does not juxtapose a copy with the original signal to create its effect. Instead, it alters the sound by sweeping one or more peaks (called notches) across the frequency spectrum. Take a frequency equalizer, boost a very narrow band by about 12 dB, and slowly move the frequency from one end of the spectrum to the other. You will have a good idea of the kind of work a phaser does.

In terms of controls, the phaser is also relatively simple. As with chorus and flanger, it offers a rate to set the speed of modulation and a depth to manage the intensity of the effect. We also occasionally encounter a mix control, a width control (for stereo width), a knob often called color (which modifies the effect's timbre), and a feedback control that intensifies the effect by reinserting it at the circuit input. That said, the parameter specific to the phaser is called notch or stage. This control sets

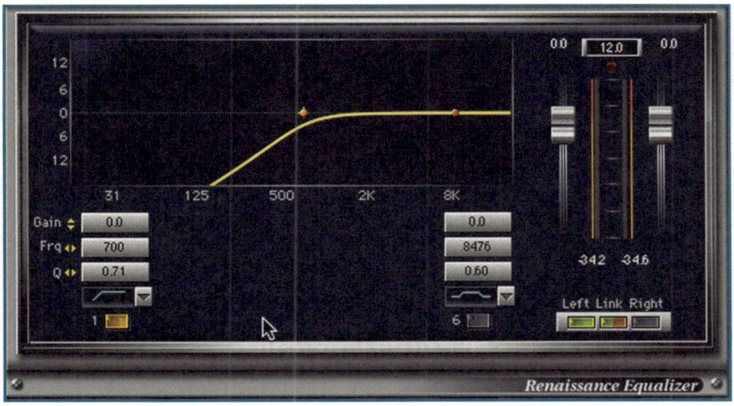

When chorus or flanger is used in send/return mode on a track, it can be useful to insert an equalizer to cut some of the low frequencies. Those frequencies contribute very little to the stereo image and can cause masking.

the number of bands that will sweep through the frequency spectrum. The graduation of this control is not of great practical use, however, since the effect changes radically depending on the number of bands used.

The phaser's highly distinctive sound limits its range of applications.

Because of its very distinctive sound, the phaser is actually used only rather rarely. It tends to thin the sound and become somewhat tiresome when overused. It is occasionally used on guitars, especially in reggae and funk, and can serve to color synthesizer sounds or create temporary effects.

Auto-pan is also a modulation effect that does not add echo to the original sound. It does not modify the signal itself, but instead manipulates its position within the stereo image. It therefore moves the signal from left to right according to a modulation speed (rate) that can be synchronized to the song tempo. A waveform selector determines how that movement will occur. Here again, the waveform icons express very clearly the panning strategy selected. The presence of a mix control will guide us in deciding whether to use it as an insert directly on the track or in send/return mode.

Auto-pan is useful when we want to create a rhythmic movement effect without altering the source's timbre. It is better suited to processing monophonic tracks, although it is entirely possible to apply it to stereo material. Unless the goal is to create an occasional effect, it is preferable to use it in moderation. The movements it generates can indeed become distracting and tiring for the listener rather quickly.

The waveform selected on the auto-pan determines how the signal moves within the stereo image.

8.6 Stereo Image Analyzers

These analyzers provide a visual representation of the stereo image in a mix. They help us assess the spatial layout of one or more elements.

Depending on the model, the analyzer will display stereo activity using either an oscilloscope or a semicircular graph. Perhaps it is simply a matter of habit, but the semicircular display seems much clearer and easier to use to me than an oscilloscope display. It is therefore with this type of analyzer that I will illustrate my examples.

It should be noted that inserting an analyzer at the very end of the output bus makes it easier to use. We can then choose the material to be analyzed by pressing its solo button.

8.6.1 THE OBJECTIVES

Objective 1: Facilitate balance and placement decisions

The visual representation provided by stereo image analyzers can help us achieve an even distribution along the left/right axis. These clues can be particularly useful if the room in which you are mixing has acoustic anomalies that alter your perception of the stereo image.

A stereo image analyzer visually represents the panorama of an element or of an entire mix.

Suppose we have two elements we want to place opposite each other within the spectrum. Let us say a guitar and a mandolin. By pressing the solo button on each track, we will be able to see their respective positions within the stereo image. More interesting still, we will be able to compare their relative levels visually. It then becomes easy to adjust their pan and relative levels in such a way as to favor an even distribution across the horizontal axis.

This method works very well to confirm the balance of identical instruments (two electric guitars placed opposite each other) or double-tracked parts (the same instrument performing the same part twice).

We can also make it easier to set up more complex placement configurations. Take the example of a three-part vocal harmony in which each part is doubled. We therefore have six harmony tracks—two soprano voices, two tenor voices, and two bass voices—to distribute evenly in space. Following the method used above, we can place the soprano voices opposite one another and calibrate their relative levels. We then do the same for the tenors and the basses. Once each of the three parts is balanced, all that remains is to link the faders by voice groups (sopranos, tenors, and basses). From then on, it becomes possible to create a balance for the whole vocal harmony while preserving the balance of the stereo image.

Here, a stereo image analyzer is used to balance two guitars placed opposite one another. In Image 1, we can see that the guitar on the left (labeled GTR1) is too loud compared with the one on the right, since the stereo image shifts to the left. In Image 2, the opposite is true: the guitar on the right is louder than the one on the left. In Image 3, the levels of both guitars are perfectly balanced. The stereo image is therefore distributed evenly on both sides.

The stereo image analyzer can also provide valuable clues about the space occupied not only by an element, but also by any stereo effect applied to it. Let us take again the example of the chorus we added to the guitar in order to clear the lead vocal. By sending only the guitar and its effect to the analyzer, we can fine-tune the width added by the chorus so that it does not mask other elements placed farther out in the stereo image.

Of course, all these decisions can be made by ear alone, but it is often useful to confirm their accuracy visually with the help of an analyzer.

Objective 2: Detect phase problems

An out-of-phase element is relatively easy to detect for a trained ear. When in doubt, an analyzer can visually indicate phase coherence between one or more tracks and, if necessary, help us make the required corrections.

So much for basic phase problems! It is, however, more difficult to assess whether a track exceeds the limits of stereophony. This is often the case with sounds generated by virtual instruments, which are frequently outrageously wide! By isolating the element in the analyzer, we will be able to adjust its panning so as to give it a more reasonable dimension.

As we have emphasized several times already, it is important to ensure that our mix and the elements composing it remain clearly audible in mono. The stereo image analyzer makes it possible to visualize the overall width occupied by a mix and thus to assess how well it will hold up in mono.

As a general rule, the width of the mix as a whole should exceed stereo limits only occasionally so as not to compromise mono playback.

The overall width of a mix should only occasionally exceed stereo limits.

I am aware that the word "occasionally" may seem vague to some here. But take a few minutes to try the following experiment. Choose a few commercial tracks, import them into your DAW, and visualize the extent of their stereo spread using an analyzer. Not only will you become familiar with your analyzer's display, but you will also notice that the vast majority of commercial tracks exceed stereo limits only very slightly, and only from time to time.

Of course, the opposite can also occur. Thus, if the analyzer reveals that your mix does not occupy enough space, you can revisit some of your panning and effects decisions or slightly correct its dimension with the help of a stereo imager.

As with over-compression, an overly wide or overly narrow stereo image is often difficult to recover. That is why regular listening in mono and the use of a stereo image analyzer will help you stay in control of your mix's dimensions.

9
DYNAMIC PROCESSING TOOLS

Several tools can help us keep control over a mix's dynamics. Some operate on principles similar to compression, while others are designed to solve specific problems related to a track's dynamics.

Simply put, compression raises the soft parts of a signal and lowers the loud parts.

9.1 The Compressor

In the 1940s, radio played much the same role that television does today. Families would gather around the radio to listen to spoken programs, radio dramas, news bulletins, music, and even live-broadcast plays or concerts.

As programming became more varied, commercial radio stations were faced with a major technical challenge: volume fluctuations. If the volume was too low, the content might become inaudible to listeners, but it could also compromise the stability and range of the station's transmitted signal. On the other hand, if the volume was too high, it could cause serious damage to the equipment used for broadcasting. Not to mention that listeners did not much appreciate having to constantly adjust the volume on their radios to counter these irritating fluctuations.

A technician was therefore assigned to correct the volume manually during broadcasts, a task far more demanding than it might seem. Imagine the stress of having to ride the volume during a comedy in front of a live audience: turning up the di-

An advertisement for the General Electric BA-5. In the 1950s. This unit was a huge success in the radio industry.

alogue and anticipating the audience's laughter! Miss a joke and you blow the station's equipment.

Engineers soon developed equipment capable of making these volume adjustments automatically. It is therefore to the radio industry that we owe the creation of two important audio-processing tools: the compressor and the limiter.

9.1.1 WHAT IS COMPRESSION?

Much like our radio technician, the compressor adapts volume according to the content it receives: it raises the softer parts of a signal and lowers the louder ones in order to make the overall level more consistent.

Despite the apparent simplicity of the concept, compression is one of the most difficult aspects of audio mixing to master. Many professionals openly admit that they do not fully understand everything that happens when they apply a compressor to a signal. It must be said that the result varies greatly depending on the instrument being processed and, of course, the settings used. Add to the equation the various operating modes of the units, their position in the signal chain, and the settings they do—or do not—offer, and we can all agree that the compressor is not a device whose use could be described as intuitive.

We will therefore explore the different facets of compression in order to make the most of what it can do during mixing.

9.1.2 COMMON SETTINGS

Threshold

The threshold sets the level above which the signal will be affected by compression. Thus, a threshold set at −12 dB means that the compressor modifies the part of the signal whose level exceeds −12 dB and leaves more or less untouched everything below that threshold. The position of the threshold therefore determines how much of the signal will be compressed.

The threshold may be variable or fixed. If it is variable, the threshold is adjusted with a clearly labeled control. If the compressor has no threshold control, then the threshold is fixed. In that case, the input level is used to reach the threshold.

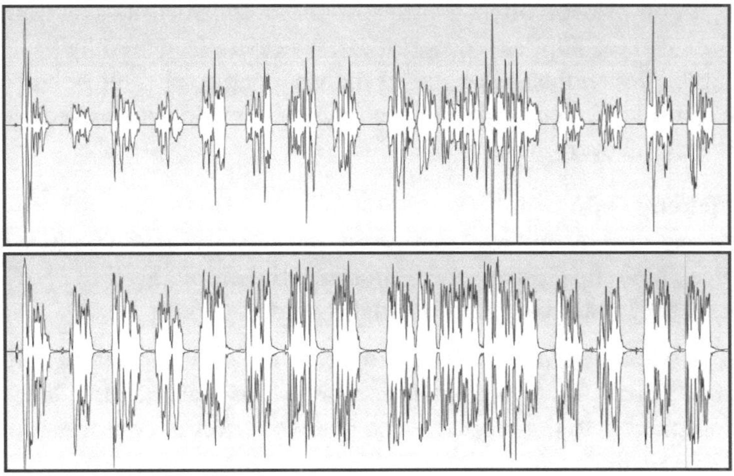

Top: a vocal track before compression; bottom, the same vocal track once compressed.

Ratio

The ratio determines the degree of compression applied to the signal. It is expressed using two numbers. The first indicates the input level and the second, the output level. Thus, a ratio of 3:1 means that a signal exceeding the threshold by 3 dB is reduced to 1 dB at the output.

Threshold determines how much of the signal is compressed—and ratio, how strongly.

Depending on the unit or plug-in, the ratio may be selected from a list of preset values or entered numerically.

Attack and Release

Let us suppose that a garden hose is spraying water at you and that you have to avoid it. Depending on the sharpness of your reflexes, some of you will move in time, others will not. Your reaction time will determine how wet you get.

The attack and release parameters are, in a way, the compressor's reaction time. They determine how quickly the compressor reacts to the signal.

A short attack setting means that the compressor will act quickly as soon as the threshold is reached. A longer setting will let part of the signal pass above the threshold before compressing it.

The same is true of the release. A fast setting stops compression as soon as the input level falls below the threshold. A long value causes the compressor to release the signal more gradually.

The attack parameter therefore sets the speed at which the compressor begins working, and the release sets the speed at which it stops working.

If a compressor offers neither of these controls, its reaction time is fixed. Optical compressors, for example, generally have rather slow reflexes because of the very nature of their operating mode. To return to our analogy, they would get sprayed by the signal every time!

The PROGAR (PROgram GuARdian), designed in 1935 by Al Towne, is said to have been the very first commercial compressor. It combined an "intelligent compressor" that automatically adjusted the volume during broadcast with a limiter that set the maximum output level.

Makeup Gain

As we saw in our explanation of ratio, compression reduces level. Makeup gain is used to increase the output level to compensate for what was lost through compression.

It also helps reduce the level difference between the before and after signals. By bringing the compressed signal back to a level comparable to the input, we can hear the effect of compression more easily.

The VU Meter

Most compressors include one or more VU meters used to display level fluctuations. They make it possible to assess the input level, the output level, and the amount of reduction resulting from compression (gain reduction).

If the unit has only one meter, it is usually accompanied by a switch that allows you to toggle between these three displays.

The gain-reduction display is especially useful. It provides three important pieces of information:

- the beginning of compression: *directly related to the threshold position and the attack setting*

COMPRESSION CIRCUITS

Optical

A light shines onto a sensor. The audio level changes the intensity of that light, and the sensor translates those changes into level information for the compressor. Since the compressor's reaction time is directly determined by this process, most of its parameters are fixed. The available controls are often limited to input level, output level, and sometimes a filter. This simple layout makes optical compressors easy to use.

It goes without saying that optical compressors are inherently fairly slow, which gives them a very musical action. They also tend to add warmth and fullness to the sound and are therefore often used for processing vocals, bass, and strings. However, they are not very effective at crushing a source. They are therefore less suited to aggressive room-microphone treatment or to parallel compression.

VCA (Voltage-Controlled Amplifier)

This type of unit bases its action on the voltage of the input electrical signal. It generally allows very precise adjustment of each compression parameter. This flexibility is in fact one of its main characteristics. VCA compressors are generally considered neutral when applying a low degree of compression. Their color becomes much more apparent, however, when more aggressive settings are used.

FET (Field-Effect Transistor)

FET compressors also base their action directly on the electrical signal. This type of transistor, commonly used to replace tubes, adds more coloration than VCA-type models, particularly in the midrange. Versatile, they are ideal for bringing an element closer to the listener, adding a touch of character to a track, and carrying out more colored processing.

Vari-Mu

This type of unit applies compression by means of tubes. Much like a guitar amplifier, the saturation generated by the tube adds richness to the sound. These compressors often do not offer a ratio control. The degree of compression, like the degree of coloration, increases as the input level is raised. There are, of course, Vari-Mu compressors that use transistors rather than tubes in their amplification or compression circuit. It is therefore the choice of components that gives the compressor its particular color..

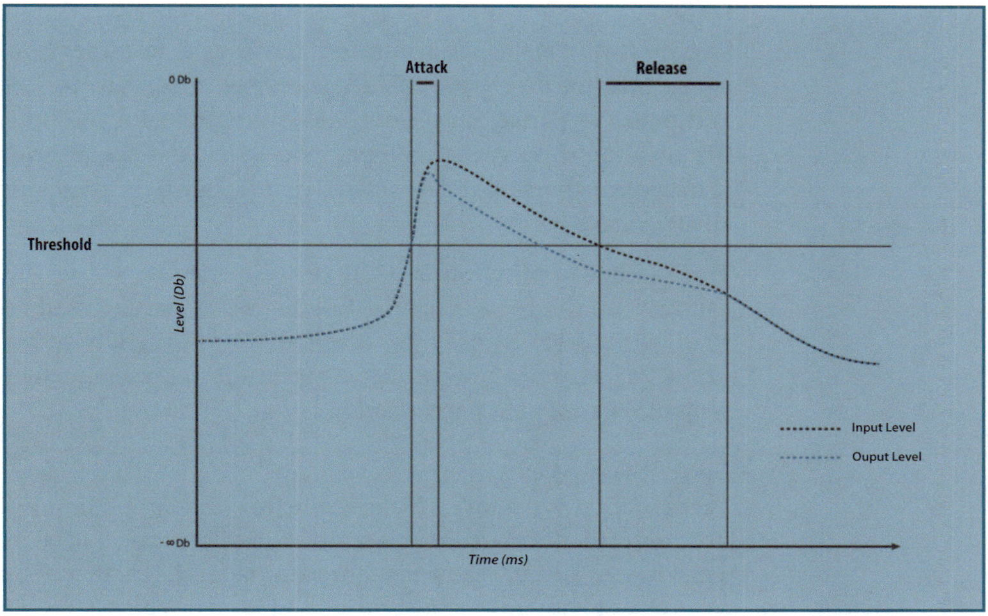

The different phases of compression and their effects on output level.

- the degree of compression: *directly related to the threshold position and the ratio*
- the end of compression: *directly related to the threshold position and the release setting.*

In gain-reduction mode, the meter therefore provides a visual representation of your compressor's work. Though less reliable than your ears, it offers valuable clues for refining the settings.

9.1.3 ADDITIONAL SETTINGS

There is an incredible number of analog and digital compressors on the market. Since the advent of DAW systems, plug-in manufacturers have competed with such zeal and ingenuity that they seem to release a new one every week.

After your ears, the VU meter in gain-reduction mode is the best way to assess the effect of your settings.

The wide range of available units inevitably brings different terminology and control layouts. Additional functions that are harder to grasp may therefore be added to the standard controls. Here is a brief overview of the various extra settings you may find on some compressors.

Auto release

As the name suggests, auto release automatically determines the optimal release according to the signal it receives. It is often effective when aiming for transparent compression, especially when processing performances with varied note lengths or irregular rhythm, such as voice or bass.

Knee

Together with the attack parameter, the knee determines how compression will be applied. The knee comes in two flavors: soft and hard. Soft knee engages compression gradually, reaching the maximum degree of compression when the signal level reaches the threshold. The attack of the signal is therefore affected more quickly.

This gradual application is often very effective on vocals. By contrast, hard knee applies the full degree of compression as soon as the level exceeds the threshold. It is generally better suited to instruments whose attack we want to preserve—that is often the case with percussion.

Auto Makeup Gain

This function is meant to make the before and after compression levels identical. Although mathematically correct, it often tends to overamplify the post-compression level. It is therefore generally preferable to adjust the output level by ear.

Lookahead

When this function is activated, the input signal is moved forward in time. The compressor can therefore, in a sense, predict the next event that will exceed the threshold. This function can help more easily tame short-lived, excessive transients—such as those of certain hand percussion instruments—that might otherwise outrun the compressor. Needless to say, this feature is found only on certain digital compressors.

The effect of the knee setting on compression. As we can see, compression is applied more gradually with a soft knee than with a

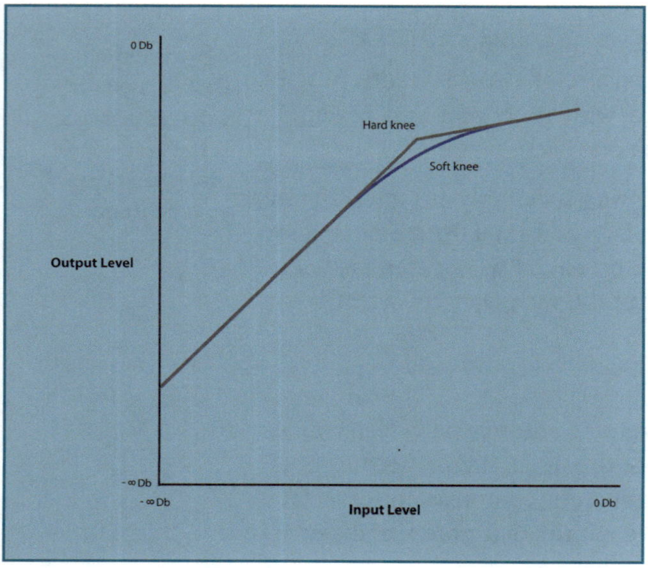

Stereo linking

Originally, stereo analog compressors consisted of two independent mono compressors. Thus, if a signal in the left channel exceeded the threshold, the right channel would not be compressed.

The stereo link option makes it possible to apply compression to both channels regardless of where the loud signal is located in the stereo image.

For example, let us place two performances of the same guitar part at opposite extremes of the stereo image. Without stereo link, each guitar will be compressed individually, preserving the distinct character of each performance and creating a sense of movement in the panorama. With stereo link, the compression of both guitars is unified, giving the illusion of a single guitar filling both sides of the stereo image. Whether or not to use stereo link therefore depends on the degree of stereo cohesion we want to achieve.

Sidechain

Normally, a compressor reacts to the signal it is meant to process. Sidechain makes it possible to apply compression to one signal not in response to its own level, but to the level of another signal fed to it. We will discuss this in detail later in the chapter.

Filters

Filter options are sometimes found on compressors in order to process a track's signal before it is compressed. These filters do not alter the track's frequency spectrum, but rather the signal being sent to the compressor.

As we saw earlier, low frequencies generate much more energy than high frequencies. Compressors are therefore naturally more sensitive to low-end content than to high-end content. Thus, when listening to certain instruments, such as bass, we will often feel that the volume of the high notes differs from that of the low notes.

Using a filter during compression can sometimes help achieve a more even level across an instrument's full range.

Mix (Dry/Wet)

The mix control, sometimes called dry/wet, allows you to set the blend between the compressed signal and the original signal. It is therefore a way of obtaining parallel compression using only a single track.

Peak-RMS

This selector focuses the compression circuit either on peaks or on average level (RMS).

Because the compressor must calculate an average of the input level, it reacts more slowly in RMS mode. As a general rule, peak mode is more effective on percussion, while RMS mode is better suited to tracks with fewer peaks to control.

Feedforward, Feedbackward

This selector refers to the order in which the compressor's internal components are arranged. In broad terms, in feedforward mode the signal is compressed before the compressor's internal amplifier, and in feedbackward mode it is compressed after that amplifier.

Although the result varies depending on the mode used, there is not really any application in which one mode has a decisive advantage over the other. We will therefore switch from one to the other and choose the one that gives the better result.

9.1.4 THE OBJECTIVES OF COMPRESSION

The compressor was originally designed to automatically reduce the level differences present in an audio signal. That is

A FEW COMPRESSION CLASSICS

Fairchild 670. With its 20 tubes and 14 transformers (!), the Fairchild has an exceptionally complex internal architecture. These components, combined with a Vari-Mu circuit, give it a warm, enveloping sound. Some engineers even use it without any compression at all, simply to benefit from the warmth added by its many components. The Fairchild is renowned for its use on vocals, but it is effective on just about any source. It also offers the possibility of working in Mid/Side, making it possible to compress the center and the sides of the signal independently.

DBX 160. Where others add color, the DBX 160 delivers power. This compressor has earned its place in studios because of the impact it brings to the material it processes. It naturally excels on percussive instruments such as kick drum and snare, but it can also work wonders on bass and synthesizers.

EL8 Distressor. Introduced in 1995 by Empirical Labs, the Distressor is an analog compressor controlled by a digital circuit. It was designed in part as an emulation of several of the models listed here. Among other things, it offers the possibility of changing the response of its detection circuit, which makes it a highly versatile unit.

API 2500. This VCA compressor has the characteristic of rounding out the low frequencies without coloring the rest of the spectrum. This quality makes it a favorite in mastering, as well as on drum subgroups.

SSL Master Compressor. This type of compressor is included by default on the main output channel of the legendary SSL consoles. It adds a great deal of bite and impact, particularly in the midrange. It also excels at gluing a drum subgroup together.

UREI/Universal Audio 1176. The sound of the 1176 is present on countless productions. This compressor stands out for its very fast attack and for its ratio selectors, which can be pressed simultaneously to obtain the aggressive sound heard on many drum recordings. The bite it adds to the sound makes it a favorite for snare drum, kick drum, and bass. It also has the characteristic of bringing the source closer to the listener, which makes it a staple for vocal processing.

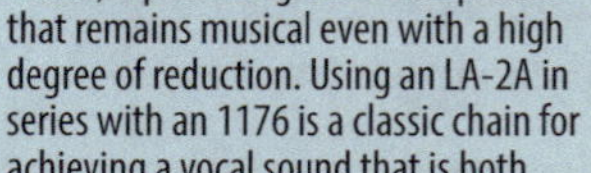

Teletronix/UREI/Universal Audio LA-2A. Its optical compression circuit and tube amplifiers give this unit a round, warm sound. Relatively slow in attack, it provides gradual compression that remains musical even with a high degree of reduction. Using an LA-2A in series with an 1176 is a classic chain for achieving a vocal sound that is both warm and present. The simplicity of its controls (two knobs!) also makes it quick and easy to use.

therefore the first use that comes to mind. However, it can do much more than even out volume.

Beyond understanding its settings, success with compression lies in the objective behind its use. The main questions to ask before inserting a compressor on a track are: "What am I trying to achieve? Do I want to even out the performance, color it, crush it, or bring it forward?" In the end, mastering compression lies less in the how than in the why.

Beyond understanding its settings, the key to successful compression is using it with a clear purpose.

Here, then, are six common compression objectives—six whys—that will help you define the task at hand and determine the best way to achieve it.

Objective 1: Volume Leveling

When we begin a mix, some instruments seem to disappear and reappear because of fluctuations in their level. In such cases, compression aims to make the instrument's level more consistent so that it remains present in the mix.

Bass and vocals are generally the elements that benefit most from volume leveling. Bass often forms the foundation of a mix. It plays both a rhythmic and a harmonic role, linking the drums to the rest of the arrangement. It therefore needs to remain clearly audible throughout the song.

For bass, a medium attack (around 50 ms) generally gives good results. The release, meanwhile, should be set so that the compressor stops working before the beginning of the next downbeat. The threshold should be placed at the base of the peaks. The ratio then determines the extent of the leveling. A good starting point is 4:1, but it is not uncommon to use a higher ratio (10:1 or more) to really flatten the bass's dynamics.

Vocals often show large dynamic variations that make some passages hard to hear while others take up too much space. This instability can compromise lyric intelligibility and make the vocal harder to follow in the mix.

Volume leveling is often intended to be transparent.

We will tend to use a short attack to control the peaks at the beginning of each word. It is generally effective to set the threshold very low so that a large portion of the signal is affected. Using a low ratio (between 2:1 and 4:1) will make the performance more even while ensuring transparent compression. The release should be set fast enough for the gain-reduction meter to return regularly to 0 between words.

Of course, many other instruments can also benefit from volume leveling. In general, we will use a low threshold and a modest ratio. The speed of the attack will determine how much attack we want to preserve, and the release will be adjusted according to the tempo of the performance. A small amount of reduction—on the order of a few dB—is usually enough to stabilize an instrument's level. Let us remember that the goal here is to even out the level transparently, not to create an effect. Thus, if the gain-reduction meter only rarely returns to 0, your compression is probably too severe.

Objective 2: Bring Out an Instrument's Details

A compressor can also be used to accentuate the details of a sound. The objective is therefore to highlight low-level elements. This technique can, for example, bring out the drummer's nuances on the snare drum, finger noise on an acoustic guitar, or the singer's breathing between phrases.

Heavy peak reduction makes it possible to bring up low-level content.

To obtain this effect, the signal's peaks will be reduced radically. The threshold should therefore be placed at the base of the peaks and a high ratio used (from 8:1 up to 20:1). Fast attack and release settings will reduce their level. We should not hesitate to apply 10 dB, 15 dB, or even 20 dB of reduction. By compensating for the loss of level with makeup gain, we reveal all the low-level content.

This technique is commonly used to accentuate the natural reverb captured by room microphones during a drum recording. It also lengthens the decay of the drums, giving them a sense of power.

It is also a common approach in parallel compression, a technique we will explore later in this chapter.

Objective 3: Modify an Instrument's Attack

Some instruments, such as acoustic guitar, often have strong peaks that can distract the listener. For example, we may hear the pick striking the strings very clearly, while the notes themselves get lost in the rest of the arrangement. In such a case, a compressor will be used to soften those peaks and make the harmonic content more audible.

The attack setting can be used both to reduce and to increase a signal's attack.

To achieve this objective, we will use a fast attack, a release in time with the tempo, and place the threshold at the base of the peaks.

Conversely, we may sometimes be faced with an instrument whose attack needs a little more bite. We may therefore aim to increase the peaks of the signal. Although this objective may at first seem contrary to the nature of compression, we must remember that the attack setting allows us to control the compressor's reaction speed. We will therefore use an attack setting long enough to let the peaks through, and a long release to attenuate the sustain. The threshold will be placed at the base of the instrument's natural attack.

Objective 4: Control an Element's Presence

The compressor also makes it possible to control how present an element feels in the mix. It can help create the impression that an instrument is either closer to or farther from the listener. For example, using a relatively high ratio (around 8:1), a moderately long attack, and a very short release will tend to bring the source closer to the listener. This technique works particularly well on vocal tracks and electric-guitar subgroups.

Overcompression pushes the track away from the listener.

Conversely, overcompression tends to push the track away from the listener. Although it should generally be avoided, overcompression can be used to advantage when the goal is precisely to push an element farther back in the mix. This approach can be particularly effective for placing vocal harmonies behind the lead vocal.

A very short attack and a rather long release will tend to push the track farther back in the mix. Using a high ratio and a low threshold will produce a similar effect.

Objective 5: Glue Tracks Together

When used on a subgroup, compression plays a unifying role. It helps create the impression that a collection of individual tracks belongs to the same whole. The compressor will, so to speak, synchronize the attack of the tracks while reducing volume disparities.

This gluing effect is often what we are looking for when using a compressor on the drum subgroup. Care should be taken to set the attack according to how much peak information we want to preserve, and the release according to the tempo. In general, the compressor should have returned to 0 dB before the next downbeat. The amount of compression needed to glue drum tracks together is often on the order of 3 or 4 dB of reduction.

The gluing effect is often achieved with only a small amount of reduction.

It is the same objective we pursue when inserting a compressor on a mix's stereo output. Here, the required amount of compression is minimal. The effect is often at its best when less than 2 dB of reduction is applied.

Ideally, the compressor should be inserted on the output bus fairly early in the mix, because it will influence your decisions throughout the rest of the process.

Objective 6: Color a Track

Compression can also be useful for giving a track a particular color. Nearly all compressors, whether digital or analog, impart some tonal character to the sound. The LA-2A, the Neve 33609, and the Fairchild are known for the warmth they add; the SSL tends to accentuate the midrange; the 1176 saturates in a pleasing way, and so on.

Every compressor has its own distinctive color.

This coloration becomes more and more apparent as the amount of compression increases. In addition, a very short release generates harmonic distortion that helps emphasize the character of the unit.

Most emulation plug-ins reproduce the saturation of analog compressors. Depending on the model, we can therefore increase the input or output level to obtain this saturation and thereby color our track

9.1.5 RECOMMENDATIONS

Get Familiar With Your Units

There are countless compressors and compression plug-ins available today. What is more, most DAWs include a broad selection of dynamics processors. Which one should you choose?

When starting out in mixing, we often tend to pick a compressor at random from the list and do our best to achieve the sound we want. In my opinion, this random selection is one of the main obstacles to learning compression.

Choose one compressor model and learn it in depth rather than jumping from one unit to another.

The first reason is that each of your compressors will have a completely different visual layout and set of controls. One may have a fixed threshold, another an adjustable one; this one may have an attack control, that one may not, and so on. To make matters even more complicated, the type of circuit used in the unit—or emulated by the plug-in—greatly influences the way it will act on the sound.

For these reasons, trying to learn several compressors at once is counterproductive. Focusing on one unit at a time makes it easier to understand the process and achieve specific results.

Of course, you can choose whichever one you like, but personally I suggest using a model that offers a limited number of controls. For example, the 1176 or one of its many emulations is an excellent model for getting acquainted with compression. Not only is its layout simple, but its controls are limited to the essentials: fixed threshold, attack, release, and ratio. It will also deliver good results regardless of the source you feed it. It is flexible enough to allow you to achieve any of the objectives described above.

But whichever unit you choose, the important thing is to try it on as many different sources as possible and in varied musical contexts until you can anticipate the result of your settings. Once you fully understand that first unit, move on to learning a second compressor and compare the results.

By becoming familiar with your compressors one after another, you will be able to determine the strengths and weaknesses of each unit at your disposal. Little by little, you will develop preferences regarding which unit to use depending on the source being processed and the objective you want to achieve.

All of this obviously takes time. But this exercise will lead you to a better understanding of the compression process. InIn fact, this method will probably get you good results faster than blindly jumping from one unit to another.

A Setup Method

1. Set the ratio to a high value (16:1 or 20:1).

2. Set the attack and release controls to their fastest settings.

3. While keeping an eye on the gain-reduction meter, lower the threshold until you reach about 20 dB of reduction.

4. Lengthen the attack until the portion of the attack you want to preserve becomes audible.

5. Lengthen the release so that compression stops before the next downbeat.

6. Readjust the ratio to set the desired amount of reduction.

7. Gradually raise the threshold until you achieve a natural result.

8. Fine-tune your settings.

Explore the Presets

The vast majority of plug-ins come with a range of presets for various instruments or applications. These presets are generally created by experienced people. Some manufacturers even offer presets designed by leading mixing engineers. When starting out with compression, it can be very interesting to browse these presets in order to become familiar with the plug-in, learn its capabilities, and see how these professionals suggest using it.

That said, the odds that a preset will perfectly meet the needs of your song are rather low. After all, there are no miracle recipes in mixing. However, these presets can provide a useful starting point for refining your settings.

Make Realistic Comparisons

Inserting a compressor on a track invariably changes its output level. This level change, whether upward or downward, influences your perception of the result. It is therefore important to use makeup gain so that the pre- and post-compression levels are comparable. By switching back and forth between the original and the compressed sound, you will then be able to judge the accuracy of your settings.

The Cumulative Effect of Compression

As I pointed out at the beginning of the chapter, compression is one of the most difficult aspects of mixing to grasp. You have to train your ear to hear its effect on sound. That is also why we all tend to overcompress elements when we begin mixing.

Overcompression is one of the problems professionals most often point out when listening to mixes made by less experienced people. Let us step back a little and look at what happens, compression-wise, in a perfectly ordinary mix.

First, we have applied compression on a few tracks to even out the performance. We have then grouped some of those tracks into a subgroup that we compressed in order to glue everything together. On the mix output, we inserted a tape simulator that also subtly reduces the dynamic range of our mix. Finally, we placed a compressor on the mix output to unify the overall sound. Once our mix is finished, we send it to a mastering engineer—and guess what? They too apply compression to make it commercially comparable to other productions in that genre.

Overcompression is one of the problems professionals most often point out when listening to mixes by less experienced mixers.

We quickly realize that compression is cumulative. As a result, an element often needs much less reduction than we might think, since it will likely pass through one or more additional stages of compression before reaching the listener.

It is therefore important to remain cautious about how much dynamic range reduction we apply to an instrument, a subgroup, or an entire mix. Remember that one of the secrets of a successful mix lies in the accumulation of many small interventions and only rarely in one spectacular move.

Fight Your Reflexes

If you are interested in mixing—which seems fairly obvious since you are reading this book—you have probably read or heard that compression is its magic ingredient. While there is some truth to that, we should not go overboard.

Not every track in a mix systematically needs compression. For example, trying to reduce the dynamic range of a heavily saturated rhythm guitar is a futile exercise. All you have to do is look at its waveform to understand that its dynamic range is already practically nonexistent.

At the risk of repeating myself, it is important to have a precise objective in mind before inserting a compressor on a track. If there is any magic at all in compression, that is where it lies. Thus, if you cannot clearly define what you want your compressor to do, there is a good chance that the track simply does not need one.

9.1.6 ADVANCED COMPRESSION TECHNIQUES

Serial Compression

Earlier, we mentioned that the different types of compressors each have their own sonic characteristics. Some add warmth, others add presence; some excel at leveling volume, others are especially effective at reducing attack, and so on.

Serial compression consists of placing compressors one after another in order to take advantage of the strengths of each unit. On a vocal, for example, we might place a first compressor to benefit from the warmth it adds to the sound, followed by a second compressor to bring the vocal closer to the listener.

Using compressors in series also makes it possible to achieve a high degree of compression without making the treatment intrusive. It is indeed easier to achieve transparent compression by spreading the work across two units rather than doing a large amount of reduction in one place.

On bass, for example, it is not uncommon to place a first compressor to tame the peaks—therefore with a high ratio, fast attack, and high threshold—and then add another unit after it to even out the whole signal—therefore with a low ratio, slower attack and release, and low threshold.

This method therefore makes it possible to target precisely the share of the work and the objective assigned to each unit.

Sidechain Compression

Whether we are aware of it or not, we are all exposed to sidechain compression almost every day. This process is in fact a favorite of advertisers. You have heard those ads in which booming music suddenly gives way to a narrator—generally just as booming—before returning to full volume once the speaking is over?

In those ads, a compressor is placed on the music track. That compressor is then sidechained to the narrator's voice. Thus, compression happens not according to the musical content, but according to the narrator's voice. As soon as the narrator speaks, the music is automatically attenuated to give priority to the voice, making the text more audible. That is exactly the principle behind sidechain compression: prioritizing one signal over another.

The procedure is relatively simple, but it varies depending on the software you are using. All you need to do is insert a compressor with a sidechain function on the track you want to attenuate. Then use a send from the source you want to prioritize in order to feed that sound into the compressor's sidechain. The source is sent either by enabling the compressor's sidechain input in the send menu, or by selecting the source directly in the compressor's sidechain menu. From that point on, the compressor reduces the level of the track on which it is inserted according to the signal it receives through the sidechain.

In mixing, this method can help us solve masking problems between two conflicting sonic elements. The source sent into the sidechain channel therefore takes precedence over the one on which the compressor has been inserted.

This technique is also used very frequently in electronic music to emphasize the downbeats of a rhythm. A compressor is inserted on the bass track, and the sound of the kick drum is fed into that compressor's sidechain. Thus, each time the kick drum is struck, the bass is reduced in level by the compressor. This ensures that the kick cuts through the low frequencies on every hit.

Besides preventing possible masking between the two elements, this approach also enhances the groove. Certainly, the bass level is attenuated every time the kick drum hits, but we can also view the maneuver the other way around: the bass level is increased between the kick hits. This alternation between the two elements creates a kind of wave in the low frequencies that has the effect of reinforcing the groove of the piece. This technique is very effective for musical styles built primarily on rhythm, such as reggae, funk, rap, and of course EDM.

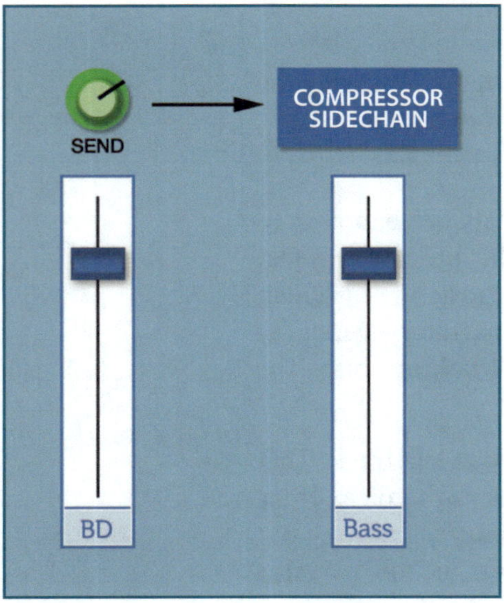

A sidechain routing setup intended to reduce the bass level so the attack of the kick drum can be heard.

Sidechain compression can also be used to counter the masking of reverb or delay. Let us suppose that we want to add delay to a guitar solo. We place a compressor on the delay and feed the guitar signal into its sidechain channel. Thus, every time the guitarist plays, the effect pulls back, then returns during the silences. We get more intimacy during the performance without losing the sense of space provided by the delay.

The same technique is also very effective on the lead-vocal/reverb combination.

We can also push the principle further by controlling the level of the entire mix according to the presence of the lead vocal. We first create a subgroup containing all the mix elements except the lead vocal. We then place a compressor on that track and feed the lead-vocal signal into its sidechain channel. Thus, as in radio advertising, the level of the musical content rises between phrases (ideally with a little more subtlety than in a radio ad!).

Sidechain compression makes it possible to prioritize one element over another.

Whatever elements we use it on, the success of a sidechain technique lies in the compressor's attack and release settings. We must ensure that the level attenuation happens transparently—neither too loose nor too abrupt.

In mixing, the amount of attenuation required is of course less than what we hear in advertising. A reduction of 1 to 3 dB is generally enough to achieve the desired effect.

Parallel Compression

At the beginning of the chapter, we broadly defined compression as a process that reduces the loud parts of a signal and raises the soft ones. A simple way to think about the effect of parallel compression is to imagine compression that would only raise the soft parts of the signal without touching the loud parts. We therefore get a fuller, more present sound while preserving the natural dynamics of the source.

Parallel compression brings up the soft parts without touching the loud parts.

Although parallel compression is far from transparent in itself, it paradoxically allows part of the sound and natural dynamics of an instrument to remain intact—something impossible to achieve by applying compression directly to the track.

The Mechanics

As its name suggests, parallel compression assumes that two identical instances of the same element—either a track or a group of tracks—will be heard simultaneously. One of these instances will be heavily compressed. On a console or in your DAW, there are three ways to create parallel compression.

For an individual track, we simply make a copy on which we place the compressor. This is very often how parallel compression is applied to vocals, snare drum, or bass, for example.

Parallel compression can also be applied to a subgroup. We first create a compression channel—either by adding an effects bus or a new subgroup—on which we insert a compressor. Using the subgroup's send, we route the signal to that compression channel. This method works well for subgroups containing homogeneous instruments, such as guitars, keyboards, or brass.

Although it is generally appropriate to apply parallel compression to an entire subgroup, it is sometimes more useful to recalibrate how much signal from each of its elements will be sent to the compressor. This is often the case with drum tracks. We can thus limit the often excessive presence of the hi-hat, cymbals, and room microphones in the compressed channel.

That leads us to the third method. We create a compression channel. Then we use the send from each track to route its signal to that channel. By doing this, we can choose how much of each element is sent to the compressor.

The effect of parallel compression is very quickly noticeable. The level of the compressed track is therefore usually set much lower than that of the original track.

Compressor Settings

Since parallel compression is primarily intended to expose the low-level information in a track, the compressor settings applied to the copy will resemble those used to bring out an instrument's details. We will therefore use very fast attack and release settings, a high ratio, and adjust the threshold to achieve between 10 and 20 dB of gain reduction.

With such heavy compression, the choice of unit is greatly influenced by the color it imparts to the track. Analog compressors and their emulations are therefore excellent choices for this kind of treatment.

Two Ways of Applying Parallel Compression.

(Left) When processing a single track, the simplest method is to make a copy of it and insert a compressor on that copy.

(Right) When processing a subgroup, its signal is routed to another subgroup or to an effects bus with a compressor inserted on it.

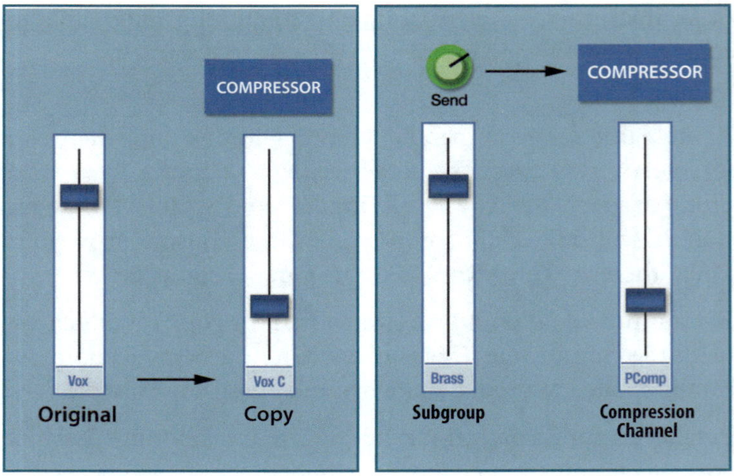

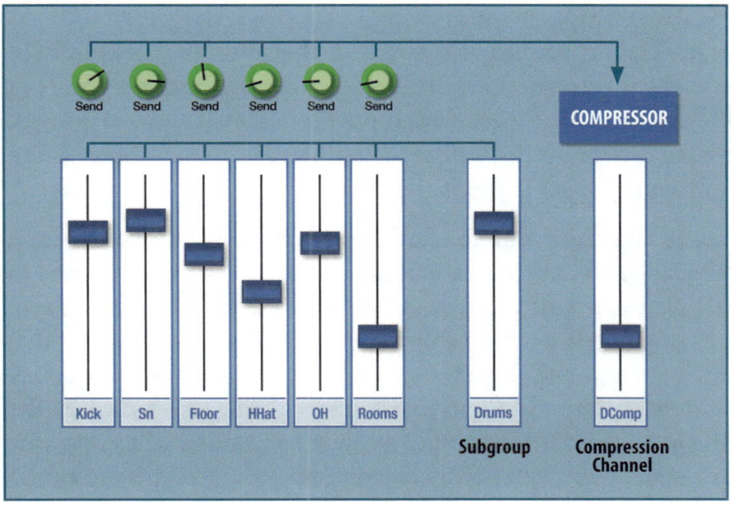

By using the send of each track to route the signal to the compression channel, it becomes possible to send the compressor an independent balance from that of the subgroup.

The Objectives of Parallel Compression

Of course, parallel compression is instinctively associated with drums. But it can also be used on other instruments. The goal, however, will differ slightly from the quest for power typically associated with parallel compression on drums.

Take, for example, an acoustic-guitar or piano solo, two instruments that are particularly dynamic. Sometimes certain passages in the performance get lost in the arrangement. Naturally, it is out of the question to alter the instrument's natural dynamics—that is a large part of its signature and the artist's. Parallel compression can then help us bring out the details of the performance and help it cut through the arrangement.

In the same vein, parallel compression can be used to reinforce an element's presence so that it always remains clearly audible in the mix. That is often what we are trying to achieve with bass or lead vocals.

The saturation generated by a heavily driven compressor adds a great deal of color to the sound. Parallel compression can therefore also be used to add energy to an instrument. This effect is particularly effective on a lead-vocal track.

It is also possible to color an entire mix by adding a compression channel to which all of its elements are routed. However, we must keep in mind that the compression channel removes most of the dynamics from what it receives. The blend must therefore be adjusted so as to add power to the mix without making it flat and lifeless. This should be thought of as the pinch of salt that enhances the flavor of a dish.

Multiband Compression

A multiband compressor is a unit that divides the frequency spectrum into sections and assigns a compressor to each of these bands. This allows each portion of the signal to be processed differently. This type of compressor is sometimes useful for treating specific problems in one or more parts of the signal.

Let us take the example of a vocal track. The singer whispers a languid verse. Their face is right up against the microphone to add as much warmth as possible to the voice. For some reason, the singer moves away from the microphone for the last two lines of the verse. There is a good chance that the low-frequency content of those last two lines will be much lower than in the previous ones. We can therefore insert a multiband compressor to reduce that disparity by treating only the lower band of the signal.

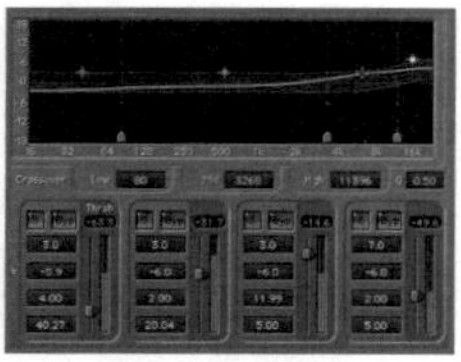

This multiband compressor divides the frequency spectrum into four parts and allows each one to be compressed differently.

The same can happen with an electric guitar whose tone becomes shrill on certain attacks. We may then try to attenuate the problem by treating only the high-frequency band.

When working with a multiband compressor, we do not need to use all the available bands. Instead, we should identify the part of the signal that actually needs correction and treat only that. The width of each band can also be adjusted, making it possible to target the area to be processed precisely.

In that sense, it is often easier to think of the multiband compressor not as a compressor, but rather as a frequency equalizer that happens to be dynamic. We will discuss the dynamic equalizer later in this chapter.

In mixing, the use of a multiband compressor should be the result of a considered decision. After all, adjusting one compressor is already no small task, so setting four or six on the same track borders on masochism! This unit should therefore be seen as a last-resort tool for correcting the dynamics of a track that resists more conventional treatment.

Mid/Side Compression (or M/S)

M/S comes from a stereo encoding technique. M stands for mid and S for side. The signal is divided into two channels: a center channel and a channel containing the information from the left and right sides, allowing each to be processed independently.

In mixing, this type of treatment can help us rework tracks that were delivered in stereo, such as virtual-synth tracks or loops. It can indeed happen that the presence or absence of reverb makes those tracks difficult to integrate into the rest of the mix. For example, an acoustic drum loop may not contain enough reverb. Since we do not have the individual tracks, we cannot raise the level of the room microphones. Of course, it is possible to add an artificial effect, but it may be more appropriate to enhance the natural ambience captured during recording. In that case, we place an M/S compressor on the track and apply heavy compression to the sides of the signal. This brings up the natural sound of the room in which the drums were recorded.

This Fairchild 670 emulation allows M/S compression.

Following the same principle, a synth track may present an adequate stereo image but not enough attack in the center to cut through the mix. With an M/S compressor, we can modify the attack of the center channel to give it more impact without necessarily altering the synth's stereo image.

At first glance, the amount of width that can be added to the stereo image with this kind of compressor may seem tempting. Like stereo enhancers, however, abusing it for that purpose risks causing significant mono compatibility problems. Just like multiband compression, M/S compression is a specialized processing tool and is therefore best used sparingly.

Independent Compression of Each Side of the Stereo Image

Earlier in the chapter, we pointed out that the stereo linking function makes it possible to apply compression evenly to a stereo source regardless of where the signal is located. There are, however, occasions when it is desirable to compress the left and right sides independently.

For example, when a compressor is placed on a vocal-harmony subgroup or on the output bus, compression without stereo linking affects the signal coming from each side according to its own energy. It can therefore sometimes flatten the volume disparities present in each channel.

It is wise to use multiband and M/S compression sparingly.

If you have a compressor that offers this function, it is worth experimenting with it to see whether this type of treatment suits the needs of your mix.

9.2 The Limiter

The limiter is a very close relative of the compressor, so much so that some units bear both names. For example, the DBX 160 is called a Compressor/Limiter, and the 1176 a Limiting Amplifier. In addition, many compressors include a selector called

Limiter, which certainly contributes to the possible confusion between these two types of dynamic processing.

A limiter is a processing module that makes it possible to apply a very high degree of compression quickly. In theory, any compressor capable of reaching a high compression ratio—say greater than 20:1—can be considered a limiter.

More recently, the distinction between a compressor and a limiter has become clearer. A range of units and plug-ins has indeed refined the definition of a limiter by incorporating an important parameter: maximum output level. This is what is called a brickwall limiter. Its near-instant attack effectively creates a brick wall that the signal can never cross.

The limiter sets a ceiling the signal can never exceed.

With this type of limiter, we no longer really think in terms of compression ratio, but in terms of ceiling. It is therefore by setting a maximum output level that we affect the dynamics.

Since it works by clipping the signal, the limiter's intervention is not what one would call a subtle tool. Truncating the part that exceeds the ceiling inevitably alters the signal. However, when used in moderation, its action is surprisingly transparent.

9.2.1 SETTINGS

Most limiters offer a limited number of controls.

The threshold works much like that of a standard compressor. It determines the point above which the signal will be processed.

Another parameter, called ceiling or output level, sets the maximum output level. This ceiling is expressed in negative dB. Thus, a ceiling of –0.2 dB indicates that the maximum level will be 0.2 dB below digital zero.

The limiter very often includes a release that determines how quickly it stops acting. Of course, one or more meters are also

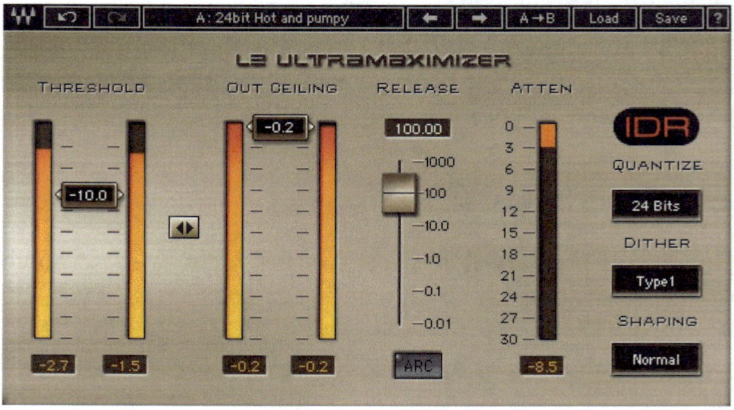

Waves' L2 Maximizer is probably one of the best-known brickwall limiters. In addition to the usual controls, it includes a function that allows the threshold and the ceiling to be adjusted simultaneously, making it possible to maintain a uniform output level regardless of the amount of reduction being applied.

provided to display input and output levels as well as the amount of reduction.

Because they are normally placed at the very end of the processing chain during mastering, limiters often include dithering selectors that make it possible to reduce the bit depth at the output—24, 20, 16, 12, and sometimes 8 bits—in order to meet the specifications of the final delivery format.

9.2.2 THE OBJECTIVES OF USING A LIMITER

Well known among mastering engineers, the limiter is often the final tool used to reduce a song's dynamic range in order to increase its average level. But limiters are not useful only in mastering; they can also provide valuable help during mixing by performing certain tasks that their cousin, the compressor, cannot accomplish as easily.

Objective 1: Attenuate Strong Occasional Peaks

During mixing, we are sometimes confronted with instruments whose dynamics do not seem to respond well to a standard compressor. The compressor simply cannot tame the peaks without overcompressing the rest of the content. In such cases, a limiter can come to our rescue by treating only the very top of the signal without touching the softer parts.

Many instruments can benefit from this treatment. Bass, for example, particularly when played slap style, is often better served by a limiter than by a compressor. The same holds true when the bass track contains wide dynamic variations because of a lack of technical control during the performance. At times, the string's contact with the pickup can also cause strong peaks.

Electric-guitar tracks without too much saturation can also become very percussive. Clipping them slightly with a limiter will often help attenuate these dynamic spasms.

As for acoustic guitar, certain playing styles are more likely than others to create sudden dynamic swings. This is often the case with fingerstyle guitar. Of course, that dynamic is often deliberate on the player's part and is part of the charm of the performance. However, to fit within the overall mix, it is sometimes necessary to temper those emotional surges. For the same reasons, snare drum and voice can also benefit from the use of a limiter to attenuate occasional peaks that distract our attention while listening to the mix.

In all these situations, adding a limiter alongside a standard compressor will ensure control over the signal's dynamic range.

The limiter will handle the excessive peaks, and the compressor will even out the rest of the signal.

Using a limiter and a compressor in series can be helpful when processing a signal with strong occasional peaks.

On many limiter models, lowering the threshold gradually increases the track's overall level. This increase disrupts gain structure and makes before/after comparisons difficult. A simple way around this problem is to link the threshold and the maximum output level so that they move together. On many limiters, a link function makes this easy. This way, we can maintain a uniform output level regardless of the amount of reduction being applied.

Objective 2: Use It in Parallel to Increase Impact Without Removing All the Dynamics

A limiter can be used in parallel with the original track to enhance resonance—of a snare drum, for example—or reduce volume disparities while preserving part of the original track's dynamics.

This technique can be useful on the instruments mentioned in the previous objective and also work well on intense vocal tracks.

Objective 3: Add Cohesion to the Bass and Kick Drum

It may happen that, despite the dynamic processing applied to the individual bass and kick tracks, they do not form the solid unit we want to hear in certain musical styles. In that case, it is possible to stabilize the dynamics of both tracks simultaneously with a limiter.

To do this, we create a subgroup, route the bass and kick drum tracks to it, and insert a limiter to process their dynamics together. Since the kick drum has stronger peaks than the bass, it will make the limiter react more quickly. This also implies that the bass level will increase when the kick drum is silent. This way, a solid low-end foundation is created in the mix. As a general rule, a reduction of around 3 to 6 dB is enough to achieve this cohesion.

A limiter gives a punchier result than a compressor for this kind of task. We must therefore judge whether this method suits the song.

Objective 4: Create an Effect

A limiter can also be useful for creating an effect. In electronic music, for example, it is common to place a limiter on the kick drum in order to obtain a waveform whose peak has a squarelike shape. In doing so, saturation is added to the signal, which helps the track cut through the rest of the mix.

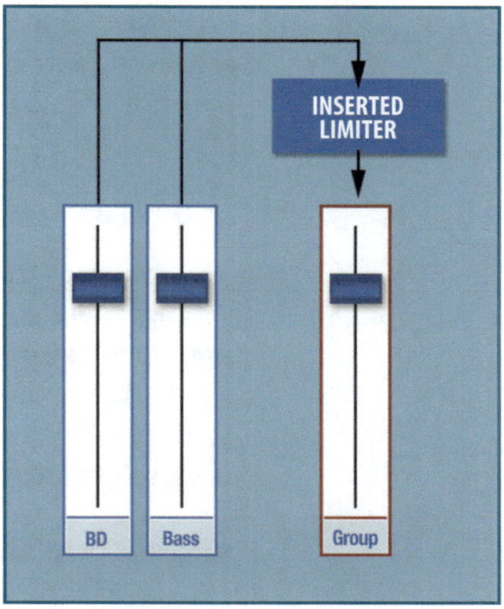

Here, the kick drum and bass are routed to a subgroup with a limiter inserted on it. The limiter acts on both signals simultaneously and adds cohesion to the low end of the mix.

Objective 5: Evaluate How the Mix Reacts to the Application of a Limiter

During mixing, the use of a limiter on the output bus should always be temporary. It is much wiser to leave final level optimization to the mastering stage. That said, a limiter can still be useful for various evaluation tasks.

For example, a limiter placed at the end of the output bus will shed light on how the mix will react once its level is maximized in mastering. The overall increase in level will also reveal problems that may have gone unnoticed during mixing, such as background noise.

Inserting a limiter also makes it possible to spot peaks that cause it to react excessively. You can then determine which element is producing them and revise its treatment, rather than letting it shape the dynamics of the entire mix more than necessary.

Needless to say, a mix in progress and a mastered track are two very different things, particularly in terms of dynamics and level. Inserting a limiter at the output of your mix reduces those differences, making comparisons with reference tracks easier.

This method therefore helps us evaluate how the mix holds up against a commercial track. It will also provide valuable clues regarding the balance of the various instruments, the level of the effects, and frequency distribution.

Objective 6: Prepare the Version of the Mix to Present to the Client

It is common practice to use a "limited" version of the mix when presenting the final version of a project to the client. This serves a purpose similar to that of the previous objective: bringing the mix closer to the commercial sound we are used to hearing.

Inserting a limiter on the output bus should always be a temporary measure.

If a client requests a version they can listen to outside the studio, it is also appropriate to use a limiter to make that version closer in level to a mastered track. In that case, it is wise to limit the reduction to 3 or 4 dB so as not to alter the sound of the mix excessively.

Obviously, once the mix has been approved, the limiter will be removed before moving on to mastering, which is the more appropriate stage for managing the final level.

9.3 The Gate and the Expander

The gate is used mainly to eliminate or reduce the level of background noise or bleed that lies beneath the main signal. Its operation is based on dynamics. It sets a minimum threshold, like a gate that opens only when the signal is loud enough to pass through. Any part of the audio that fails to cross that threshold is therefore attenuated or rendered inaudible.

9.3.1 SETTINGS

A gate, like an expander, generally includes the following parameters.

Threshold: the level above which the gate lets the sound pass at full level. Sometimes this parameter is divided into two parts: Gate Open and Gate Close. Together, they define the level range within which the gate remains open. This type of operation therefore allows more precise adjustment, although in the vast majority of cases a simple threshold is enough to calibrate a gate properly.

Attack: the speed, in milliseconds, at which the gate opens once the threshold is reached.

Release: the speed, in milliseconds, at which the gate closes when the level falls below the minimum threshold.

Floor (range or reduction): determines the amount of level reduction applied to the signal.

Hold: the delay, in milliseconds, during which the gate remains open before entering the release phase.

A VU meter: although the display varies depending on the model, a gate includes at minimum a meter to assess the amount of level reduction applied to the signal. On analog units, this meter is often a graduated series of LEDs. In digital form, it is more often a continuous meter with a precise numerical indication of the reduction being applied.

A graph: plug-ins and digital consoles offer a graph similar to that found on some compressors. It makes it possible to visualize the threshold position and compare input and output levels.

THE EFFECTS OF A GATE'S PARAMETERS

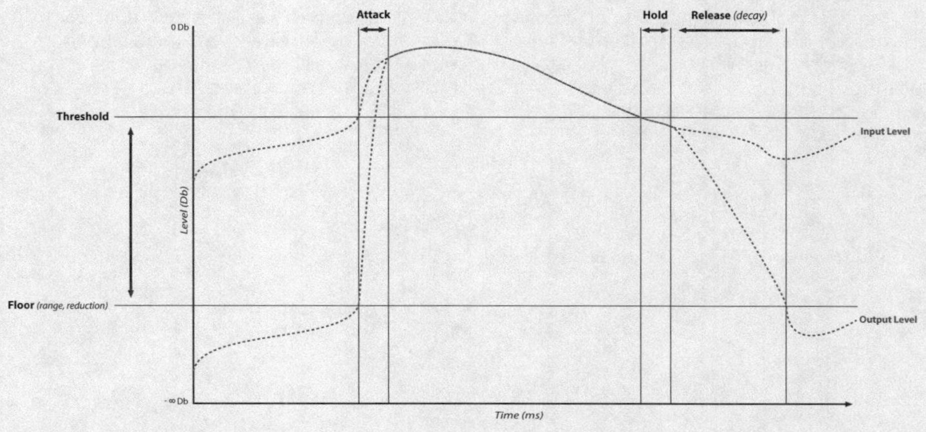

Some gates also include **a frequency selector** that allows only part of the signal to be treated. Like the filters found on certain compressors, this selector does not alter the signal itself, but rather the way the gate analyzes and processes it. Thus, it focuses the gate's action on a specific frequency area without affecting the rest of the signal.

9.3.2 THE OBJECTIVES OF USING A GATE

Objective 1: Attenuate Background Noise

To achieve this objective, we determine the level above which the signal is considered important and attenuate everything below that threshold.

In spoken narration, for example, it is usually easy to find the level at which the voice opens the gate. We can therefore eliminate a good deal of ambient noise, page turns, distracting breaths in pauses, and so on.

That said, this line between useful and useless is rarely so clear, especially when dealing with an amplified instrument such as guitar or bass. The hiss of an amplifier can become difficult to eliminate, especially in quieter passages such as the end of a sustained note or chord.

That is where the release setting becomes especially meaningful. It should be adjusted to determine the point at which the background noise becomes more distracting than the sound of the instrument. When available, the hold parameter inserts a

THE EXPANDER

Many gates also offer a function called expander. Unlike a gate, which reduces the signal uniformly regardless of how far below the threshold its level is, an expander applies gain reduction according to the signal's relative distance from the threshold. Thus, the closer the level is to the threshold, the less it is attenuated. Conversely, the farther it is from the threshold, the more it is reduced.

Because its action is more gradual than that of a gate, the expander provides more transparent processing on sources with a great deal of low-level nuance. It is therefore appropriate when we want to minimize the loss of musical content while managing background noise or bleed.

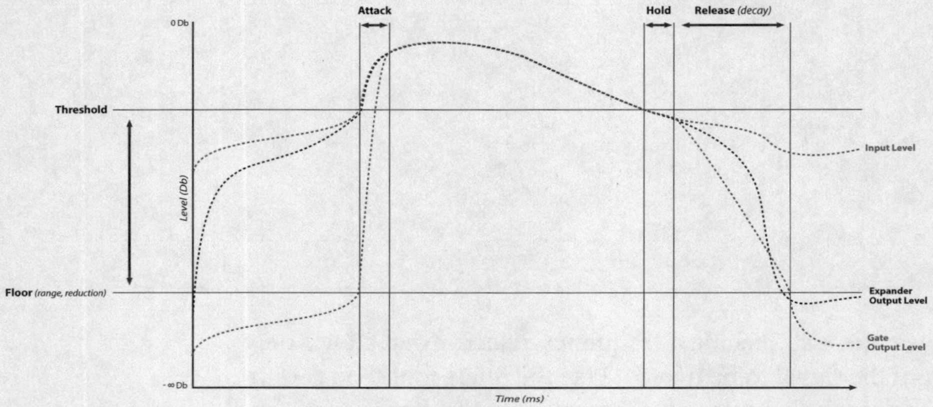

delay before the gate closes, which can help preserve the full length of a note even when its level is low.

The attack setting requires similar care. We will try to find an opening speed fast enough not to reduce the level of the transients and slow enough to prevent the gate from opening for no reason during quieter passages. For this type of work, a gate offering an expander function generally produces a more natural result.

In some cases, background noise is mainly present in a specific part of the frequency spectrum. Take the hiss of a reel-to-reel tape machine, for example. This hiss is generally found in the upper part of the frequency spectrum. Gates equipped with a filter then become useful for attenuating that hiss in the high frequencies while leaving the lower part of the signal largely unaffected.

Background noise is unfortunately almost unavoidable in recording. We must therefore avoid the trap of trying to eliminate it at all costs. In the vast majority of cases, a certain amount of noise is acceptable.

Adjusting the floor allows us to determine the degree of reduction sufficient to attenuate the background noise without compromising the musical content.

You can therefore see that setting a gate is not always particularly simple. In fact, when working digitally in a DAW, the gate is not always the most effective way to manage background noise. Without going so far as to say that it is an archaic tool, let us say that it is no longer as useful as it once was. It is often much simpler—and above all more reliable—to delete the unnecessary parts manually right in the project window and apply fades to silence at strategic points. In that way, we can decide case by case what is acceptable and what is not.

Objective 2: Attenuate Bleed in an Acoustic Drum Kit

The gate becomes a more useful tool when used to reduce bleed, such as that found in drum recordings. Let us be honest: the drum kit is not exactly the most discreet instrument. The sound produced by a snare hit, for example, will inevitably be captured by the microphones placed on the other parts of the kit. In addition, when a drummer plays, all parts of the kit vibrate whether they are struck directly or not. By placing a gate on each drum element, we reduce both the bleed between microphones and sympathetic resonance. In doing so, we not only make the sound of each element more precise, but also simplify its individual processing.

The release setting is particularly important when processing drum elements. It should generally be adjusted to cut the bleed while preserving as much of the element's natural resonance as possible.

As with background noise, it is preferable not to systematically eliminate every trace of bleed. Not every musical genre requires such a defined drum sound. In styles with a more organic sound, such as jazz, blues, or folk, the drum kit is perceived as a whole rather than as a collection of individual elements.

We should avoid trying to eliminate background noise at all costs.

Rock, heavy metal, and even pop often call for a more precise sound. Even in those styles, however, it is rarely appropriate to set the floor high enough to remove the bleed completely. A lower degree of reduction, between −10 and −20 dB, will in fact give a more natural result.

In any case, reducing bleed is not the only way to increase the definition of a drum kit. Adding samples—especially of snare drum and kick drum—is a common method for achieving that objective.

PREVENTING UNWANTED GATE OPENINGS

Despite all the care taken in setting its threshold, a gate may still open where it should remain closed. These unwanted openings are called false triggers. This situation is particularly common (and irritating!) with acoustic drums. In a DAW, it is of course possible to automate the threshold to correct these occasional mishaps. However, it is generally simpler to solve the problem directly in the edit window.

We select the portion of the signal that causes the gate to open unexpectedly and lower its level enough for it to fall below the gate's threshold. By treating each problematic area this way, we avoid having to readjust a threshold that already works well for the rest of the piece.

In the snare-drum track shown opposite, a tom hit exceeds the threshold, causing the gate to open.

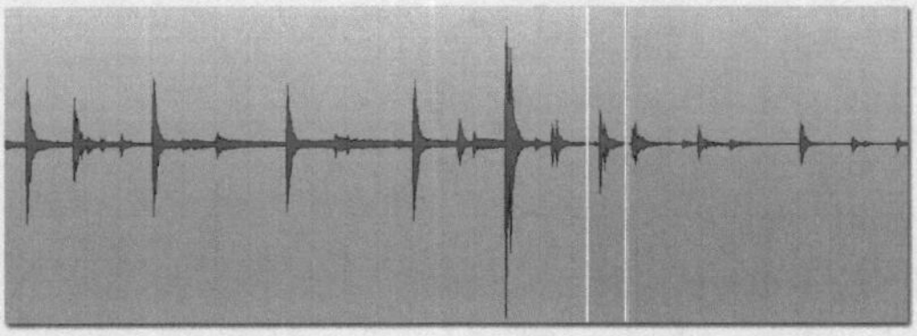

In the project window, the cut tool is used to split the track on either side of the offending sound.

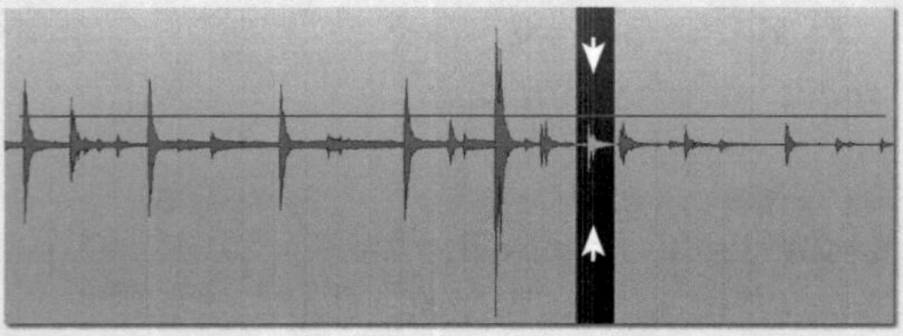

Using clip gain, the level of the newly created segment is reduced so that it falls below the gate's threshold, preventing the gate from opening inappropriately. This process can be repeated as needed to deal with other exceptions elsewhere in the song.

Objective 3: Attenuate Bleed From Several Instruments Recorded Simultaneously

In the same way, it can be useful to use a gate or an expander to reduce bleed in live recordings or studio sessions where several instruments were recorded at the same time.

We must be aware that removing bleed between instruments will inevitably affect the overall sound of the recording.

In these types of recordings, it is essential to listen carefully to the effect of the gate, not only on the track being processed, but also on the other tracks. A live recording is a whole. We can clarify certain tracks, but we must be aware that removing the bleed between instruments will inevitably affect the overall result. For these reasons, For these reasons, mixing a live recording can sometimes be challenging.

It is nevertheless possible to clarify certain elements without losing the sense of cohesion that gives a live recording all its charm. The elements we want to bring closer to the listener—typically kick drum, snare drum, and voice—can be cleaned up using a gate in parallel. We make a copy of the track on which a gate will be applied and use the original unprocessed track as well. This method makes it possible to be a little more radical in suppressing bleed, which greatly facilitates the use of effects.

Take the example of a lead-vocal track. By using a copy with an aggressive gate, it becomes easier to add effects such as delay and reverb without also feeding the sound of the other instruments into them. We can blend in the original ungated track to preserve the sense of ensemble. We can also mute that copy by lowering its fader and then use its sends in pre-fader mode to feed the lead-vocal effects.

As for drums, adding samples generally does a better job of bringing the main elements forward than using a gate. That does not exclude the possibility of cleaning up the original tracks to remove some of their bleed and complementing them with samples in parallel.

Objective 4: Synchronize the Ends of Vocal-Harmony Phrases

When recording multiple vocal harmonies, a great deal of attention is often paid to the beginning of the words so that everyone sits correctly in the rhythm. In some cases, however, there may be differences in the note lengths of the various harmonies.

By using a gate in sidechain mode, it is possible to better synchronize the vocal harmonies with the lead vocal.

Using a gate in sidechain mode will make it possible to synchronize those overly long notes at the ends of phrases. We first route all the harmony tracks to their own subgroup. We insert a gate on it and activate its sidechain function. Then we use a send from the lead-vocal track to trigger the gate's opening. Notes that were previously too long now match the duration of the lead vocal.

As for settings, the threshold should be chosen so that the singer's notes open the gate, but not their breaths. If some breaths are too prominent, they can be reduced in the editor in the same way as drum false triggers.

Generally, the attack should be set to its fastest position so that the attack of each note passes through clearly. The release should be short enough to reduce the note length, yet long enough for the note endings to remain as natural as possible.

This method does not work only on vocal harmonies. It can also be used on any type of ensemble whose note endings we want to synchronize: brass, strings, double-tracked guitars, and so on. The key is to choose the element whose rhythm is the most appropriate and make it responsible for opening the gate.

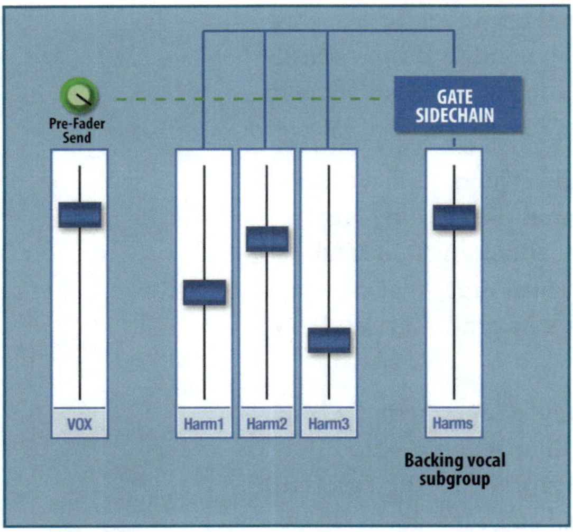

In this example, the lead vocal is used to synchronize the vocal harmonies. The three harmony tracks are routed to a subgroup with a gate inserted on it. The lead vocal triggers the gate through a send routed to the gate's sidechain. Pre-fader mode is used to ensure that the gate does not react to volume adjustments made on the lead-vocal track.

Objective 5: Add a Gate to a Reverb

A gate can also be used to shape reverb. The gate is placed immediately after the reverb effect, and the threshold and release are adjusted so as to cut its duration abruptly. We therefore keep only the impact of the dense part of the reverb.

Although this effect had its heyday in the 1980s, it can still be useful for adding dimension to a snare drum. Of course, today we would generally apply it with a little more subtlety.

Objective 6: Add Color to a Rhythmic Element

The idea here is to add a sound to one or more existing rhythmic elements. To do so, we choose a continuous sound and insert a gate on its track. We then use a rhythmic element—often the kick drum or snare drum—and, by assigning it to the gate's sidechain, make it responsible for opening and closing the gate. Thus, every time the rhythmic element is struck, it opens the gate and lets the continuous sound be heard. The gate's release sets how quickly that sound stops being heard. In general, the effect is more effective when the attack is set to its fastest position and the floor to its maximum value so that the continuous sound is completely inaudible when the rhythmic element is not heard.

This technique was very common in snare processing in the 1980s and 1990s. The continuous sound used was generally white noise or pink noise. Most DAWs include noise and waveform generators that can be used to create this effect.

Using a gate in sidechain mode is also very effective for adding very low frequencies to a kick drum. We can use a waveform generator or synthesizer to produce a very low-frequency sine wave, typically between 30 and 60 Hz. By applying the method described above, this wave will be added to the kick drum each time it is struck.

Objective 7: Create a Rhythmic Effect

Using a gate in sidechain mode also makes it possible to create a wide range of rhythmic effects that add movement and color to an existing groove. As in the previous objective, one or more drum tracks are generally used to control the opening and closing of the gate.

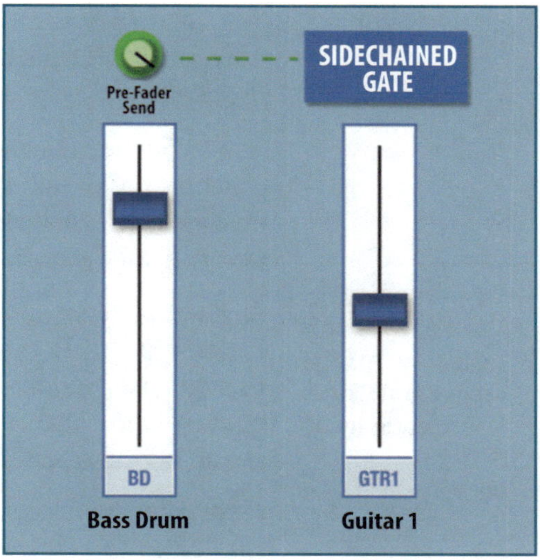

Here, the kick drum controls the gate on the guitar track via sidechain. Each time the kick drum is hit, the gate opens to let the guitar signal through.

Although it is entirely possible to use noise or a waveform generator, it can be interesting to choose tracks already present in the mix. We might, for example, select a keyboard track to work in tandem with the kick drum, or a guitar that will be triggered by the snare drum. Thus, every time the snare or kick is struck, it is colored by the tone and note of the instrument assigned to it.

Of course, nothing prevents us from adding effects to the instruments being triggered by the rhythmic elements. In this respect, a delay synchronized to the song tempo often creates a very interesting effect. In addition, by using a send in pre-fader mode to feed the gate's sidechain, we can also make the rhythmic elements themselves inaudible so that only the instruments they trigger are heard.

In short, the possibilities are limited only by the imagination.

9.4 The De-Esser

Despite all the care taken during recording, vocal tracks often still contain sibilance. Sibilance is a hiss produced by certain consonants such as s, sh, and ch, and similar sounds.

When excessive, these hissing sounds can become distracting because they generally occupy the same frequency areas that add presence and intimacy to the important elements of the mix.

As its name suggests, the de-esser is designed to eliminate that hiss. In fact, the de-esser can be thought of as a compressor that reacts only to high frequencies. It is also possible to use a multiband compressor or a dynamic EQ to perform the same task But since this specialized tool is included by default in most DAWs and is simple to use, it is well worth knowing its settings and how it works.

9.4.1 SETTINGS

Threshold, as usual, is used to determine the point above which the signal will be processed.

The frequency selector is the heart of the de-esser. It allows the exact part of the signal to be selected for treatment. It generally extends from 2000 Hz to the end of the audible spectrum, thus covering all the areas likely to contain sibilance.

A de-esser is designed to treat excessive sibilance in a vocal track.

A filter selector, similar to the one found on an equalizer, makes it possible to define the extent of the area being treated. In high-pass mode, it treats the region from the chosen frequency to the end of the spectrum. In bell mode, it focuses its action on the selected frequency.

A compression selector determines whether the compression is applied to the entire signal or only to the targeted frequency area. In sidechain or split position, the reduction is applied only to the selected frequencies. In broadband position, it affects the whole signal. In other words, the de-esser's response to sibilance reduces the level of the entire signal. This way of applying compression can sometimes produce a more transparent result.

A reduction-amount control is sometimes provided to specify the maximum amount of reduction the de-esser can apply to the signal. In its absence, the threshold position determines the depth of the treatment.

A listen button is often present so that only the selected frequency area can be heard. It may help pinpoint the problematic frequency or frequencies.

A meter completes the unit by indicating the amount of reduction being applied.

9.4.2 THE OBJECTIVES OF USING A DE-ESSER

Objective 1: Reduce Sibilance

It goes without saying that the most common objective of a de-esser is to reduce vocal sibilance. It is important to note that, in order to achieve this objective, it is advantageous to place the de-esser at the very beginning of the insert chain on the track. This limits the amount of sibilance that reaches the treatments that follow, especially compression and EQ.

The main challenge is identifying the frequency or frequencies that contain the sibilance. This phenomenon depends on an incalculable number of factors: the microphone used, its placement, any added processing, the lyrics themselves, and even the singer's mouth physiology. There is therefore no miracle recipe.

When the problematic frequency is difficult to pinpoint, we lower the de-esser threshold enough to make the meter show some reduction. We then use the listen function and sweep through the frequency spectrum with the selector. By watching the reduction meter, we can determine which frequencies trigger the strongest response from the de-esser. A frequency analyzer can also provide useful clues for identifying the problem areas.

Selecting the frequency is often easier by choosing a section of the vocal track where the sibilance is especially prominent. We then create an audio loop so that this section plays continuously during our search.

It is entirely possible—and even common—to find more than one sibilant area. Typically, s sounds are often found above 5000 Hz, while sh and ch sounds tend to be lower in the spectrum, around 3000 Hz. A single de-esser will generally not succeed in treating both zones simultaneously. It may therefore be appropriate to use one de-esser per zone. A good starting point is to use one de-esser covering everything above 5000 Hz with a high-pass filter and, if necessary, another one targeting a frequency around 3000 Hz with a bell filter.

Using more than one de-esser is sometimes necessary to target sibilant areas more precisely.

Once the sibilant frequency or frequencies have been identified, it is useful to check whether the treatment should be applied to the entire signal or only to the sibilant area itself. There is no hard rule in this regard. Only listening will determine which option gives the most natural result.

There is no fixed target for the amount of reduction, since it varies from track to track. The goal is to keep the vocal as natural as possible. Once again, numbers alone can be misleading. Too much reduction often sounds worse than the sibilance itself, so careful listening remains essential.

Objective 2: Reduce Sibilance Feeding into Effects

Sometimes sibilance can draw undue attention to the effects assigned to the signal, especially delay and reverb. In the case of delay, the sibilance will be repeated, and in the case of reverb, it will excite the high frequencies, which does not suit certain musical styles. Excessive sibilance in these types of effects can also make it harder to manage the high frequencies of the mix.

To counter this situation, it is possible to insert a de-esser at the input of the effects track. We generally process everything above 5000 Hz with a high-pass filter in order to limit the amount of high-frequency content in the signal before it reaches the effect. This helps prevent those frequencies from competing with the ones that make the mix's important elements feel closer to the listener.

Objective 3: Attenuate Excessive High-Frequency Peaks in an Instrument

Although the de-esser was originally designed for vocal treatment, nothing prevents us from using it on other types of instruments. Since its effect is similar to that of a multiband compressor or a dynamic equalizer, it often allows us to solve certain frequency problems just as easily as those types of treatment.

Although it was designed for voice, the de-esser can be useful for processing other types of instruments.

Percussion can often benefit from a de-esser. Drum overheads or hi-hat, for example, may contain certain frequencies that seem to cut through the mix excessively. For overheads, we generally target a region around 7 or 8 kHz. For hi-hat, we are more likely to aim between 8 and 11 kHz.

Hand percussion such as tambourines, shakers, suspended cymbals, and triangles may also require the use of a de-esser to temper excessive brightness. In terms of settings, it is often appropriate to choose a broad frequency area using a high-pass filter. Although it is not uncommon to address everything above 10 kHz, it is a good idea to begin the search around 8 kHz.

Finally, acoustic string instruments such as acoustic guitar, violin, or mandolin sometimes exhibit harsh frequencies. These may be caused by a lower-quality instrument or by poor microphone selection or placement during recording. A similar problem may also occur on electric-guitar tracks, especially when the tone is saturated. For these types of instruments, we will inspect the spectrum between 2 and 6 kHz using a bell-shaped filter to target the area to be treated.

Whatever instrument we use it on, it is important to listen carefully to the result of the treatment and use the reduction meter as an indicator. As with voice, the optimal amount of reduction varies from track to track. The effect of the de-esser must be judged by ear, case by case.

9.5 The Transient Designer

Until now, I have deliberately avoided discussing dynamic expansion, a process in which a compressor is used to increase a signal's dynamic range rather than reduce it. Instead of lowering the level when it exceeds the threshold, we raise it. In practice, however, dynamic expansion with a compressor is only rarely necessary. There are, in fact, more flexible tools for increasing a signal's dynamic range precisely.

The transient designer is one of those tools. As its name suggests, it makes it possible to shape an instrument's envelope by increasing or decreasing the amplitude of its initial portion.

As we saw in the section on compression, a similar task can be carried out with a compressor. So why use a transient designer for that job? Simply because it is a specialist that compares an instrument's attack with its sustain and makes it possible to alter their proportions. This way of approaching the signal allows it to do the job more simply and more precisely than a traditional compressor, and without adding too much color to the sound.

A transient designer makes it possible to modify the balance between a signal's attack and its sustain.

9.5.1 SETTINGS

There are several transient designer models, and each has its own way of naming and presenting its parameters. However, we can identify the generic functions they share.

An attack control, often labeled attack or punch, increases or decreases the initial portion of the signal. It generally takes the form of a rotary knob, often graduated in decibels. Turning it to the left reduces the attack; turning it to the right increases it.

Sustain is used to increase or decrease the part of the signal that follows the initial attack. It too is accessible via a rotary knob. When this control is absent, the transient designer works using only one parameter: attack.

An output level, often labeled output or level, makes it possible to compensate for any level decrease or increase resulting from the processing.

These are therefore the three basic controls found on the vast majority of models. Of course, some units offer additional functions or allow the signal to be processed in a more specific way.

Some models also include a control that specifies the duration of the action on the attack. It is often presented as a switch with two or three positions (slow, mid, and fast) or as a control calibrated in milliseconds.

Another frequently offered function is a filter that determines which part of the frequency spectrum will be affected by the treatment. Let us note that, in the absence of such a control, most transient plug-ins do not distribute their action evenly across the frequency spectrum. They tend to favor the low frequencies when amplifying transients and the high frequencies when reducing them.

In the late 1990s, the German company SPL was the first to market a specialized tool for transient processing.

An integrated limiter may also be included to ensure that the output level never exceeds digital zero. Some models also offer saturation options.

9.5.2 THE OBJECTIVES OF USING A TRANSIENT DESIGNER

Objective 1: Add Presence to a Percussive Instrument

If you make electronic music, you already know how much presence a transient designer can add to a kick or a snare. By increasing the amplitude of their attack, these elements will cut through even the densest mix.

This technique can also be used in almost any musical style. Of course, in most cases, we must avoid applying it with as much force as in electronic music so as to preserve the natural sound of the original source.

What is nice about transient designers is that the effect of their controls is often easy to hear. For this type of application, we increase the attack until the element finds its place in the mix. Generally, a neutral or slightly reduced sustain gives good results.

Objective 2: Add Dynamics to an Instrument

We are sometimes faced with a track that lacks dynamics, either because of a restrained performance or because of overcompression during recording. We can therefore use the transient designer to accentuate the level difference between an instrument's attack and sustain.

Although many elements can benefit from this type of treatment, drums are of course the first thing that comes to mind. A somewhat lifeless drum performance can be brought back to life by inserting a transient designer on the entire drum subgroup or on certain individual elements.

This type of treatment can also help restore the internal balance of a drum kit more effectively than using only the track faders. For example, a drummer may have an appropriate dynamic on the cymbals, hi-hat, and kick drum, but strike the toms and snare drum with less conviction. We would then treat those elements so as to achieve not only a coherent level balance, but also a more consistent dynamic across the entire kit.

Objective 3: Lengthen or Shorten the Sustain of a Percussion Instrument

A transient designer can help restore impact to a somewhat lifeless performance.

A transient designer can of course modify an instrument's attack, but it can also help us work on the next part of its envelope: sustain.

Fast double-kick passages can sometimes become blurry because of excessive sustain. A transient designer makes it possible to shorten the note lengths and sharpen the articulation of those passages. We therefore reduce the sustain setting in order to minimize the overlap between the sustain of one note and the attack of the next.

The opposite situation can also arise. For example, a snare drum may have such a short envelope that it seems to lack dimension. Increasing the sustain setting can sometimes restore a sense of depth.

A similar treatment can be used when we want to enhance the ambience of a recording. By increasing the sustain setting, we emphasize the natural reverberation present in a signal. This possibility should be kept in mind when processing room microphones or when trying to give a track natural depth without adding an artificial reverb effect.

Objective 4: Bring a Loop Back to Life

The transient designer is a very powerful tool for processing loops. Loops are often overcompressed or have a dynamic that does not quite suit the piece we are working on. We can therefore process the entire loop or, where possible, some of its individual elements, using the same techniques as for traditional drum tracks.

Let us point out here that multiband transient designers are better suited to working on full loops because they allow us to target specific frequency ranges. As in the case of the compressor, we must keep in mind that setting a multiband unit is always delicate and that it is often better to reserve them for situations in which simpler treatments do not work.

Objective 5: Reduce Strong Peaks in a Signal

As we mentioned earlier, excessive peaks in a signal can be attenuated with a compressor, a limiter, or a de-esser. A transient designer can also be added to that arsenal, especially models with a speed control. In that case, the speed is adjusted so that only the peaks are affected, and their amplitude is reduced by lowering the attack setting.

Even if using a transient designer for this kind of application is not what first comes to mind, its often transparent action makes it an option worth considering.

Objective 6: Enhance the Dynamics of an Overcompressed Track

A transient designer can also be used in parallel to shape the envelope of a track while preserving part of its natural dynamics. This approach is particularly suitable for processing overcompressed tracks. As with parallel compression, it is often preferable to exaggerate the treatment and then blend it in parallel with the original track until a suitable result is achieved.

That said, decompressing a track—or worse, an entire mix—is no walk in the park. It is in fact extremely difficult to bring a flat-lined track back to life. Using a transient designer in parallel can, however, produce a more natural result than inserting it directly on the track.

9.6 The Dynamic Equalizer

Although its layout resembles that of a standard parametric equalizer, the dynamic equalizer is, in a way, a de-esser that can be placed anywhere in the frequency spectrum.

Dynamic EQ makes it possible to modify the gain of a frequency area, but also to manipulate its dynamics.

Dynamic EQ allows us to work on frequencies on two levels: volume and dynamics. We can therefore adjust the gain and bandwidth of a frequency area as we would with a standard equalizer, while also processing its dynamics using compression.

9.6.1 SETTINGS

At first glance, dynamic EQ looks very much like a classic parametric equalizer. Each filter therefore includes a frequency control, a Q control, a gain control, and a filter type selector.

Each filter also has a threshold that sets the point above which the dynamic processing kicks in. Attack and release controls are regularly provided to govern how quickly compression

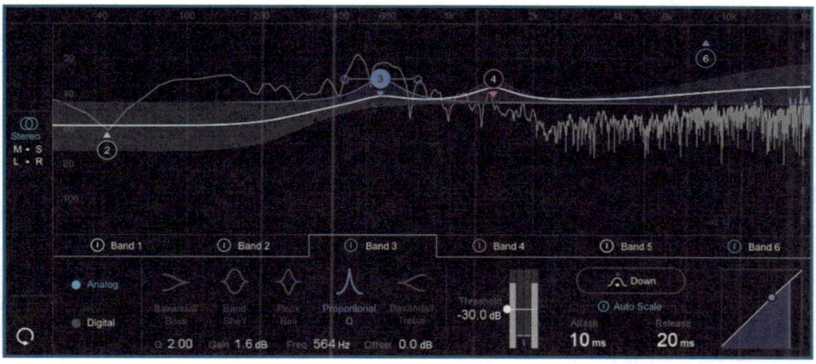

The visual layout of iZotope's dynamic equalizer.

takes place and, occasionally, a ratio that sets the degree of compression being applied. A graph also makes it possible to assess the amount of reduction being applied.

Most dynamic EQs use a graph similar to that of a digital equalizer to display the filters and gain changes. Very often, a frequency analyzer is displayed in the background. The dynamic variations themselves are shown by moving curves.

Dynamic equalizers generally make it possible to perform dynamic expansion. In that case, instead of reducing the level when the signal exceeds the threshold, the signal is increased. Some models also allow the processing to be applied in stereo or in mid/side mode.

9.6.2 THE OBJECTIVES OF USING A DYNAMIC EQUALIZER

Objective 1: Reduce Inconsistencies Within an Instrument's Range

We sometimes notice that certain notes of an instrument are louder than others within its range. This phenomenon may be due to the quality of the instrument or its mechanical setup, or simply to the way the player attacks the note. On string instruments, for example, we often notice a level difference between an open-string note and the same note played with a fingered position on the neck.

Dynamic EQ can process a specific area of the frequency spectrum without altering the rest of the signal.

As we saw in Chapter 7, frequencies are directly related to pitch. It is therefore possible to modify the level of a specific note using an equalizer. Altering the frequency of that note with a standard equalizer will, however, affect the entire track. The dynamic equalizer makes it possible to reduce the dynamics of that note without altering the rest of the signal. We simply set the threshold so that compression brings the level back to something comparable to the other notes in the range. Of course, we can also use dynamic expansion to increase the level of a note that is too quiet.

In the same spirit, certain elements in drum overheads sometimes take up more space than necessary. Dynamic EQ can, for example, be useful for reducing an overly present cymbal or hi-hat by intervening only when the level of their respective frequencies exceeds a certain threshold.

Objective 2: Even Out the Frequency Response of a Vocal Performance

A vocal recording can often be enough to make your head spin. A singer caught up in the rhythm may dance during the performance. Another may glance at lyrics laid out on a music stand. Yet another may move close to the microphone to whisper a mellow passage and then pull away to belt out a primal scream.

During a vocal recording, the distance between the microphone and the singer will inevitably vary throughout the performance. Although this is generally not a problem, there are occasions when the frequency distribution of the vocal track fluctuates too much as the singer moves. It then becomes difficult to process those uneven passages with a standard equalizer without compromising the rest of the performance.

Dynamic EQ can be useful for managing occasional frequency variations in a vocal recording.

Take the example of the mellow whisper followed by the primal scream. Because of the closer microphone position, there is a good chance that the low frequencies will be more present in the whisper than in the scream. If we use a standard EQ to reduce the low frequencies of the whisper, we will end up with a primal scream that lacks body. In this kind of situation, dynamic EQ can come to our rescue by reducing the dynamics of the low frequencies only when their level becomes excessive.

In the same vein, we sometimes detect resonances that differ depending on the part of the singer's range being used or the force with which the voice is projected. Certain words may therefore cut through the mix a bit more than desired. Once again, dynamic EQ makes it possible to process only the excessive frequencies of those words without altering the rest of the performance.

Dynamic EQ can also be used to reduce excessive sibilance. Thus, instead of resorting to several de-essers to treat the various sibilant frequencies, dynamic EQ allows us to gather all those treatments in one place.

9.6.3 RECOMMENDATIONS

Use Dynamic EQ as a Last Resort

Dynamic EQ is a wonderful tool for treating problems localized in a very precise area of the frequency spectrum without affecting the rest of the signal.

Despite its attractive possibilities and its apparent similarity to a conventional equalizer, dynamic equalization is a complex process whose true mastery requires a long learning period. It is therefore risky to rely on it for everything. Most of the time, using processing tools whose operation is more familiar to us, such as a de-esser, a conventional equalizer, or a compressor, allows us to tackle the same types of problems more instinctively.

Dynamic EQ can often be replaced by other tools we are more familiar with.

What is more, dynamic EQ, though well known in mastering for several years, is still relatively new in the world of audio mixing. Remember that thousands of albums were successfully mixed without this type of processing. It is wise to reserve it for the rare occasions when conventional tools cannot accomplish the task at hand.

10
SATURATION

In 1983, a new audio format was born: the compact disc. Small and durable, it was expected to consign the vinyl record—the primary commercial format for music up to that point—to oblivion. More than 200 billion compact discs have been sold: quite a commercial success!

Of course, albums released on this new format were produced with analog equipment. It must be said that the digital technology of the time was certainly not as accessible or as capable as it is today. In 1981, the Sony PCM-3324, a 24-track digital tape recorder, promised the pleasures of 16-bit, 48 kHz recording for the modest sum of about US$150,000! No wonder so many studios hesitated to make the digital leap! What is more, many engineers criticized digital for its rather sterile sound and lack of depth, a view shared—often with good reason—by many audiophiles, who far preferred the sound of their vinyl records to that of those awful little pieces of plastic!

And yet, digital offered undeniable fidelity and clarity, not to mention its incredible dynamic range. So what could possibly have been wrong?

10.1 What Is Saturation?

As digital audio continued to develop, it became increasingly clear that the coldness often attributed to the medium was actually due to its excessive... fidelity. Analog equipment does in fact generate a range of anomalies that give sound a very pleasing

The Sony PCM-3324, a 24-track digital tape recorder.

warmth and roundness. A large part of these anomalies comes from saturation.

Without getting lost in needlessly complex mathematical and electrical explanations, saturation could be defined as a process that adds to the sound a rich collection of harmonics generated from the original signal. These may be induced by the electrical hardware used in the construction of a device (transistors, tubes, wiring, etc.) or, of course, produced digitally. Functioning as both an equalizer and a compressor, saturation affects both a signal's frequency spectrum and its dynamic range.

But beyond the technical explanations, saturation is character. In small doses, it has the gift of adding roundness and depth to the sound; in larger doses, it can bring an element to life.

10.2 Description and Settings of the Main Saturation Generators

Settings vary greatly depending on the type of device or plug-in used to generate saturation. Here is an overview of the main sources of saturation and their most common parameters.

Analog Devices

Analog devices are, of course, one of the ways to obtain saturation. This equipment can take many forms: preamps, compressors, equalizers, tape machines, etc. As soon as the signal passes through a series of transformers, tubes, or any other physical electrical component, a certain degree of saturation is added to the signal.

Beyond the technical explanations, saturation is character!

That saturation will be more or less noticeable depending on whether the equipment is being driven hard or not. If you are a guitarist and use a tube amplifier, this principle is already very familiar to you. Audio processing analog devices behave much the same way. In fact, engineers often set the level of a tape machine or the channels of an analog console beyond the 0 mark on their VU meters in order to take advantage of the saturation added to the signal.

The saturation produced by analog devices also has the property of being nonlinear. Both the amount and the color of the saturation vary with how hard the electrical components are driven, though not in a uniform way. For example, once a device's level has been set to 75% of its capacity, it is entirely possible that the final 25% will add no further saturation to the signal. That does not mean, however, that the signal's tone will not continue to change in that last portion of the level range. This nonlinear response partly explains why two units of the same analog device model can have different sonic signatures.

In general, the harder an analog device is driven, the more saturation it generates. The same is true of most digital emulations.

Emulations of Analog Processing Devices

As we noted earlier, the lack of saturation in digital audio was one of the main reasons—if not the main reason—for its sonic coldness. Plug-in manufacturers quickly understood this and created a wide range of tools to compensate for that shortcoming. As a result, the vast majority of digital emulations of common analog processing devices—whether equalizers, compressors, or channel strips—reproduce the saturation characteristics of the original hardware. Faithful to those originals, some of them color the sound simply by being inserted in the chain, even when they are not applying any obvious processing to the signal.

Given the variety of analog devices available as emulations, it is difficult to know exactly how saturation is introduced into the signal. One constant remains, however: the harder a device is driven, the more it reveals its distinctive color. Increasing the input or output level of these plug-ins will therefore very often generate saturation.

Above, a 1000 Hz sine wave as it appears on the frequency analyzer. Below, the same wave passing through this analog compressor emulator, even though it is not applying any apparent compression to the signal.

When these emulations are used for routine track processing, it is often advantageous to do so with a cumulative effect in mind. Conservative settings are therefore recommended, since their mere presence is often enough to add subtle coloration.

In parallel processing, however, the plug-in should be driven harder to bring out as much color as possible. The choice of the emulated device will then determine the character being

HYBRID MIXING

Provided you have access to analog equipment, other methods can also be used to generate saturation.

Many mix engineers, in fact, incorporate analog hardware into their digital processing chains. This method, often referred to as hybrid mixing, is said by many to give digital sound some of what it may otherwise lack. Others question the value of this approach because it requires the signal to be converted twice—from digital to analog and then back again—and makes revisions after client review more cumbersome.

added. Naturally, it may sometimes be necessary to address gain staging issues by reducing the output level.

Console Emulators

Analog consoles are an integral part of what might be called the analog sound. Each of the major brands—Neve, SSL, Trident, API, Universal Audio, and others—has sonic characteristics of its own. Console emulator plug-ins seek to reproduce that sonic signature.

They often provide two types of plug-ins: one to recreate the effect of the channel (its name will contain the word "channel") and another to emulate the summing process (the word "bus" will appear in its name).

Channel-type plug-ins are inserted at the beginning of each track's signal chain. On first listen, some users may be surprised—or even disappointed—by the very subtle processing they often bring to the track's sound. What must be understood is that channel emulators are designed to create the cumulative effect mentioned earlier. It is therefore by lightly saturating each track that they add color to the mix as a whole.

In general, console emulators consist of two plug-ins: one to be placed on the tracks and one for the mixbuss.

The other part of the equation, the summing emulator, is used to reproduce the specific effect produced by combining the signals of all the individual tracks at the output of an analog console. The action of bus-type plug-ins is added to that of the channel plug-ins to complete the emulation process. Although the summing emulator can sometimes work well on a subgroup, it is generally placed in the first insert of the main output bus.

These plug-ins, whether channel or output bus models, generally include a limited number of controls. First, a console type selector lets us choose which brand of console will be emulated. (It should be noted that the brand name is never stated clearly on the selector, probably for legal reasons. You therefore need to consult the manual to determine which console brand the abbreviation or selector name refers to.) An input control plays the same role as a standard gain setting and determines the level going into the emulator. A knob, often called drive, determines how hard the channel is being pushed.

The input and drive controls both determine the amount of saturation added to the track. A 6 dB increase in the input level therefore has the same effect as a 6 dB increase in the drive control. However, the input level directly affects the output level, whereas the drive control does not. If, for example, we want to add more saturation by raising the input by 3 dB, those 3 dB are added to the track's current output level. It quickly becomes clear that this increase may create gain staging problems, especially when the processed track is already loud. It is therefore often preferable to reach the desired amount of saturation by means of the drive control and thus preserve the original level of the track.

Most console emulators make it possible to group processing by track categories (called groups). The group selector is built into the channel plug-in on each track. Once a track is linked to a group, its settings are no longer directly accessible. This makes it possible to adjust the console simulator's settings on all the group's tracks from a single location. If, for example, we assign all the drum tracks to group 1, we will be able to switch from one console model to another in order to compare their respective effect on the drum signal. We can also adjust the drive setting on all the tracks in the group at once to control how much saturation is added to it.

Console emulators create a cumulative saturation effect by lightly coloring each track in a mix.

Console emulators are perfect for giving warmth and depth to a mix without becoming too obtrusive. Even at their default settings, their mere presence seems to make mixing easier, especially with regard to the equalization process. The consistent color they bring to the sound also helps the tracks blend into a coherent whole.

Tape Machine Emulators

Tape machines have colored—and still color—a large portion of commercial recordings with their distinctive saturation. Whether we realize it or not, that color has been an integral part of our musical experience since early childhood. Its saturation is so familiar that most of us find it pleasing to the ear. That is why tape machine emulators occupy such an important place in digital music production.

These emulators include settings that may require a few clarifications, especially for anyone who has never used this type of machine.

Let us begin by pointing out that the most decisive control is, of course, drive. It determines the gain at the tape machine's input. As always, the more this setting is increased, the more saturated the signal becomes.

There is also a selector used to define tape speed. Graduated in ips (inches per second), it generally offers three options: 7.5,

15, or 30 ips. The slower the speed, the more pronounced the tape effect becomes.

Another selector sometimes allows us to choose the tape width being used. Traditionally, 2-inch tape is used for multitrack recording, while narrower tape (1/4 or 1/2 inch) is used to record the mix output. Even though this practice is not required in digital production, it is still common to use a wide tape for an individual track or subgroup and a narrow tape on the output bus, if only out of respect for tradition. It should also be noted that the wide tapes used for multitrack recording are typically run at slower speeds (7.5 or 15 ips) than the narrow tapes intended to receive the final mix (30 ips).

The tape machine emulator generates a type of saturation that is familiar to us.

We also often find a selector that changes the characteristics of the emulated tape ("Tape Type" or "Formula"). The effect of this selector is noticeably subtler than that of the previous two. It is still worth moving from one type to another to hear the nuances of each of the tape formulas offered.

Like most analog device emulations, tape machine emulators reproduce the background noise generated by the machine and the tape itself, and a "Noise" control lets us adjust how much is added to the signal. It should also be noted that many engineers feel that this noise helps unify the mix. In a digital context, of course, we are free to set its presence as we wish.

Two other parameters, more esoteric for beginners, are bias and wow and flutter. Without getting unnecessarily complex, bias relates to the magnetization process of the tape. This setting has a marked influence on frequency distribution and the overall quality of the sonic result... at least in analog. In digital emulations, the effect of bias varies depending on how it has been modeled. Most plug-ins offer bias selections in 3 dB increments ranging from 0 to +6 dB. In theory, a higher bias causes the tape to saturate less quickly and softens the high frequencies. Once again, it is best to experiment with the emulator's bias setting and assess its effect in each possible position.

Wow and flutter, for their part, reproduce anomalies caused by the mechanics of the machine. Pitch modulation generated by variations in motor speed (wow) and volume fluctuations caused by the movement of the tape against the playback head (flutter) can therefore be simulated. Since these anomalies are part of the machine's sonic signature, these settings can often be left in their original position.

The tape machine emulator is extremely useful for wrapping an element or an entire mix in saturation that is pleasing to the ear. Inserted on a track, it increases the sense of closeness to the element and reinforces its frequency distribution. On the output bus, its saturation brings a warmth to the sound that seems both to help define the elements of the mix and to blend them into a whole.

The emulator also gives low frequencies more body by making them rounder and deeper. When used more aggressively, tape machine emulators are, of course, perfect for recreating the vintage sound of albums from the 1960s and 1970s.

Saturation Plug-Ins

In addition to these options, there are also plug-ins designed specifically to create saturation. Some draw inspiration from the analog world, others from the digital realm, and each has its own flavor and sonic signature.

Unsurprisingly, the drive control, found on most of these plug-ins, defines the amount of saturation being added. We also find simple equalizers for filtering the extremes of the frequency spectrum. Finally, they often provide a mix control, allowing us to set the balance between the original signal and the saturation, as well as an output level. These plug-ins can be used either as inserts directly on the track or in parallel processing.

As with compressors, it is therefore better to explore the possibilities of each saturation plug-in progressively rather than choosing one blindly. Some will shine on drums, while others will be better suited to saturating bass or vocals. A good deal of experimentation will help us become familiar with the distinctive color of each one and the kinds of tracks and instruments it serves best.

Lo-Fi Plug-Ins

Lo-fi (low fidelity) plug-ins reproduce saturation and other characteristics associated with older analog or digital media.

Vinyl simulators are meant to evoke the glory days of scratched records and dust on the stylus. They generally allow us to define the amount of damage using parameters such as "Wear," "Dust," "Scratch," mechanical or electrical rumble ("Noise"), and sometimes even record warp ("Warp"). Most allow users to choose among the playback speeds typical of the medium (33, 45, or 78 rpm) and include a decade selector (generally ranging from 1900 to 2000).

This type of plug-in is generally used to give part of a song—or the entire song—an aged quality. Vinyl simulators do in fact have a gift for creating a distinctive atmosphere that quickly transports the listener to another era. The effect is common in rap music, where it is used to color the entire instrumental section or some of its individual elements.

Recording through a consumer device is an excellent way to achieve a lo-fi effect.

Re-recording is also an excellent way to obtain a lo-fi sound. We can, for example, record our mix or one of its elements onto a standard cassette recorder and then bring that recording back into our mix. After all, what better way to recreate the sound of a telephone than by recording the track directly into... a telephone? Other devices—a portable radio, a laptop, or even a walkie-talkie—will likewise bring a lo-fi flavor to your recording.

Still in the lo-fi category, bit crusher plug-ins draw their inspiration from the digital realm. Their action is therefore based on reducing the resolution of the encoding of a digital signal.

Their main parameters naturally refer to concepts specific to digital conversion. A "Sample Rate" control, expressed in kHz, affects the signal's sampling rate, while a "Sample Depth" control, expressed in bits, reduces its resolution. There is also often a control that reduces the anti-aliasing effect (a filter ensuring that a frequency exceeding the representational limits of the sampling rate will not be falsely reproduced elsewhere in the frequency spectrum).

The saturation produced by a bit crusher is generally harsher and colder than any type inspired by the analog world. That is why some plug-ins also include an analog saturation component to temper, so to speak, the coldness of the effect.

Digital-inspired saturation plug-ins produce a harsher, colder effect than analog-inspired ones.

Its ability to simulate the sound of the earliest digital music production devices, such as samplers and drum machines (808, 909, Linn, etc.), makes the bit crusher a favorite in hip hop, where it is used to give old-school flavor to drum loops and samples. Also very common in electronic music, its biting saturation can also prove useful in other genres for creating occasional effects, coloring certain rhythmic elements such as bass or kick drum, or processing delay effects.

Amp Simulators and Reamping

These simulators reproduce the sonic characteristics of electric guitar and bass amplifiers. They offer emulations of a wide range of common amplifier and speaker cabinet models. Some allow users to fine-tune every detail of the variables involved in a real recording session: the microphones used, their position relative to the amp, their respective levels, and so on.

Originally designed for guitar and bass processing, amp simulators offer a variety of effects that can also be used on other elements in the mix.

In addition to the countless saturation flavors these virtual amps offer, these plug-ins also give us access to many stompbox effects drawn from the guitar world: chorus, flanger, delay, reverb, etc. So although they are primarily designed for amplified instruments, they offer such a wide range of possibilities that not using them on other elements in a mix would almost amount to negligence. The wide palette of colors these pedals provide makes them excellent candidates for creating unusual effects. Why not run the vocal through a wah-wah pedal or send the drums into a guitar amplifier?

Of course, reamping through a physical amplifier or real effect pedals is also an option worth considering. If we want to use an amplifier, we naturally need microphones to record it and, ideally, a reamping box to change the impedance of the audio interface's output. To send a signal directly to effect pedals, we once again need a reamping box on the way out and then recover the analog signal on the way back in by using our audio interface's Hi-Z input or a DI box. We discussed reamping techniques in detail in Chapter 4.

It is also possible to obtain analog saturation by routing the signal to a microphone preamp, a method that works particularly well on bass tracks, whether virtual or not. In this case, no additional equipment is generally required. We simply need to use the appropriate routing.

All of these methods are particularly effective for processing tracks generated by virtual instruments and giving them both color and naturalness.

10.3 The Objectives of Using Saturation

Objective 1: Blend an Element into the Mix

Bass is probably the instrument that benefits most from saturation. Thanks to it, even the dullest bass lines, whether they come from an electric bass or a virtual instrument, will manage to find their place in the mix. It is always surprising, in fact, to hear how much saturation a bass can take before it begins to distract the listener.

It is also a very interesting option to consider when trying to resolve the traditional conflict between kick drum and bass, or when two bass lines are competing with each other. Reamping also works very well on bass tracks because of the touch of naturalness it imparts to them.

It should also be noted that saturation can help make instruments rich in low frequencies (bass, an 808, or a kick drum, for example) audible on playback devices with limited reproduction capabilities (computer speakers, mobile phones, earbuds, etc.).

The activity within the mix may also guide our choice of saturation. Inserting one or more analog device emulations directly on the track will allow a bass line to settle subtly into a sparse arrangement, whereas a saturation plug-in will help the bass claim its place in denser arrangements.

Certain elements are extremely difficult to integrate into a mix without a good dose of saturation. Tracks performed by several people at once (group vocal harmonies, claps, foot stomps, etc.) or occasional sound effects (gunshots, explosions, tire squeals, etc.) are generally usable only once their emotional charge has been amplified through saturation.

Adding saturation or using reamping are excellent ways to lend a more natural quality to virtual instrument tracks.

Tracks generated by virtual instruments are also often difficult to blend into a song with an organic sound (an acoustic ballad, folk, country, etc.). Once again, a touch of saturation will make these elements better suited to the sonic landscape in which they take part. And do not hesitate to saturate choirs or orchestral sections generated virtually. Even if at first you feel you are committing a sacrilege, it may be exactly what those tracks need in order to blend into the mix. A light saturation with a natural tone, such as that of a microphone preamp, a tape machine emulator, or a saturation plug-in set to a minimal effect, is generally enough to do this kind of work.

Objective 2: Simulate an Analog Processing Chain

Even if we do not have access to analog equipment, it is entirely legitimate to want to give an analog color to certain projects that lend themselves well to it (a classic rock album, blues, jazz standards, folk songs, etc.). We can, of course, insert a saturation plug-in here and there, but the saturation associated with analog sound is of a very different nature.

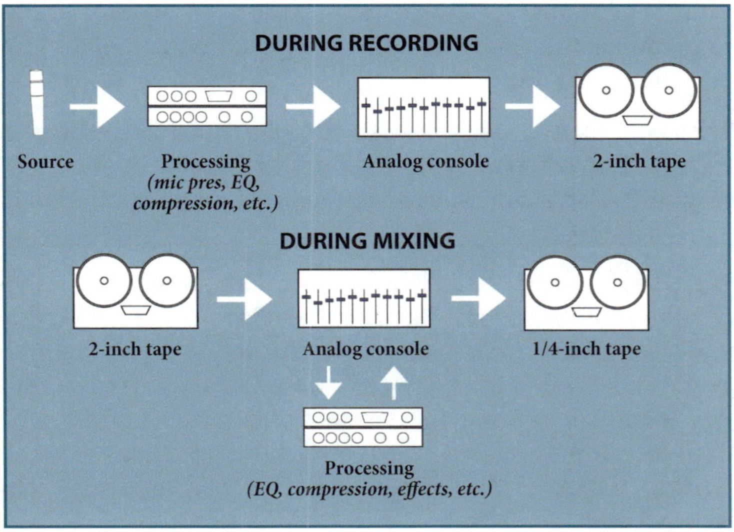

The signal path of a typical analog chain.

Let us pause for a moment on the typical path taken by the signal in a fully analog production. At the very beginning of the chain, a microphone is placed in front of an instrument. Its signal is first routed to a mic preamp, then, very often, to a processing chain (compressor, equalizer, or others). It then goes to the console and ends its journey on 2-inch tape. During mixing, the sound coming from that tape goes back into the console, passes through a second processing chain, returns to the console, and finally ends up on the tape of another tape machine. It therefore becomes clear that analog saturation is added in small doses at every stage of the chain.

So if our goal is to get closer to the saturation associated with analog, it makes perfect sense to proceed gradually. Simply inserting a tape machine emulator on the output bus is not enough.

Although emulations allow us to reproduce each of the devices in the chain, doing so would inevitably lead to using an excessive number of plug-ins on every track in the project. The solution, then, is not to recreate the entire chain, but rather to take inspiration from it by placing our emulations in an order that follows the same logic. The processing chains shown in the margin suggest combinations of emulators that can help us move closer to the analog processing approach.

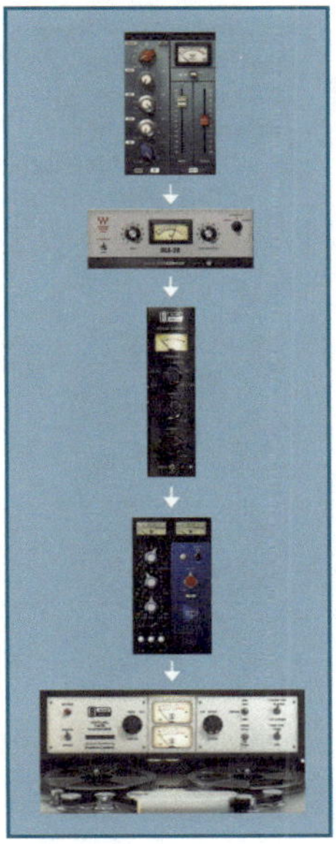

Simulating an analog chain on a track

In this simulation, the signal first passes through a preamp, then a compressor, a console emulator, an equalizer, and ends its path on the virtual 2-inch tape of a tape machine emulator.

Objective 3: Increase the Emotional Impact of an Element

Adding a good dose of saturation gives a track size and personality. Let us take the example of a song we all know: We Will

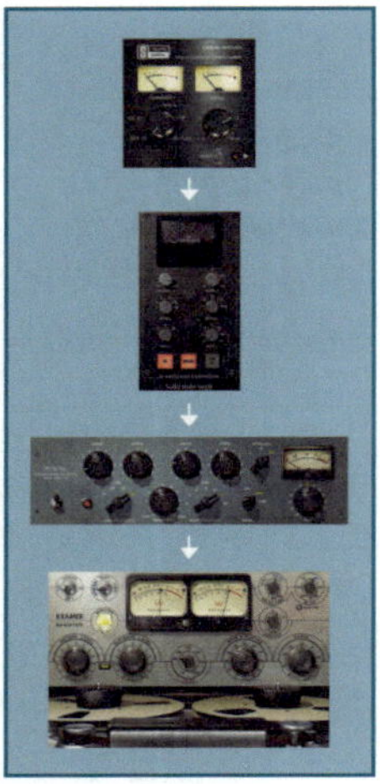

Simulating an analog chain on the mixbuss

The summing process is recreated by a console emulator, followed by a compressor, an equalizer, and a 1/4-inch tape machine emulator.

Rock You by Queen. Now imagine that song without the heavy saturation on the drums and group vocal harmonies. Much less convincing, is it not?

That impact, that character, is what saturation brings to the track. In fact, when using saturation with this goal in mind, the focus is less on technical considerations than on the emotion it adds to the track.

On vocals, saturation adds a sense of closeness because the compression it applies to the signal tends to bring out all the low-level information, such as breaths between phrases and subtle variations in tone. Very often, a small amount of saturation is enough to bring out the emotional nuances of the performance. It only takes a little more saturation to set the vocal on fire. The voice then becomes grittier and suddenly feels more vibrant and intense.

The type of saturation chosen, and its level relative to the original signal, therefore reflect the feeling we want to enhance. To reach this specific goal, it is often easier to use in parallel, allowing us to compare different saturation colors quickly and set the level of the saturated version independently.

Objective 4: Process Delay Returns

It is common to add saturation to delay effects, particularly those used on vocals. Adding saturation to echoes helps prevent masking by giving them a sonic signature different from that of the lead vocal.

Although this technique can be applied to slapback effects, vocal throws and other echoes that are further removed in time from the source benefit from it the most. This processing can also be used to make a delay intended to fill empty spaces more interesting. In that case, the goal is to draw the listener's attention momentarily to the echo so that it is no longer perceived as a mere ambient effect, but rather as a point of interest in the mix. The type of saturation chosen defines the color of the echo, and its amount determines how strongly we want it to stand out in the mix.

Objective 5: Support the Song's Structure

Besides creating occasional effects, saturation can sometimes help clarify the transition between different sections of a song. This technique helps maintain the listener's attention by changing the character of the song according to its structure.

We are all familiar with arrangements in which the acoustic guitar in the verse gives way to a saturated electric guitar in the choruses. This strategy, which is highly effective, can inspire us in the treatment of other elements in the mix.

For the lead vocal, for example, we might use one type of saturation in the verses and another in the choruses. For rhythmic elements—bass, drums, or one of their individual components—varying the amount of saturation from one section to another will help enhance the impact of transitions. We might increase the amount of saturation on the drums in the bridge or choruses and reduce it during the verses. This section-based saturation approach can also be used in the processing of delay effects.

Saturation is an amplifier of emotion.

Objective 6: Salvage a Track with Faulty Tone

We are sometimes faced with a track that has so many sonic flaws that it seems unusable. Integrating a track with phase problems, excessive background noise, or intermittent distortion can indeed become a real headache, especially when it is supposed to play an important role in the song.

In such a situation, the best way to salvage the track is often to degrade it even further so that its sonic problems come to be perceived as a deliberate effect.

Further degrading the sound of a track is sometimes the best way to save it.

Naturally, saturation plays an important role in this deliberate sonic degradation. It is therefore applied in sufficient quantity to mask the problems in the track. Strong equalization and a bold choice of saturation (real or virtual saturation pedals, lo-fi, bit crusher, etc.) are often called for in this type of work.

10.4 Recommendation

Take Into Account the Compression Inherent in Saturation

If you regularly work with guitar tracks, you have probably noticed that the more saturated a guitar sound is, the more stable its dynamics become. It therefore becomes clear that saturation inevitably induces a certain degree of compression in the signal.

Unlike compressors, saturators do not allow us to control precisely how the signal's dynamics will be modified. Every device or plug-in that generates saturation has its own dynamic signature. What we do notice, however, is that saturation reduces transients more quickly than most compressors. In addition,

THE COMPRESSION GENERATED BY SATURATION

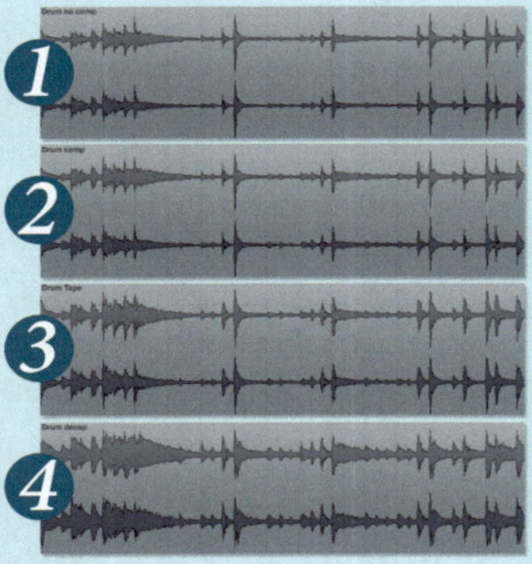

1) The original drum recording

2) The same recording passing through a compressor applying 4 dB of gain reduction

3) The same recording after moderate processing with a tape machine emulator

4) The same recording after moderate processing with a saturation plug-in

By comparing these waveforms, we can see that both the tape machine emulator (3) and the saturation plug-in (4) apply more compression than the compressor (2). It should also be noted that the saturation plug-in is the one that reduces the signal's transients most quickly.

It is therefore important to keep saturation's inherent compression in mind and, when necessary, revisit any other processing affecting the dynamics of the saturated element.

the amount of compression applied is directly related to the amount of saturation affecting the signal.

In the same spirit, when a high degree of saturation is added to an element that remains present throughout the mix, it is often worthwhile to use it in parallel. Not only do we preserve part of the track's original dynamics, but we also give ourselves the option of adjusting the amount of saturation to the needs of the song.

As we saw earlier, compression is cumulative. The compression generated by saturation is also part of that equation. The presence or absence of a saturator in a processing chain therefore has a significant impact on the other components in that chain. For example, if a compressor used to level the volume is already in the chain, it is appropriate to reassess its settings and even question whether it is still needed, since saturation is already doing part of its job.

11
SMART TOOLS

IT IS IN THE VERY NATURE OF TECHNOLOGY to be constantly evolving. The world of audio is obviously no exception. A great many so-called smart tools have, in fact, stormed the plug-in market. Let us take a quick look at the main families of these tools and what they are used for.

11.1 "Smart" or AI-Based?

Let us first make a brief distinction between tools based on the application of algorithms and tools that rely on artificial intelligence.

A large share of so-called smart processing tools are based on spectral analysis algorithms. They scan the characteristics of the element being processed and modify it, often in real time, by applying the algorithm defined by the manufacturer. These tools are generally used to correct anomalies in a signal. In this chapter, we will focus mainly on one of the most commonly encountered smart tools: the resonance suppressor. Oeksound's Soothe2 is probably the best-known example in this category. Several manufacturers, including Slate Digital, SSL, and iZotope, to name just a few, have also developed tools that perform similar work.

It is fairly easy to see here that the label "smart" often has more to do with marketing than with technological reality.

Behind the label "smart tool" there is often nothing more than a collection of advanced algorithms, whose evolution is tied mainly to computer processing power rather than to any genuine intelligence. In reality, applying an algorithm is the basic operating principle of any software tool. Released in 1997, Auto-Tune, for example, applies an algorithm that processes pitch in real time. In that sense, it too could be described as smart, although at the time the preferred term was "automatic." The label should therefore be taken with a grain of salt.

The label "smart" often has more to do with marketing than with technological reality.

Tools that rely on artificial intelligence, for their part, are instead based on the analysis of thousands of existing musical works. From these analyses emerge predictive statistical models that enable the software to suggest processing solutions. For example, an AI EQ inserted on an acoustic guitar track will attempt to bring that guitar's spectral characteristics closer to those observed in earlier productions featuring similar acoustic guitars.

AI-based tools are useful for offering processing suggestions that can serve as starting points for a mix. Profile-based operation is also particularly well suited to cleanup and stem-separation applications.

11.2 Resonance Suppressors

Resonance suppressors are in fact adaptive dynamic equalizers that analyze audio material and target excessive peaks present in the signal. They can be thought of as a collection of de-essers spread across the frequency spectrum, each acting automatically within user-defined ranges.

11.2.1 THE OBJECTIVES OF USING RESONANCE SUPPRESSORS

The resonance suppressor is particularly effective for correcting localized problems that are difficult to treat manually, such as those caused by a musician moving in relation to the microphone, by an instrument's uneven response across its range, or by the sudden appearance of isolated frequencies.

The resonance suppressor is effective for correcting localized problems that are difficult to treat manually.

Although it can be used on a subgroup or even on an entire mix, it is often more effective on individual tracks. It is generally inserted at the beginning of the chain, before compression.

Taming harsh frequencies or excessive peaks in a vocal track is one of the most common uses for a suppressor. It can, for example, be used to stabilize low-frequency fluctuations caused by the singer's movements or to attenuate midrange resonances that can make the voice sound muddy or nasal. It is also very effective at softening harsh frequencies between 2.5 kHz and 5 kHz.

The resonance suppressor is also highly effective on percussion. On a drum kit, it can calm overexcited hi-hats and cymbals. It can complement compression on hand percussion such as tambourine, and may even replace it on certain instruments such as glockenspiel or xylophone.

Some acoustic guitar tracks present resonances that are difficult to treat because they vary depending on the note being played. A suppressor will track them more easily than a conventional dynamic EQ. For the same reasons, the violin often benefits from this tool as well.

Certain modulation effects, such as phaser or flanger, can amplify or generate moving resonances in the sound. Placing a suppressor after the effect makes it easier to even out the frequency response than manual correction.

Most suppressors also offer a sidechain option. Unlike most traditional compressors, a suppressor can be set to act only on specific frequency ranges. In a sidechain relationship between kick drum and bass, for example, it can reduce only the low end of the bass track without affecting the rest of its spectrum. This preserves its attack while freeing up space for the kick drum in the low end of the spectrum. This targeting ability can make the suppressor useful for countering masking.

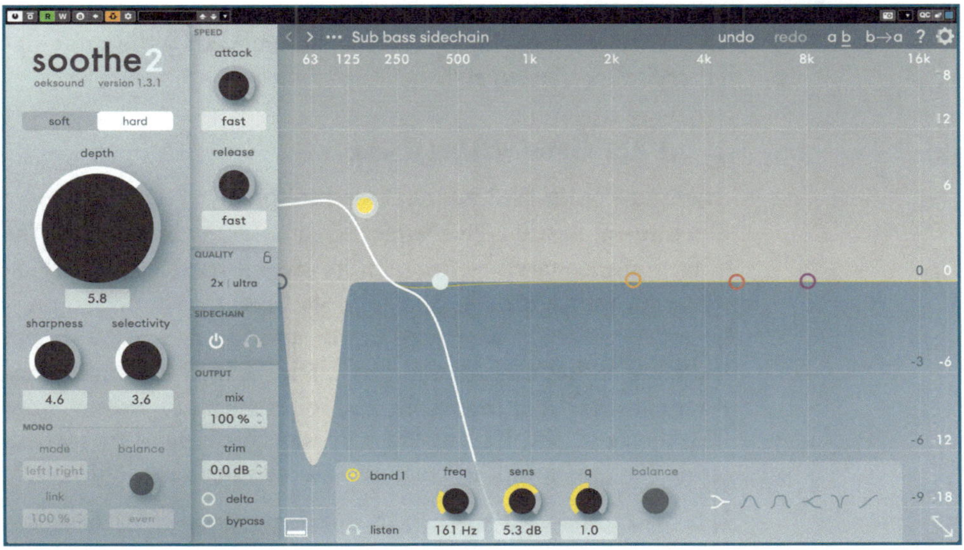

Oeksound's Soothe2 resonance suppressor allows sidechain use targeting a specific frequency range. Here, the low frequencies of the bass make room for those of the kick drum, which drives the sidechain.

11.2.2 RECOMMENDATIONS

Have a Goal in Mind

Despite what one may read on some discussion forums and hear in tutorials, resonance suppressors are not magical. Not all resonances necessarily need to be removed. Some may contribute to the personality of a sound; others help it find its place in the mix.

Resonance suppressors remain powerful corrective tools, acting on both the dynamics and the EQ of a track. Like all algorithm-based tools, they have neither aesthetic judgment nor musical sensitivity. They therefore cannot be used indiscriminately. They are beneficial only when we take the time to understand how they work and use them with a specific goal in mind.

11.3 Mix Assistants

A mix assistant works by comparing a given track with a series of reference profiles organized by instrument family. The plug-in analyzes the frequency and dynamic characteristics of the track being processed and applies various treatments to bring its attributes closer to those of a reference target. In most cases, the user can select that target from a menu, and the proposed processing remains fully editable.

Mix assistants compare a track's frequency and dynamic characteristics to those of a similar AI-learned model.

More advanced plug-ins can also integrate tracks into a broader sonic aesthetic. To do so, they generally require the user to group similar tracks into broad categories and select a musical style. At that point, the applied treatments no longer rely solely on instrument profiles, but are also influenced by the sonic signature of the chosen style.

11.3.1 RECOMMENDATIONS

Starting Points, Not a Final Destination

Once again, the adjective "smart" may be a bit exaggerated. The plug-in understands nothing on its own: it must be told which direction we want to go in. And even then, that direction must be generic enough to be listed in a drop-down menu. We should therefore expect a result that flirts with the lowest common denominator of the chosen style. The solutions it proposes will not help us stand out. Rather, the very way this type of tool works tends to align us with the references learned by the plug-in.

It is also important to keep in mind that even if we treat the suggestions made by these plug-ins as starting points, mixing can quickly turn into a major correction job. We will constantly have to revisit the processing in order to recover the original intent.

iZotope's Neutron includes a mix assistant that analyzes the instruments in a mix and compares them to AI-learned reference profiles in order to suggest processing starting points.

Mix assistants, like most so-called smart tools, "listen" to a song only statistically. They replace neither the critical judgment nor the musical sensitivity of a mixing engineer. They should therefore be regarded as tools that can inspire processing ideas for tracks that are giving us trouble.

Keep Your Software Up to Date

The size of an AI-based tool's reference library helps ensure that its suggestions remain both relevant and up to date. If the manufacturer stops enriching its machine-learning models, the tool may begin suggesting targets that no longer reflect recent trends. Keeping these libraries up to date is therefore crucial to the quality of the tool's performance.

Users must also make sure to keep their tools up to date so that performance does not stagnate. These updates obviously come with their share of inconveniences, especially in terms of cost, compatibility, and system stability.

11.4 Cleanup and Repair Tools

Because smart tools analyze the makeup of an audio signal rather than the musical meaning of a song, they are particularly well suited to cleanup tasks.

Plug-in-based tools make it possible to attenuate common audio problems in real time. Background noise can easily be reduced when its signature is relatively stable, such as ventilation hiss, amplifier noise, or tape-machine whine. Likewise, it is possible to reduce short transient noises, such as clicks and pops, if they have caused only moderate damage.

Offline tools make it possible not only to clean up a signal, but also to reconstruct it.

By combining algorithmic processing with models learned through artificial intelligence, offline repair tools can go much further. No longer constrained by real time, they can not only attenuate problems, but also reconstruct damaged audio. This opens the door to much more complex repairs, such as removing occasional noises or crackles, reconstructing a clipped signal, or restoring an old recording.

Several offline tools can also analyze a signal in order to separate its sources. Although the results vary, this decomposition of the signal allows for much more effective cleanup than a real-time plug-in. This type of separation also makes it possible to extract an element from a loop or rebalance the instruments that make it up.

11.4.1 RECOMMENDATIONS

The Side Effects of Cleanup

In our discussion of the gate in Chapter 9, we pointed out that it is wise to avoid systematically eliminating background noise. That recommendation also applies to all uses of cleanup plug-ins.

These tools do not merely lower the volume of an annoying noise: they base their action on directly modifying the sonic signature of a track. This manipulation inevitably generates artifacts, which can sometimes be more insidious than the problem we are trying to solve. Thus, although they can reduce a variety of audio problems, it is important to find the right balance between repair and the anomalies generated by the tool.

Do Your Cleanup at the Very Start of the Mix

Cleanup plug-ins can quickly become very resource-hungry. It is therefore worth considering whether it would be better to render the processing rather than keep the plug-in active throughout the mix.

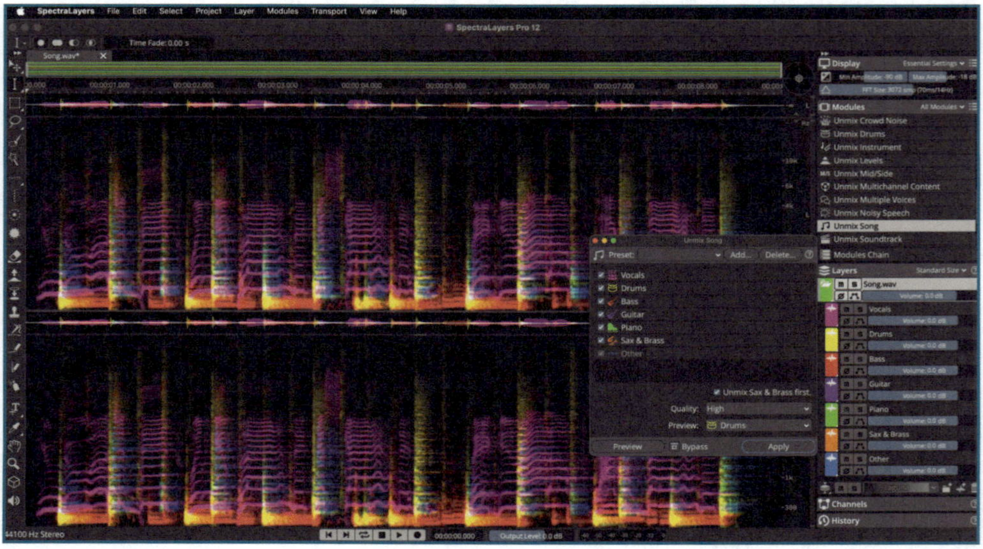

Steinberg's SpectraLayers is a tool that relies on AI to carry out advanced audio cleanup and restoration tasks.

Offline repair work, for its part, requires leaving your editing software. It is generally a lengthy process that requires careful attention. If you resort to this type of treatment, it is crucial to carry it out at the very start of the mix so as not to lose momentum once the mixing process is underway.

Judge for Yourself Whether a Plug-In Is Useful

The vast majority of these so-called smart plug-ins are presented as the cure-all for every problem you have. Seasoned mix engineers will describe them as game changers that will instantly improve the quality of your mixes without any effort. Unfortunately, or perhaps fortunately, that kind of plug-in does not exist. These tools sometimes serve as starting points, but rarely as solutions. Some of them may, however, help by simplifying your work or speeding it up. It is up to you to decide whether what a given tool offers truly suits your way of working.

12
MIXING STRATEGIES

As we mentioned in the very first chapter, "mixing aims to draw out a piece's full potential—both technically and emotionally—in order to move the listener, capture their interest, and hold their attention." So beyond the mastery of processing tools, the real work of mixing lies in how we transform a series of individual tracks into what we call a song. In that sense, this chapter proposes strategies that take us to the heart of that transformation process and seek above all to put technique at the service of the music.

12.1 Technical Strategies

12.1.1 LISTENING LEVEL AND PERCEPTION

At the beginning of the last century, Bell Telephone Laboratories employed a handful of researchers dedicated to fundamental research in sound recording and transmission. Among them, Fletcher and Munson tackled the notion of sound level and the way it is perceived.

The tests are relatively simple. A subject is played a 1 kHz tone followed by a 2 kHz tone and is asked whether the first sound is louder or softer than the second. The test is then repeated using different frequencies in order to continue the evaluation across the entire audible spectrum.

The study led to an important discovery: the human ear does not perceive loudness linearly. In other words, our perception of loudness varies according to the frequency being heard. For example, a 1 kHz tone at 40 dB seems to us to be the same loudness as a 100 Hz tone at 60 dB. And yet there is an actual level difference of 20 dB!

Not only is human hearing non-linear, but it also varies with the listening level.

Another important revelation: not only is human hearing non-linear, but it also varies with the listening level. To go back to the previous example, if both tones are heard at a level of 90 dB, they will be perceived as equally loud. Fascinating, is it not?

The fact that the human ear perceives frequencies differently depending on level raises two fundamental questions for our work. First, at what listening level should we mix in order to make informed decisions? And above all, how can we reach listeners when we know nothing about their listening level?

By examining the Fletcher-Munson graph, we see that our perception of frequencies is most uniform at high listening levels, around 90 dB. However, if you set your monitors to reach that level, you will quickly realize that prolonged exposure at such a volume is fatiguing and may also damage your hearing.

Since maintaining such a high level is hardly realistic, one option would be to use a lower but constant listening level. Habit should allow us to extrapolate the proper amount of frequency content across the spectrum. Even though that assumption seems reasonable, it is difficult to apply in mixing, because tracks are delivered to us at different levels and our manipulations constantly alter signal amplitude.

The graph summarizing Fletcher and Munson's findings regarding the perception of sound frequencies as a function of listening level.

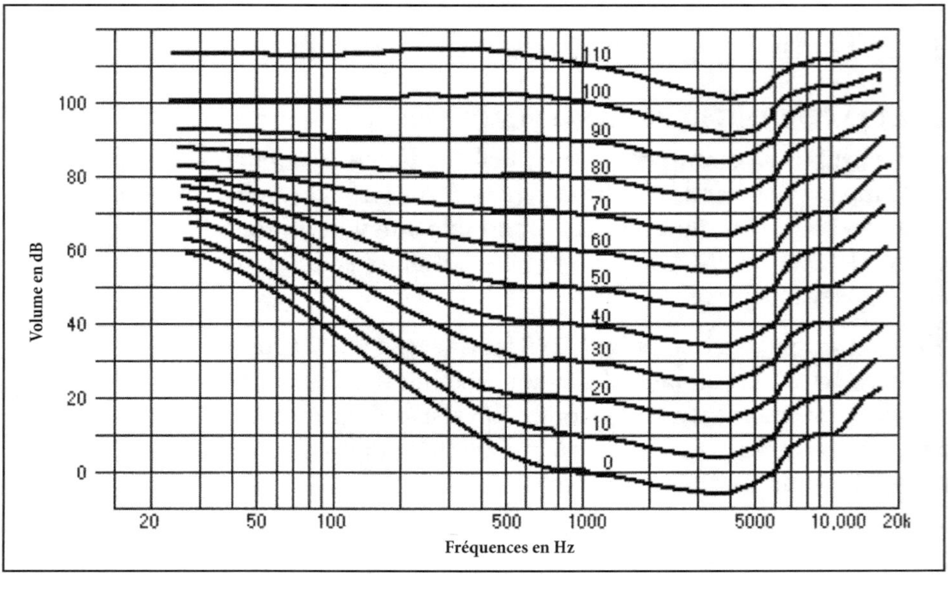

The Lowest Common Denominator

To continue this line of thought, let us add the listener to the equation. After all, this is who we are doing all this for!

Try the following experiment. Choose a commercially released track known for its sound quality. Start listening to it at a high level and gradually turn it down. You will hear the low frequencies disappear little by little. Continue lowering the volume until the track resembles a whisper. If you listen closely, you will notice that you can still hear the harmonic instruments, the attack of the percussion, and distinguish every word the singer is saying. As you slowly raise the volume again, you will find that although the low frequencies gradually add body to the track, the midrange remains perfectly well defined.

Our perception of the midrange remains uniform regardless of the listening level.

This phenomenon also illustrates another major conclusion of the Fletcher-Munson study: changes in level hardly affect our perception of the midrange. More specifically, the ear's response between 700 and 4000 Hz is particularly uniform across listening levels. To borrow an expression dear to mathematicians, we might say that the midrange is "the lowest common denominator" of music reproduction!

Varying the Listening Level

If there is one thing we do know about how listeners will hear our work, it is that we have no idea! So for a mix to hold up at any listening level, we must make sure that its midrange adequately represents all the essential elements of the piece. The best way to achieve this is to mix at low volume as often as possible.

But what do we mean by "low volume"? Well, accomplished mixers who use this method do most of their work at a level low enough to carry on a conversation without having to raise their voice (for those who like statistics, let us note that the average level of a conversation is around 60 dB).

Mix at low volume as often as possible, and raise it to better judge the low frequencies.

Using a low listening level while mixing also makes it possible to work for long periods without ear fatigue and partly reduces the effect of flaws in the surrounding acoustics.

Of course, it is impossible to judge the amount of low-frequency content without a fairly high listening level. So all we need to do is raise it occasionally in order to make it easier to process instruments that sit in that frequency range and to evaluate how effective the low end is within the mix as a whole.

Level and Before-and-After Comparisons

Going back to our friends Fletcher and Munson, we understand that the louder the level, the more uniform the frequency distribution and the more present the low end. Which leads us to an extremely important perceptual distortion that we cannot ignore: between two signals, we will always prefer the louder one.

That preference has nothing to do with sound quality. It is purely a matter of level. When we think about it, that makes perfect sense, because a loud sound necessarily has a richer frequency signature than a quiet one. The greater the level difference between the two signals, the more distorted our perception becomes.

Matching levels for before-and-after comparisons helps us evaluate our processing more objectively.

In mixing, this illusion can subtly influence our decisions, especially when we apply processing to a track. The only way to defeat it is to always set a processor's output level as close as possible to its input level. When you bypass the processor, you should not hear any significant change in level. That way, you will get a realistic before-and-after comparison, allowing you to judge more accurately what your processing is doing to the sound.

Of course, not every device and plug-in includes an output level control. When that is the case, a gain plug-in can be inserted after the processor to match levels.

12.1.2 MAKING A LARGE PROJECT EASIER TO MANAGE

Aside from manipulating level during mixing, it is essential to establish a strategy for handling large projects.

In analog mixing, the number of tracks in a project, no matter how large, must first be reduced to match the number of channels available on the console. So a 70-track project, for example, cannot be mixed on a 48-channel console without a serious slimming-down process first! This may seem paradoxical, but that limitation is often an advantage.

In digital, that constraint does not exist. It goes without saying, however, that the greater the number of individual tracks, the harder they are to locate, which undermines the fluidity of the mix. Mix preparation therefore becomes a determining factor.

The best way to proceed is to approach these projects as we would in analog. Very often, grouping tracks into subgroups and assigning VCAs during preparation will allow us to achieve that goal. But sometimes certain projects are so large that these techniques are no longer enough. Faced with such monsters, we will have to make choices!

Creating Stereo Tracks

Sometimes stereo tracks are delivered as two mono tracks or, if you prefer, as dual mono, one track for the right side and another for the left. Some virtual instruments or grouped sections, such as backing vocals, horns, strings, or choir, may indeed be presented this way. We can easily export each of these pairs as stereo tracks to replace them in the project.

Limiting the number of individual tracks in a project makes it easier to manage.

Also, some mono elements are in a sense inseparable from one another. The overhead tracks of an acoustic drum kit recorded with two microphones, for example, are often not very useful individually. The same goes for room tracks, which are often recorded to recreate a stereo space. Certain instruments, such as piano or acoustic guitar, may also have been recorded in stereo. These tracks can be replaced by exporting them in stereo once they have first been phase-aligned and balanced as needed.

Reducing the Number of Microphones Used

To reduce the number of tracks in a project, it is worth checking mono recordings made with multiple microphones.

Let us admit it: electric guitar recordings can quickly get out of hand! During tracking, the engineer may have placed more than one microphone on the amplifier. When that approach is deliberate, we will usually be given a track that combines the selected microphones. The situation becomes more complicated when the use of multiple microphones is intended to leave more flexibility for the mix, results from experimentation, or, worse yet, indecision. It then falls to us to choose which microphones will be used and in what proportions. A few factors can help guide that process.

In a rock song, it is common to double performances so that they can be placed on either side of the stereo panorama during mixing. Now imagine that each performance was captured with three microphones. We then end up with six guitar tracks. With four or five occurrences of that kind of doubled part, the number of guitar tracks quickly becomes gigantic! Even though they can be grouped into subgroups, it is often worth reducing the number of microphone tracks being used.

Superfluous tracks are obviously not limited to electric guitar. The abundance of microphones placed on a drum kit and those set up to capture the ambience of various instruments are not always useful in a mix. In some cases, we may also receive effect tracks or subgroup exports that overlap with individual elements we already have. In most cases, these tracks only make the project heavier and should be set aside.

Just because a track is delivered to us does not mean we absolutely have to use it.

So just because a track is delivered to us does not mean we absolutely have to use it. We must first assess the relevance of each element and determine whether or not it contributes to the mix.

12.1.3 SPLITTING TRACKS INTO SECTIONS

You are working on the vocal track. You set the EQ and compression, and everything is working perfectly. Then the chorus hits. The singer is now belting and apparently moved away from the microphone during recording. The melody, once in the low register, is now much higher. The sound lacks body, and the compression needle seems ready to bend as it pins the meter!

In this kind of situation, we can of course try to find middle-ground settings. But why compromise on such an important track when it is so easy to split it? This is called "multing." The technique consists of splitting a recording into sections so that they can be placed on separate tracks. That enables us to process them differently to suit the needs of the song. In the previous example, we would have one vocal track containing all the verses and another containing all the choruses.

Splitting a recording into sections and placing them on separate tracks helps us avoid compromises.

Multing also allows us, when needed, to change the processing chain as well as send destinations and send levels, not just the settings. That freedom is useful when applying some of the contrast strategies we will discuss later.

So this technique can be used whenever the sound of an element changes enough over the course of a piece to make it difficult to treat as a single track. A drum kit played with brushes and later with sticks, a clean guitar that becomes distorted, or a synthesizer that changes patch during the song are all situations well suited to multing.

12.1.4 FREEZING PROCESSING

Many DAWs offer a freeze function, often represented by a snowflake icon, that temporarily renders a track with its insert processing. When this function is engaged, the original track is temporarily set aside and replaced by a processed version. From that point on, it is no longer possible to change the insert settings or edit the track. When the freeze function is disabled, all our processing is restored exactly where we left it.

Since the track's processing is no longer being applied in real time, this function frees up computer processing power. That makes it easier to reduce latency for recording or for using virtual instruments during production.

Freezing a track's processing frees up computer power and encourages us to move on with the mix.

Beyond its practical usefulness during production, freezing a track can also serve a psychological purpose during mixing. By locking in our decisions, it encourages us to live with our choices and move on. Sometimes that is exactly what we need to return to the big picture of the mix and keep it moving forward.

12.2 Mixing Strategies

12.2.1 THE WHOLE IS MORE IMPORTANT THAN ITS PARTS

When we begin mixing, sound quality is our only concern. We strive to make everything perfect with generous doses of EQ and compression until every element in the mix sounds as good as possible. Who among us has not spent long minutes adjusting the sound of an instrument in solo? Completely thrilled by the presumed effectiveness of the processing, we disengage the solo button only to realize that the track simply does not fit in with the rest of the mix. Why? Simply because mixing is much more than an accumulation of individual elements: it is a whole!

The sound of a track in solo is of no interest; it is the overall sound that matters.

The truth is that the sound of a track in solo is of no interest whatsoever, because it will never be heard that way. The overall sound is far more important than any of the tracks that make it up. So processing is always best adjusted while listening to all the tracks in the mix or, at the very least, its main elements. We should therefore reserve the solo button for certain specific tasks, such as setting a gate threshold, the tempo of an echo, the length of a reverb, or checking for masking between two important tracks.

12.2.2 HIERARCHIZING TRACKS

One common misconception is to believe that all the tracks in a mix are equally important. That assumption not only makes mixing extremely difficult, but also reduces our ability to capture and hold the listener's attention. Whatever piece we are working on, some elements are more important than others because of their role in the arrangement or their ability to convey emotion.

Normally, it is possible to grasp the essence of a piece in a handful of tracks.

Normally, it is possible to grasp the essence of a piece in a handful of tracks. Very often, the song itself tells us which elements to prioritize. Obviously, the lead vocal almost always sits at the top of the list. But beyond that, what is or are the driving elements of the piece? Is it the rhythm, a guitar line, a bass line, or a keyboard line? A good way to assess the importance of an element is to ask the following question: "If I mute it, does the mix collapse?" If the answer is yes, that track is essential. If not, it is a secondary element.

The direction of a piece is largely defined by the tracks that are brought forward. Imagine, for example, a song like Uptown Funk by Bruno Mars if its bass line had not been emphasized. In the case of With or Without You by U2 or Uprising by Muse, it is instead a pulse that serves as the foundation for the entire mix.

The character of a piece is largely defined by the tracks that are brought forward.

This form of hierarchy is remarkably effective for structuring the way we approach a project, especially when it is a large one. At the beginning of the mix, we make only the essential tracks audible and build a mix that works with those tracks alone. We then add the secondary tracks one by one according to the importance of their contribution to the piece. Priority is therefore always given to the tracks that were already audible before the addition. We make sure that every new element we add complements the ones already there without ever overshadowing them. We then apply the same principle to the effects.

This way of proceeding lays a clear foundation for our decisions regarding level and panning within the mix. It also simplifies the resolution of masking problems between tracks or caused by effects. It helps establish the overall direction of the song and quickly tells the listener what genre it belongs to. Not to mention that by varying the presence of secondary elements over the course of the mix, we create countless opportunities to keep the listener engaged.

12.2.3 STARTING A MIX WITH THE CHORUS

It is the nature of arrangements to change gradually over the course of a song. For example, the introduction and first verse, although they may sometimes clarify the driving elements of a piece, generally contain only a stripped-down version of the arrangement.

Starting a mix from the very beginning of a song therefore presents several obstacles simply because it does not provide us with enough information. At that stage, it is also very difficult to establish a gain structure that can be maintained once the arrangements grow denser. In addition, the processing applied to the tracks does not take into account the masking issues that will arise as the piece develops. As a result, we lose a great deal of time continually revisiting decisions that were, all in all, made too early in the mix.

Beginning a mix is a bit like planning an itinerary: the trip is simply impossible if you have not defined your destination! In the case of the vast majority of songs, that destination is the chorus. As the saying goes, "That's where the money is!" It is indeed the most important part of the song for the listener, the part that resonates with them and, hopefully, the part they will remember. If the introduction and verses set the tone of a song, the chorus IS that tone!

Starting a mix is like planning an itinerary: simply impossible if you have not defined your destination!

In that sense, the final chorus of a song is probably the best place to begin a mix. It generally contains the densest arrangement, which helps us establish the hierarchy discussed in the previous section. The simultaneous presence of many of the mix elements will reveal most of the masking issues, which will clarify our decisions regarding mix processing and the placement of elements in the stereo field. The final chorus is very often the moment when the level of a song is at its highest. It therefore becomes easy to establish the upper limit of our gain structure and use it as the basis for the rest of the mix.

To return to our analogy, once we have established the final chorus as our destination, we can work backward to define the itinerary we will use to get there. It then becomes easier to define the role of the tracks in each of the song's other sections and the processing needed to highlight them while clarifying the structure of the piece.

So even though beginning the mixing of a song with its chorus is more demanding than starting with its opening, this way of working allows us to choose more effectively how we will present the piece to the listener in order to lead them, with us, toward the same destination.

12.3 Contrast Strategies

In everyday life, some things catch our attention more than others. It is hard not to notice fireworks in a dark sky, an ocean liner among sailboats, or someone dancing in a bank lineup! In short, as soon as something contrasts with the linearity of its surroundings, it inevitably draws our attention.

Of course, this phenomenon also applies to audio. In fact, that was the whole point of the blaring television commercials of the 2000s: to grab viewers' attention through a sudden increase in level. Fortunately, contrast does not have to be that pronounced to capture our listeners' attention.

At the same time, we know that music is now consumed in a completely different way. The listener's focus is fleeting and must be continually stimulated or it will be lost. That is why contrast strategies may be necessary to disrupt linearity and thus improve our chances of keeping the listener engaged.

As we saw in Chapter 6, automation makes it possible to modify any mix parameter with precision as the piece unfolds. It will therefore be very useful in putting several of the strategies presented here into practice.

12.3.1 ENHANCING THE ARRANGEMENTS

Contrast strategies help break the sonic linearity of a piece.

Of course, a song's arrangements generally contain contrasting elements. The move from a fairly sparse introduction to a denser section is, of course, one of the most common arrangement techniques and, let us admit it, a remarkably effective one. Breaks, tempo changes, and shifts in the harmonic instruments are also contrast devices that demand very little from us, aside from making sure we do not interfere with their natural effect.

Bringing Something New to Each Section

However, when the arrangements are too linear, it becomes essential to find ways of adding movement to the piece. Let us illustrate the point by taking one of the best-known works in the classical repertoire: Ravel's Boléro. This fifteen-minute work is, all things considered, based on the repetition of two main motifs. Now imagine that, instead of revealing themselves to us gradually, all the instruments were playing full blast from the beginning. It would be deadly dull, wouldn't it? It is the introduction of a new element with each repetition of the motifs that moves the piece forward and makes it interesting. Even if the example of Boléro is admittedly a bit extreme, this idea of slightly altering repetitive sections is essential to breaking a song's linearity.

In mixing, we will often achieve that goal by leaving certain elements out. For example, we might mute some of the backing vocals in the first chorus and introduce them only in the second. We may choose to make the synthesizer or acoustic guitar audible only during the verses. We may reserve the hand percussion for the choruses, and so on.

Some will argue that it is not the mixer's role to intervene in the arrangement. In reality, I have never met a client who was closed to suggestions that could improve the quality of the final result. After all, we are aiming for the same objective: to bring out the song's full potential. And since every one of our suggestions will, in any case, have to be submitted for approval, it would be negligent on our part not to propose ways of reaching that shared goal.

Directing the Listener's Attention

Another way to inject movement into a mix is to shift the listener's attention from one foreground element to another. In certain cases, this is an integral part of the arrangement. In traditional blues, for example, the vocal often carries on a dialogue with the guitar. The soloist, in a sense, answers each of the singer's phrases. In soul music, a similar effect is created when backing vocals and lead vocal exchange the foreground.

This concept can be very useful in many other musical styles. The idea is to fill the space between phrases by subtly directing the listener's attention toward another element in the arrangement.

Concretely, we might slightly raise the level of the rhythm guitars in a rock song whenever the vocal falls silent. In a more pop-oriented piece, it may be a keyboard line that moves forward to fill the gap. In a ballad, it might be a piano chord that is temporarily brought up. These manipulations do not need to be exaggerated: a subtle increase in level is enough for the listener to perceive movement in the foreground.

Subtle adjustments are enough to keep the listener engaged.

Accentuating Interesting Passages

In our discussion of vocal automation, we pointed out that it is possible to manipulate level in order to highlight certain phrases or key words in a vocal performance. That approach can, of course, also be applied to other elements in the mix. A drum fill, a bass line, a keyboard line, or a guitar line can be brought forward in order to draw the listener's attention momentarily to that performance.

Accentuating Transitions

Transitions play a crucial role in articulating the structure of a musical piece. They certainly mark the move from one section to another, but they also serve to build the listener's anticipation for the section to come.

We have all heard, many times over (perhaps a few too many times!), the typical synthesizer or percussion rise just before the chorus in an EDM track. Although this type of transition is not exactly subtle, it is highly effective and can be carried over into other musical styles.

In many cases, it is possible to emphasize a transition with a gradual increase in the level of the instrumental section or, as noted earlier, by raising the level of one of its elements.

It is sometimes necessary to add a new element to mark a transition.

Sometimes, however, transitions require a slightly stronger intervention in order to give them more drive. Several techniques can then be considered depending on the musical style involved. We can, for example, add an instrument to mark the transition. A wind chime glissando is a classic in soul ballads; guitar feedback works well in rock; and that is not to mention the many effects that can be created with synthesizers.

Another very effective method is to reverse the waveform of an element so that it is heard backward. A cymbal, a guitar or piano chord, or even vocals work well for creating this kind of effect. The attack of the reversed instrument is then aligned with the downbeat of the following section. The reversed element can come from a sound library, but the effect is particularly interesting when it can be drawn directly from the tracks of the project itself.

Of course, a sweep-type filter effect placed on one or more mix elements can also create the movement needed to mark the transition into another section of the piece.

12.3.2 BREAKING THE MIX'S SONIC LINEARITY

Enhancing the arrangements therefore takes us a good part of the way toward keeping the listener's attention. Several purely technical tricks can also help us reveal a song's full potential.

Raising the Level of the Choruses

We might as well begin with the classic of classics: raising the overall level of the chorus. Not very original, of course, but always tremendously effective.

Since it is generally unthinkable to raise each element of the chorus individually, the increase must take place on the output bus. If the mix never leaves the computer, we obviously cannot use the output bus fader without risking clipping during export. So if the routing does not include an overall subgroup, a pre-master, we use the gain control of the output bus or place a trim plug-in in its first insert.

Typically, the increase is around 1 dB, although that value may vary depending on the compression on the mix output.

If a compressor is present on the output bus, using the output gain control will drive that compressor harder. Not only will the applied increase in level be reduced, but we will also have to determine whether the extra work imposed on the compressor contributes positively to the final result. If not, the increase in chorus level will have to be performed after the dynamics insert.

That said, this maneuver only makes sense if it can be repeated for every chorus. So the main challenge is generally not raising the level, but lowering it again for the following verse. If the level difference cannot be concealed, we will spread the decrease over a longer period so that it becomes less noticeable. But with a bit of luck, it may be possible to highlight an element during the transition in order to mask the drop in level. Since the level of the output bus is likely already in motion, it is clear that great care must be taken when manipulating the element in question.

Lowering a mix's level after raising it requires great care.

Changing the Stereo Image According to the Song's Sections

Thanks to automation, it is relatively easy to manipulate the space elements occupy in the stereo panorama in order to increase contrast when moving from one section to another.

As we pointed out earlier, choruses generally feature denser arrangements than verses. They therefore naturally tend to occupy more space in the stereo field. That contrast also contributes to their impact when they arrive. It is therefore worth considering ways to heighten that difference.

Our first instinct is, of course, to try to widen the chorus. We must keep in mind, however, that when every element occupies its full stereo width, their positions become harder to distinguish, especially in dense arrangements. As always, the mix must be approached as a whole, not as the sum of its parts. In that sense, widening every element is rarely the best way to make a chorus feel wider. More often, it is better to narrow the stereo image of certain instruments and distribute them more effectively across the full panorama.

A mix's stereo panorama must be considered as a whole.

Piano and stereo-recorded acoustic guitar are two examples that quickly come to mind. These instruments have wide frequency ranges that can very quickly conflict with other elements in the chorus. By narrowing their stereo image, we define their placement more clearly and increase not only their own clarity, but also that of all the other elements.

Since the very notion of contrast implies that at least two elements are involved, the most effective way to give a chorus width is often to reduce the width of the verses. We therefore focus on narrowing the stereo image of the main elements in order to pull the whole verse closer to center. In doing so, the reverb naturally fills the freed-up space, giving the verses an open ambience that also helps heighten the contrast with the choruses.

Varying the Effects According to the Sections

Though subtler, varying the effects on the lead vocal can also help break the mix's linearity. Most of this maneuver is carried out by creating effect channels, or buses, depending on the DAW, into which the effects for each section of the piece are inserted. Automation then makes it possible to activate or alter the level of the lead vocal's sends according to the section.

Many scenarios are obviously possible. Using vocal throws in the verses, increasing the amount of doubler in the choruses, opting for a tempo-synced echo in the bridge, varying the amount of reverb used from section to section, and so on. In short, we simply have to define the mix of ingredients that will best season each section of the song.

Varying the Frequency Distribution

Another technique, somewhat bolder this time, consists of temporarily altering the frequency distribution of an element or even of an entire mix in order to create a powerful contrast effect.

Placing a saturation effect on the lead vocal for a passage or even an entire section of the performance is a common example of this kind of strategy. In fact, this technique is frequently used in introductions to capture the listener's attention from the very start of the song.

Saturation can serve a similar function when it is temporarily placed on another mix element, such as the drums or bass. One would normally choose a moment when the instrument is especially exposed, during a solo passage, for example.

The use of a filter that slowly sweeps across the frequency spectrum is a common device in pop and EDM. The effect is generally applied, in whole or in part, to the accompaniment instruments in order to mark a transition or radically change the mood of the piece. It can therefore be an option worth considering, provided the musical style lends itself to it. The important thing is to keep in mind that overuse of this type of effect can quickly become tiring. Not to mention that the piece risks becoming too quickly associated with a particular era because of its fashionable flavor. That kind of song tends to age very poorly.

13

REFERENCE TRACKS AND CRITICAL LISTENING

SUPPOSE YOU LIVE in a tiny village in Nauru, in Oceania. As a child, you were known at the village school as the fastest kid on the track. The gym teacher, having recognized in you an incredible aptitude for long-distance running, suggests that you focus all your efforts on the 5,000 meters. So you throw yourself into it whole heartedly!

A few years later, your many hours of training have paid off. No one in the village, or even in the Republic, can match your times of 18:45. You are recruited to the Olympic team, where they even nickname you "The Nauru Reed Warbler" because of your small build and remarkable agility!

In Paris, on August 10, 2024, you step onto the starting line for the 5,000 meters qualifying heat. With your feet firmly planted in the lane 8 blocks, you are both nervous and confident. At the sound of the starter's pistol, your heart pounds and you take off. A superb start!

At the first 1,000 meters, you are in fourth place. There is no doubt the race will be tougher than you had expected. Halfway through, a Jamaican runner, who looks fresh as a daisy, pushes you down into fifth place. As you begin the final lap, the leaders are now out of your sight. You resign yourself to finishing dead last.

"The Nauru Reed Warbler" crosses the finish line in 16 minutes, 43 seconds, and 22 hundredths... a full 3 minutes behind the leader!

As you catch your breath, your mind swings between surprise and disappointment. "Why wasn't I told that runners from other countries were so fast? I could have adjusted my training, worked on my technique... changed my sneakers!"

13.1 Reference Tracks

This little sporting fable nicely illustrates the importance of comparing our work with what is being done elsewhere. Otherwise, how can we know whether our mix holds up against the competition?

Of course, we can carry out this exercise after the fact, but then we run the risk of ending up disappointed and surprised, like our "Nauru Reed Warbler"! After all, once the mix is finished, it is often difficult to go back. That is why using one or more reference tracks during the mixing process allows us, in a way, to make sure our mix will meet Olympic standards.

Reference tracks help us assess how well our mix holds up against the competition.

Comparing our work with acclaimed productions is one of the most powerful techniques in mixing. This exercise allows us to take a brutally objective look at how a mix behaves when placed side by side with a high-level commercial production. This comparison, often a great lesson in humility, highlights, among other things, the gaps in balance, frequency distribution, stereo spread, and effect calibration. In doing so, it forces us to push our technique and listening skills further.

It also makes it possible to assess and, when needed, correct certain perceptual errors caused by acoustics or monitors, thereby increasing the chances that the mix will remain effective in any listening context. Active listening techniques are very useful for making this comparison. We will discuss them a little later on.

13.1.1 CHOOSING REFERENCE TRACKS

Tracks can be drawn from several sources. Music magazine lists (such as Rolling Stone or Billboard), lists of awards given by the industry (such as the Grammy Awards, the Junos, or the Tech Awards), as well as the résumés of renowned producers or engineers, are good places to begin your search. In addition, any track in which you detect something particularly interesting in terms of mixing or atmosphere is a good addition to your library, regardless of its musical style.

Selecting tracks requires a good deal of objectivity. It is essential not to confine yourself to the kind of music you prefer. The idea is to choose tracks whose sonic quality is praised by the industry or the public in order to set the bar as high as possible.

When choosing reference tracks, the idea is to set the bar as high as possible.

It is worth noting that MP3 files or tracks from streaming sites are perfectly adequate as references. Streaming services also make it possible to group tracks into playlists. It is therefore an excellent place to keep your library and make it accessible anywhere, anytime.

13.1.2 INTEGRATING REFERENCE TRACKS INTO YOUR PROJECT

Generally speaking, we select one or a few tracks that match the musical style of the project at hand.

In fact, the artists you work for often suggest songs or albums that resemble their own material (and if they do not, it is an excellent idea to ask them for a few!). Although this is not essential, comparable orchestration and tempo will make the comparison easier.

The chosen reference track or tracks are then imported directly into your project. Since a commercial track is mastered and your mix is not, the reference will inevitably have a higher output level. It is crucial to reduce its level so that it matches that of your mix.

The level of the reference must be adjusted so that it matches that of our mix.

We can then switch quickly and without interruption from one to the other by using the solo and mute buttons on the reference track. I insist here on the word "quickly." Listening for a maximum of 2 seconds ensures that the ear does not have time to become accustomed to the frequency distribution of the reference, thus making the differences easier to perceive.

13.1.3 RECOMMENDATIONS

Create a Reference Library

Reference tracks that match the genre of the project at hand are, of course, essential. But reference work can extend far beyond the needs of the moment.

A reference library contains about ten tracks in a variety of musical styles. The idea is to develop such a deep familiarity with them that we will be able to anticipate how they will sound in every imaginable listening context.

Such a library is, for example, very useful for assessing the impact of a change in the physical layout of your studio or for acclimating yourself more quickly to new monitors. Likewise, if you are working in a studio that is unfamiliar to you, listening to it will help you tune your ear to that new environment. It also comes in handy for comparing monitors or headphones before making a purchase.

Reference tracks can also help us better anticipate how different listening situations affect sonic reproduction.

This library can also help us in the final stages of the mix. It makes it possible to better understand how a device (a laptop, a television, a car, etc.) reproduces tracks whose sound we know well. We are then in a better position to assess the qualities the mix should have when we test it on one of these devices.

13.2 Critical Listening

A piece of music reveals very different kinds of information depending on the perspective from which we approach it. In classical music training, for example, composers support their listening by following along with scores. This allows them to go deeper in their analysis of a piece's melody, harmonies, orchestration, and structure. They learn how to achieve certain sonorities, discover how other composers approach music, identify differences between styles and periods, and so on. It is therefore no surprise that music programs always include several courses on this subject.

Traditional musical analysis is less suited to our profession. After all, the recognition of instruments, structure, and arrangements is, in most cases, sufficiently explicit. Access to scores, assuming they even exist, is obviously exceptional. Thus, in the field of mixing, analysis is carried out primarily through listening, more precisely through what is commonly called critical listening.

The kind of listening we are discussing here has very little to do with the way a music lover or a music critic listens to a track. We use it to compare our work, refine our decisions, and deepen our knowledge. We will sometimes use tools to focus it more precisely. It is therefore a more engaged, more precise, and more deliberate kind of listening.

13.2.1 THE FOUNDATIONS OF ACTIVE LISTENING

Suppose you are with a friend in the lobby of a large concert hall. Hundreds of people are gathered there, talking, laughing, drinking, and so on. Despite the incredible commotion around you, you have no difficulty carrying on a conversation with your friend. Our brain is indeed capable, through a simple act of concentration, of isolating one element from a whole with striking precision. In the same situation, you could just as easily ignore your friend's voice and focus your attention on the conversation of the people nearby or on the clinking of glasses at the bar, thereby experiencing—admittedly in a slightly antisocial way—the power of what psychology calls selective attention.

Critical listening takes advantage of the principle of selective attention.

Critical listening takes advantage of this remarkable ability. It allows us to go beyond superficial listening by focusing our attention on specific aspects of a track in order to understand its construction and how it works. We can also enrich our analysis by using certain processing tools while listening.

13.2.2 CRITICAL LISTENING AND REFERENCE TRACKS

Critical listening is, in itself, a highly rewarding activity. But it is particularly valuable when comparing a mix with a reference track. Here, we will outline the aspects to focus on during this comparison and the information we can draw from it.

The Level of the Main Elements

Every style of music has its own code when it comes to instrument levels. One of the undeniable advantages of applying critical listening to a reference track is that it reveals that code and lets us compare our mix against it.

Critical listening goes hand in hand with listening to reference tracks.

To set the levels of the main elements in a mix, we switch very quickly and without interruption between the mix and the reference while focusing on one instrument at a time, adjusting each fader until no significant level difference is perceived. This gradually brings the balance of the mix closer to that of the reference track.

The Individual Elements

In the same vein, focusing our attention on the technical attributes of a specific instrument in the reference track tells us about its frequency distribution, its degrees of compression and saturation, and the effects assigned to it. We can therefore draw inspiration from this information to fine-tune our own processing.

Panning

Listening to the reference from the perspective of its spatial distribution reveals the position of each element in the mix along the left/right axis.

Stereo listening, of course, gives us a general sense of the panning used in the reference track. But we can also deepen the analysis by listening to only one side at a time. The position of each instrument then becomes much more obvious. By alternating from one channel to the other, we can also spot the elements that have been deliberately placed in opposition within the stereo image. In the case of doubled tracks, it is sometimes possible to tell whether each performance was recorded and processed in the same way.

All this information can be useful in developing our own panning strategies.

Effects and Ambience Management

Critical listening can also tell us a great deal about effects, particularly when using an M/S (mid/side) plug-in during playback.

Critical listening can be enhanced by the use of certain processing and analysis tools.

Although some effects are easily audible, others are not. It is sometimes difficult to clearly define the space they occupy in the stereo field, an important variable in the overall ambience of a track. By muting the centre channel (M) of the reference and listening only to its sides (S) with an M/S plug-in, we gain a wealth of information about how effects are managed. This type of listening often reveals the type of reverb placed on the lead vocal and its decay time. The same goes for effects used to add size to the snare drum, vocal harmony processing, modulation effects, the use or non-use of a global reverb, and so on. Not to mention that M/S listening always comes with its share of surprises! It often reveals things that escape our attention during conventional stereo listening.

An M/S comparison of the various sections of our reference is also very revealing of the contrast strategies used to enhance its structure. Besides making it easy to detect the elements added during the choruses, it is often possible to tell whether the effects used in the verses differ from those in the choruses. We can also identify variations in stereo width from one section of the track to another.

Listening to the centre channel is not without interest either. And since we are only one click away from accessing it, it would be negligent not to give it a listen! We can identify the elements that sit only in the centre of the mix and get a more accurate sense of their respective levels.

Frequency Distribution

Placing a frequency analyzer at the output of both our mix and the reference track allows us to visually compare their respective frequency distributions. If our output bus contains an equalizer, this comparison can be used to fine-tune its settings.

We can even push this exercise further by restricting our analysis to specific frequency ranges. To do so, we insert a multiband compressor before the analyzer on each track, making sure, of course, that no compression is being applied. By listening to each of the four bands individually, we can assess how the frequency distribution of our mix compares with that of the reference in each area of the spectrum.

The analyzer display helps detect which elements in our mix are responsible for discrepancies in a specific area of the frequency spectrum. It can therefore guide us in revising their level or equalization.

This focused listening also helps us assess how well we have handled the issues associated with each range, such as the relationship between the kick drum and the bass, the depth of harmonic instruments, the character of the vocal in the midrange, or its degree of sibilance in the high frequencies.

Listening to the midrange is also particularly interesting because it effectively simulates some of the worst real-life listening conditions. If the essentials of our mix are well represented there, the game is practically won. If not, we can make the necessary corrections to the balance or equalization by drawing inspiration from the reference track.

13.2.3 RECOMMENDATIONS

Practice Critical Listening Regularly

Of course, the more regularly we practise this kind of exercise, the easier it becomes. It is a bit like auditory weight training!

Critical listening is an inexhaustible source of inspiration and learning.

Critical listening is not only useful for comparing our mix with a reference. The vast musical repertoire is an inexhaustible source of inspiration and learning. It allows us to discover how renowned mixing engineers tackle certain problems, as well as the techniques and strategies they use to give a track character and move listeners.

Of course, you can examine tracks in the area with which you are most familiar, but it is essential to extend your listening beyond your comfort zone. Every style of music, from traditional jazz to pop, has its own unique way of conceiving balance, sound, and its manipulation. The techniques you discover there will enrich your toolkit and prove useful to you, whatever musical context you are working in.

Explore the Internet

The Internet is incredibly rich in material for practising critical listening. Simply type "isolated track" into YouTube and an astonishing number of isolated tracks from well-known songs will appear. The quality and reliability of these sources can vary, however, so they should not be assumed to be accurate in every case. Even so, these tracks can still be real mixing lessons for those willing to listen to them carefully. In some cases, every track of a song can be heard individually. With a little patience, you can even assemble them into a multitrack version and analyze them directly in your DAW.

Several websites devoted to music production also offer the possibility of downloading the individual tracks of an entire project. These tracks will give you the opportunity to experiment with styles and recording methods that are less familiar to you. In addition, they are often used in mixing or remix contests. Whether you take part or not, you can still compare your mix with those of other mixing engineers and see how they approached certain tasks.

Some software applications use artificial intelligence to separate the elements of a song. Although they are less detailed than true multitracks, they still make it possible to appreciate certain aspects of their sonics and processing.

There are also many interviews with renowned mixers and engineers explaining their work on a specific song or album. They often reveal detailed information about the recording and mixing techniques used, and sometimes even a list of the equipment associated with that particular project (type of console, plug-ins, processing chains, etc.). More than enough to make your critical listening of their work even more revealing.

14
FINALIZING THE MIX

"WHEN DO YOU KNOW a mix is finished?" That is, without a doubt, one of the questions I am asked most often. It is, of course, a legitimate question. The discomfort is all the more real for those working on their own projects, with no time constraints, no budget constraints, and no one's approval to obtain but their own!

The well-known mixing engineer Dave Pensado often says that he would still be working on the very first mix of his career if he could! It is true that in mixing, it can sometimes be difficult to know where and when to stop.

Any project, whatever it may be, must come to an end; that is the only way to make progress.

The French poet Paul Valéry captures the feeling very well: "A poem is never finished, only abandoned." Although finalizing a mix does not always end so dramatically, this kind of letting go is necessary. Any project, whatever it may be, must come to an end; that is the only way to make progress.

14.1 Finalizing the Mix

14.1.1 SIGNS THAT A MIX IS FINISHED

Here are a few signs that strongly suggest the mixing stage is over. Some of them are unmistakable; others appear as warning signals that should not be ignored. You will also find a few suggestions for avoiding the pitfalls that can slow down the completion of your mix.

The budget or the deadline has run out

It is amazing how much a release date or a limited budget helps bring a mix to completion! When working for a client, knowing when to stop is rarely a problem.

If you are working on your own projects, setting a deadline is an excellent way to keep the mixing process from dragging on indefinitely. All that remains is to be disciplined enough to stick to your deadline.

Your latest moves are not adding anything truly meaningful to the mix

When too much time is spent on a mix, it becomes very easy to get lost in the technical side of things at the expense of the song's overall direction. We then fall into a kind of obsessive state where we pay disproportionate attention to details that are, all things considered, insignificant.

Another sign: you suddenly realize that some of your latest adjustments contradict earlier decisions. Rest assured, every mixer has gone through this painful experience. This is known as "going past the mix," proof that the situation is common enough to have a name.

The best solution is to take a break and go back to an earlier version of the mix or, if necessary, to one of the project's automatic backups.

You lose sight of the song's intention

Mixing is a demanding exercise in concentration. It is physically impossible to keep a fresh ear and a clear perspective without taking regular breaks. In fact, many well-known mixers do not finalize their mixes until after a good night's sleep, so they can gain enough distance to evaluate their decisions objectively.

It is impossible to keep a fresh ear and a clear perspective without taking regular breaks.

Regularly comparing your mix to a reference track is also an excellent way to put things back into perspective. Your attention will then shift toward the whole rather than the parts.

Likewise, listening to the rough mix makes it possible to appreciate the progress that has been made and brings the song's original direction back to mind.

You no longer react to the song

Mixing is certainly technical work, but its essential aim is to convey emotion to the listener. That goal becomes extremely difficult to achieve when we have worked on a song so much that it no longer affects us.

This situation is especially common when the preparatory stages are neglected. Our attention is then constantly diverted toward basic editing problems, causing us to lose track of the work at hand.

Admittedly, repeated revision requests from clients can sometimes lead to a similar state of mind. We will see later in this chapter how client presentation techniques can help us limit the number of revisions.

You feel that you have reached the song's full potential

But finalizing a mix is not always an exercise in inner torment! Quite often, we simply feel that we have gotten everything the song has to offer. Mission accomplished!

It is also important to keep in mind that mixing cannot always overcome the shortcomings of a recording, a performance, or an arrangement. Sometimes, our only option is to do the best we can with what we have. It is certainly frustrating, but it is nevertheless a fact we must accept. We must then focus on the primary goal of mixing: to bring out a song's full potential... no matter how great or small that potential may be.

Our goal is to bring out a song's full potential... no matter how great or small that potential may be!

14.2 Finalization Techniques

Once it has been established that the mix is finished, it is worth making a brief review of its settings and evaluating its effectiveness in different listening contexts.

In analog production, the number of processes that can be applied to a track is limited by several factors, the main one being the amount of outboard gear available.

In a DAW, however, nothing prevents us from filling the insert column of every track. Of course, that kind of overprocessing comes at a price. It lengthens the mixing process by complicating navigation, settings adjustments, and gain staging management. It is also essential to understand that every time we process a signal, we compromise its integrity to some extent. It is therefore in our interest to evaluate the relevance of each intervention so as to touch the signal as little as possible.

Every time we process a signal, we compromise its integrity to some extent.

Reassess the work of the equalizers

We have seen that it is possible to apply serial processing to a track by using two different devices in order to take advantage of their respective strengths. However, there is no benefit in using the same device or plug-in twice in a processing chain unless each instance has its own specific purpose. The usefulness of that kind of duplication must therefore be evaluated carefully.

The instinctive nature of mixing and its cyclical process make these kinds of duplicates especially common in EQ. For example, we may have inserted an equalizer on a track that worked well at the beginning of the mix but lost some relevance along the way. A second equalizer may then have been inserted in the same chain to compensate for the now-incomplete work of the first one. Likewise, processing applied to a subgroup can sometimes be redundant with the processing placed on the individual tracks it contains.

Thus, EQ moves can pile up. For example, one EQ boosts 200 Hz by 3 dB and another adds 1.5 dB at that same frequency later in the signal path. EQ settings can also be contradictory. A 3 dB boost at a given frequency becomes pointless if another equalizer cuts that same frequency by 4 dB farther down the chain.

It is important to track down these instances of double EQ and see whether they can be combined into a single move.

The mix output level

Once the settings review is complete, we must ensure that the mix output level leaves enough dynamic headroom for the mastering stage.

Peaks between -3 dB and -7 dB will give the mastering engineer enough headroom to do their job.

It is nearly impossible to define precisely the ideal level a mix intended for mastering should have. In fact, very few engineers agree on the issue. They do, however, all agree that it is both unnecessary and risky to deliver a track whose peak level approaches 0 dBFS.

Peaks between -3 dB and -7 dB will provide enough headroom for the mastering work.

There is generally no need to worry about the average level of your mix. As long as you have not overused compression, it will not compromise the mastering process.

Inspect the mix bus

As we saw earlier, it is common to place EQ, compression, or saturation processing on the mix bus from the very beginning of the mix. Their broad, generic action helps simplify and lighten the amount of intervention needed on the individual tracks. Their settings should, of course, be reassessed once the mix is finished.

This reassessment naturally begins with a look at the gain structure. If the level feeding the mix bus needs to be adjusted, the simplest method is to use the mix bus gain control or place a trim plug-in in its first insert slot. If you have used a subgroup—a premaster bus—that receives the entire mix before routing it to the mix bus, the fader of that subgroup becomes the actual gain control for the mix bus.

The plug-in settings will obviously need to be revised to match the new level they are receiving. Naturally, you must also pay attention to automation data affecting the mix bus and its components, and to the way your level adjustments interact with the existing automation.

Processing on the mix bus should generally be subtle. Thus, if the compressor is showing too much gain reduction or if you hear its action too obviously, the threshold setting needs to be reassessed. Saturation tools should also be checked to ensure their dosage is still appropriate. As for EQ, it is better to identify and correct the tracks causing the problem than to try to solve it by adding an equalizer on the mix bus. Heavy EQ correction on the mix bus is always suspicious and should be examined more closely.

Vary the listening context

Everything is now in place to test the mix in different listening contexts. It should be noted here that some mixers prefer to add a limiter to the mix for these tests. About 3 dB of gain reduction and a ceiling set at -0.5 dB are more than enough to give a good preview.

Of course, if you have several sets of studio monitors, this is the time to listen to your mix on them, if you have not already done so. That said, just about any playback device can be used: headphones, earbuds, cellphone, tablet, computer, television, and so on.

The car, if you have one, is one of the best testing grounds. Since most of us listen to music in our own cars all the time, we have, in a sense, learned what a properly mixed song sounds like there.

Another trick I consistently use for every mix is to play it in the studio, open the door, and listen from outside the room. That allows me to evaluate the mix balance in a monophonic context.

All of these tests make it possible to evaluate how the mix performs in listening situations closer to those in which it will actually be heard. By removing everything related to your studio from the equation—its monitors, its acoustics, and so on—they allow you to validate certain crucial aspects of your mix, such as mono balance, the proportion of low frequencies, the level of the lead vocal, and its intelligibility.

Listening on various devices helps identify recurring problems and correct them.

Each listening context tested offers a different perspective on the mix. The more of them you try, the more information you gather about how it behaves. It then becomes possible to spot recurring problems and correct them so the mix performs as well as possible, regardless of how it is played back.

14.3 Presenting the Mix to Clients

Presenting a mix to clients—what an exhilarating moment! I love sitting back and watching their reactions as they discover the mix. Without the slightest doubt, it is the moment I enjoy most in my work.

14.3.1 PREPARING THE PRESENTATION MIX

A mix and a mastered track differ significantly in terms of level and dynamic range. Although we are aware of these differences, they are often much less clear to our clients. After all, most of them are only rarely exposed to anything other than commercially released songs.

A limiter should be used on the version presented to the client so that it more closely resembles the sound of a commercial release.

The goal here is not to master the song, but rather to make the evaluation process easier for clients. That is why it is common to place a limiter at the end of the mix bus. Its action does not need to be excessive. Just as when evaluating different listening contexts, a ceiling set at -0.5 dBFS and 2 to 3 dB of gain reduction are generally more than sufficient to produce a result that is a little closer to what they are used to hearing.

Of course, the use of this limiter is temporary. It must be disabled when it is time to prepare the version of the mix that will be sent out for mastering.

14.3.2 THE ESSENTIAL VALUE OF CLIENT REVISIONS

Since they are hearing the proposed version of their song for the first time, your clients have a fresher ear than you do. You need that distance, especially after having spent long hours working on the mix in minute detail. It is therefore important to understand that your clients' comments are essential to improving the result.

Whether or not you agree with the conclusions your clients reach is, all things considered, of very little importance. Even if you have invested a great deal of time and energy in your work, the fact remains that the project has only been entrusted to you: it is not yours. After all, it will not be your picture on the album cover—it will be theirs!

Your role when presenting the mix is not to impose your vision, but to help your clients bring the project to completion. It is therefore completely pointless to become defensive and take their comments as a personal attack or a challenge to your competence. Not only is that unprofessional, it is counterproductive.

14.3.3 THE GOAL OF PRESENTING THE MIX TO CLIENTS

Arriving at a final version

Presenting the mix to clients is often one of the rare occasions when we have direct contact with the creators and other contributors to the project—songwriter, producer, musicians, and so on.

Personally, my main objective during that presentation is to leave with a final version of the mix. In every project where this is possible, that intention is clearly stated to the clients before the presentation and often before the contract even begins.

There are several reasons for working this way. First, face-to-face contact with clients allows us to gather their immediate reactions. It then becomes much easier to interpret their comments. Being able to exchange with them ensures that the suggested revisions are understood, explored, tested, and, if necessary, applied.

Moreover, we all know the saying: "Anything left lying around gets dirty." That is just as true of a project. In fact, it is very risky to give a client a complete version of the mix. They will inevitably play it for a whole range of people with no direct connection to the project and whose opinions will therefore be more or less uninformed (why does the name Yoko Ono suddenly come to mind?). Despite everyone's good intentions, the fact remains that the more people involved in a decision, the harder it is to make. The completion of the project then drags on, the revisions become more extensive, and the motivations behind them are often vague.

The client presentation is intended to arrive at a final version of each mix.

In that sense, it is even more reckless to give the client an excerpt or a version of a mix that is still in progress. You run a strong risk of having to debate decisions that have not yet been fully worked out or of receiving revision requests based on a mix that is still evolving.

Lastly, approval of a final version guarantees payment of part of your fee. Even if we assume that most clients act in good faith, the fact remains that leaving a client with a mix they can use as they please carries a very real risk of losing, or at least delaying, payment of your invoice. It only takes experiencing that kind of situation once to understand that it must be avoided at all costs! The agreement with the client must therefore be very clear: nothing leaves the studio until the mixing is finished, a final version has been approved, and payment has been received. Simple, clear, and effective!

Reaching an agreement with a client in advance is the best way to avoid any misunderstanding.

It goes without saying that this way of working is harder to apply when clients cannot come to the studio, as is the case with projects carried out over the Internet. However, it is entirely possible to hold a finalization meeting online using a service such as Zoom. Songs can also be shared with clients for final approval through Mixup, Samply, or even SoundCloud without providing a downloadable file. Several software solutions also make it possible to stream high-quality audio so that revisions can be tried out and heard live as they are suggested. Once again, the idea is to agree on a final version as easily as possible.

14.3.4 MANAGING REVISIONS

When presenting a mix directly to an artist or producer, managing revisions is relatively simple. We discuss things person to person and make the final adjustments so the project aligns as closely as possible with their vision and expectations.

When several people take part in the presentation, as in the case of a band, for example, the revision process often has far more to do with psychology and communication than with technique. Each person has their own idea of what the ideal mix should be and therefore pays attention to different aspects of it. Musicians, for example, often tend to judge the mix based on the sound of their own instrument and performance. It is hard to blame them: it is a natural reflex. Obviously, those concerns are not always aligned with what matters most: the overall result.

There can be many reasons that justify the sound and level of an instrument in the mix balance, ranging from the direction of the song to the quality of the performance and the recording.

Trying to explain those reasons is a bit like opening Pandora's box. A better way to deal with this situation is to ask a few clear questions:

— Bassist: *"I don't like the sound of my bass. I don't think it is present enough."*

— You: *"OK, but how do you feel about the song overall?"*

— Bassist: *"The song is fine. It is actually excellent! It is just my bass I don't like."*

— You: *"OK. What do the rest of you think?"*

The sound of the mix as a whole is always more important than that of any of its individual parts.

With those questions, you have just achieved two important objectives. First, you remind everyone involved, including the bassist, that they need to focus on the song as a whole rather than on its individual parts. You also give the other band members the chance to speak and discuss the issue among themselves. What comes through in your intervention is that your goal is to meet their expectations as well as possible—which is indeed the case.

The artistic leader

Of course, each person present has their own personality and way of communicating. Some will intervene only rarely in the conversation, while others will take up much more space.

But whether the group is aware of it or not, there is always one person whose opinion carries more weight than the others. Often, the other participants will wait for that person to speak before offering a comment themselves. Although the producer is normally the one whose opinion carries the most weight, that is not always the case.

It is important to identify the most influential person and ask them to state their opinion clearly in more delicate situations or when disagreements arise within the group.

If you handled the recording, you should already have a good sense of each person's role in the group's dynamic. Otherwise, careful listening will quickly reveal who the leader is when it comes to artistic decisions.

Interpreting comments

Very few of your clients will have enough technical knowledge to express clear comments about specific aspects of the mix. In fact, you are far more likely to hear something like "the snare needs more snap" than "I'd add a 2 dB bell at 1.6 kHz on the snare EQ"!

A remark such as "the vocal isn't present enough" can be approached in many different ways. There may be too many effects on the vocal, the accompaniment instruments may be too loud, the EQ may need more high frequencies... unless the problem is simply that the vocal itself isn't loud enough!

It is important to phrase your comments in clear language that describes the result rather than the techniques used to achieve it.

At times, interpreting comments will therefore require a little investigation. The idea is to question the client in order to pinpoint the source of the problem so it can be addressed.

Naturally, you must also understand that the communication problem exists in both directions. Outrageously technical jargon will probably not be understood by your clients and may even be perceived as a condescending display of your knowledge. It is therefore important to express your comments in clear language that describes the result rather than the technique used to achieve it. If you mixed the project in keeping with its original direction and if each of your technical interventions was motivated by a goal, you should have no trouble explaining, very briefly, why you arrived at that solution.

Disagreements

As in any kind of teamwork, clients do sometimes disagree among themselves about the revisions to be made.

Sometimes the debate seems to go nowhere. Discussions may even become heated and voices may rise. In that kind of situation, experience has taught me that it is much wiser to let them hear the proposed change than to get lost in explanations. So we make the necessary adjustments on the spot and listen. Comparing the original mix with the revised version generally allows the clients to reach a conclusion on their own.

When discussions drag on, we ask a closed question to try to bring the debate to an end: "OK, should I put the synth back in or not?", "the drums +2 dB or not?", "distortion on the vocal or not?"

When opinions split into two camps, every possible effort must be made to let the clients decide. But this kind of situation shows that democracy, too, has its limits! So if no one is willing to compromise, we ask the producer or the leader of the group to make the call.

Harmless revisions

Normally, when presenting a mix to clients, we have devoted several hours of heartfelt effort and energy to it. We have weighed each decision carefully in order to achieve the best result possible. It is therefore normal to develop a certain attachment to the project and to our work.

After trying one of the suggested revisions with your client, you may feel that the change is entirely insignificant. For example, raising the vocal or hi-hat level by a quarter of a decibel has, all things considered, no real impact on the mix balance. Clearly, most people—including us—would not hear any meaningful improvement from such a subtle change.

It is much easier to make a correction quickly and let clients hear the result than to get lost in explanations.

Even if our ego—and we all have one!—may sometimes push us to point out the futility of that kind of revision, it is best to set it aside. If your client is convinced that the change substantially improves the result, it is better to go along with it. That way, you make your client happy, which is, after all, one of the goals of the exercise.

14.4 Mastering

Originally, mastering had one sole purpose: to make mixes conform to the technical specifications of the destination medium so they could be duplicated. Although that role is still important, mastering is now used to put the finishing touch on the sonic result so the material is ready for commercial release.

Mastering therefore provides the final adjustments to frequency distribution and optimizes the output level. It ensures that the material holds up against what listeners are used to hearing commercially and that it remains effective in any listening context.

Mastering is the final audio stage before distribution.

In the case of an album project, mastering engineers make sure the songs share a consistent sonic signature. They insert fade-ins and fade-outs where needed and manage the length of the gaps between songs. They also embed the metadata associated with each track into the files.

The work ends with the creation of one or more master files, which will be used for mass duplication (vinyl, compact disc, videos, and so on) or digital distribution (Tidal, Spotify, Apple Music, and other digital platforms).

14.4.1 PREPARING MIXES FOR MASTERING

The mix bus

If you placed a limiter on your mixes for client presentation, it is obviously essential to remove it from the mix bus. Let the mastering engineer handle the output level instead. They are in a better position to do so, since they are taking into account the processing they themselves apply to the mix.

As for the other processing on the mix bus, the earlier it was placed during mixing, the more it contributed to your decisions and helped shape the overall sound. It should therefore remain active. Of course, its settings may still need one last revision following the client's requested changes.

Exporting and fades

Since the engineer modifies the mix's dynamic range, the tail of certain elements—cymbals or reverb, for example—may remain audible for longer. If you are working with a mastering engineer, it is good practice to leave enough space at the end of the mix to ensure that instrument and reverb tails are not cut off. A simple trick is to place the export marker at least two seconds after the complete decay of the reverb.

For the same reason, most mastering engineers prefer to handle fade-ins and fade-outs at the beginning and end of songs themselves. In the case of a progressive fade-out that affects the musical content, it is enough to indicate where it begins and how long it lasts (for example: "fade-out from 4:18 to the end").

Audio resolution and file types

Changing a file's resolution is irreversible. The final files delivered for mastering must therefore always be exported at the same resolution that was used during mixing. The engineer will take care of matching that variable to the specifications of the destination medium.

As for file type, only .wav and .aiff formats are suitable for mastering.

14.4.2 IDENTIFYING THE MATERIAL

Mastering engineers handle a large number of projects every year. If there is one thing that exasperates them, it is poorly labeled material! It makes their work harder and increases the risk of mistakes.

Naming the files

Clear labeling of each track is essential in order to avoid any ambiguity. The name of each file must indicate the title of the song and, if necessary, its position on the CD ("3-Find Your Way"). There is a strong chance that this name will be copied directly onto the master used for duplication or digital distribution. Its spelling must therefore be checked...twice rather than once!

Mixes sent for mastering must be clearly labeled.

The project sheet

Again, in order to avoid any ambiguity, a document containing the essential information about the project must accompany your files. It should be as clear and concise as possible. Once again, some of this information may be copied onto the final masters. The spelling must therefore be impeccable.

The document will, of course, contain the artist's name and, where applicable, the album title. For each song, it should indicate:

- its exact title,
- its position on the CD, if applicable,
- its ISRC,
- its duration,
- precise instructions concerning fade-ins and fade-outs.

In the case of an album, the duration of the spaces between songs is generally determined by the mastering engineer. However, if two songs must run together without a pause, you need to indicate that clearly in your document.

It is also essential to include the contact information of the person responsible for mixing and, if necessary, the person supervising the mastering.

The ISRC Code

The International Standard Recording Code (ISRC) is used to identify a sound recording and facilitates the management of the rights and royalties associated with it. Made up of 12 characters, a track's ISRC must be encoded into the medium during mastering.

Producing a new version

Sometimes, mastering reveals problems that would be easier to fix in the mix. A file cut off too abruptly, excessive sibilance, or a frequency problem tied to a specific instrument are all issues that are difficult to correct in mastering. The mastering engineer may therefore ask you to produce a new version of a mix. In that case, it must be clearly identified (for example: "3-Find Your Way Version 2").

Album : Put My Genes On
Artiste : The Plasterers of Happiness

Track	Title	Lenght	ISRC	Notes
1	For a Moment	3:46	CAPL01500001	
2	She Loves Me All the Same	4:10	CAPL01500002	Fade-out from 4:01 to end
3	Put My Genes On	3:51	CAPL01500003	
4	Love Odyssey I	3:18	CAPL01500004	No break before next track
5	Love Odyssey II	4:18	CAPL01500005	No break before next track
6	Love Odyssey III	2:52	CAPL01500006	Fade-out from 2:43 to end
7	Forget About It	3:56	CAPL01500007	
8	The Room Is Empty	5:34	CAPL01500008	
9	Stellar Interlude	6:21	CAPL01500009	Fade-out from 6:05 to end

Eric Noel : 418-123-1234
eric@musiqueprod.com

An example of a brief project sheet for an album.

14.4.3 CHOOSING A MASTERING ENGINEER

Very often, it is our responsibility to suggest the mastering studio that will finalize the project. Aside from budget and availability, what are the main things to check when choosing a mastering engineer?

The catalog

The first thing to check is, of course, the quantity and especially the quality of the projects the engineer has completed. A substantial catalog is a sign of experience and confirms that other people have entrusted their projects to that engineer. The presence of work by established artists is often a sign of quality work.

A review of the catalog also makes it possible to discover whether the engineer seems to specialize in a particular style of music. Even if that does not necessarily make them less capable of tackling something different, chances are they will be more comfortable with projects in their niche.

But an impressive catalog means very little if none of the listed works has ever been released! A quick search on streaming platforms will allow you to identify the commercial projects and, of course, listen to them.

The equipment and the working environment

Like me, you have probably noticed that the number of studios offering mastering services has literally exploded in recent years. Yet mastering approaches audio in a way that is completely different from mixing. So not only is an excellent mixer not automatically a good mastering engineer, but they probably do not have the necessary equipment to do the job properly. An SSL console, impressive as it may be, is of no use in mastering. Nor is owning a set of plug-ins called "Mastering Bundle" and a LUFS meter enough for the task!

A mastering engineer's catalog and facilities offer good clues as to their ability to do the job properly.

The equipment and working environment available at a mastering facility are often good indicators of quality. Excellent monitors, a room with optimal acoustics, a generally limited number of specialized processing devices, coupled with a few computer tools specifically dedicated to mastering, form the core of a mastering studio's setup. It should also be noted that most professional mastering houses rarely offer any other type of service.

Communication

The mastering engineer is the last of the many contributors involved in the making of an audio project. Their role is to bring the material up to release standards without altering the project's original artistic intention. They are part of the team. The way they interact with their clients is therefore an important point to consider when selecting one.

A good mastering engineer understands that their interventions go far beyond numbers and technique. Some mixing decisions may lead them to question how they should intervene on the audio. For example, if you listen to the song "Darkness" from Peter Gabriel's album *Up* (an excellent mix, by the way!) you will understand that the very low level of the introduction and the deliberate overcompression that follows may leave the engineer puzzled. In that specific case, this is the work of Tchad Blake, a mixing engineer known for his boldness. Of course, not all of us have that kind of reputation! In such a situation, the engineer should contact you to make sure that this is truly intentional. That way, they can better choose how to intervene on the audio without working against the project's artistic intentions.

The way a mastering engineer communicates with clients is a very important factor to consider.

Since mastering processing affects the entire audio signal, it is obvious that problems tied directly to a single instrument are easier to correct at the mixing stage. Thus, if the engineer believes that a change in the mix could improve the quality of the final result, they should get in touch with you and let you know. You will then be able to determine together how extensive the correction should be and prepare a new version that will make their work easier and improve the final result.

14.4.4 RECOMMENDATIONS

Do not hesitate to ask for revisions

Mastering engineers often carry an aura of audio gurus, especially in the eyes of beginners. Rest assured, however: they are not audio deities with supernatural hearing, nor do they hold the ultimate truth on every aspect of sound. Like the rest of us, they are human—which means they can be wrong too. So do not assume that the mastering result is automatically perfect and immutable just because the engineer delivered it to you. If you or the team feel that the result of a master is not quite right, do not hesitate to ask for changes.

Of course, it must be understood that the action of mastering on a mix's frequency distribution and dynamics will necessarily affect its balance, timbre, and stereo image. In most cases, those changes help improve the final result and the flow of an album.

It is nevertheless possible for the processing to alter certain aspects of the mix or its original intention too much. In that case, it is essential to discuss the matter with the engineer and determine what can be done to reduce their impact.

Be wary of stem mastering

In the same spirit, it is worth being cautious about stem mastering. Stems are tracks that group the elements of a mix into families. In a rock project, for example, you might have one stem containing all the drum tracks, another for the bass tracks, one for the guitars, one for the lead vocal, and a final one for the background vocals. Once all of these stems are imported into a session and each respective fader is set to zero, the original mix is, in a sense, recreated.

Stems are individual tracks that group the elements of a mix into families. Playing all of these stems simultaneously, in a sense, reproduces the original mix.

Stem mastering therefore replaces the traditional stereo file with a set of tracks grouping the elements of the mix. It makes it possible to process each of them individually without affecting the rest of the track. A sibilance problem on the vocal, for example, could be reduced without changing the high frequencies of the other families.

Stems are very often used in advertising and video production because they also make it possible to adjust the levels of individual elements in the mix. It is, for example, possible to lower or completely mute the vocal level of a song so that it does not interfere with dialogue on screen.

When it comes to mastering, however, this method raises a number of serious issues. First, creating the stems themselves is not always as simple as it seems, especially when processing is placed on the mix bus. That processing is set to react to the mix as a whole, not to one part of it.

Particularly complex projects also make it difficult to create coherent track groupings. We then have to produce either a large number of stems or place tracks in a stem that does not really represent them.

In short, producing stems is a process that requires a great deal of attention and, unfortunately, time! It is therefore necessary to discuss the matter with the client in order to determine whether the time required to create stems fits their schedule and budget.

Another problem arises. Let us assume that you have spent days, weeks, or months working with your clients on a project. By the end of the process, you have arrived at final versions that everyone involved can agree on. Is it really a good idea to give the mastering engineer the ability to intervene at will on a specific element of the mix—or worse, to change its level?

Unfortunately, this regrettable situation is becoming increasingly common. A growing number of applications now make it possible to separate the elements of a mix with artificial intelligence. Some mastering engineers do not hesitate to use them in order to create stems themselves, with varying degrees of success, and then modify them as they please. Even if the engineer sees this initiative as a way to work more efficiently, they have no legitimacy whatsoever to override the decisions agreed upon by the producer, the mixer, and the artist.

A stereo file approved by the client remains the best way to prepare a project for release.

Let us be frank: those decisions are the very essence of the mixing work and are not the mastering engineer's responsibility. Personally, I would be very reluctant to give that much latitude to a single person at the final stage of a project, either for my own sake or for my clients'. Especially when the mastering engineer grants themselves that freedom!

For these reasons, using a stereo file approved by the client remains, in my view, the best way to prepare a project for release.

Furthermore, the decision to use stem mastering should always be yours, not imposed by the mastering engineer.

Ask the engineer to share their impressions

A mastering engineer focuses on aspects of audio that are often quite different from those we pay attention to in mixing. It is therefore a good idea to ask them for a brief summary of their overall impression of the project and, most importantly, which aspects of the audio they worked on, and to what extent.

The vast majority of engineers are happy to do this. Their observations not only help us grow as mixers, but can also reveal problems in the acoustics or monitoring of our listening environment that could be corrected. It would be negligent not to take advantage of their perspective!

Be loyal!

It may take a few tries to find the engineer who will handle your projects professionally and with whom you feel comfortable working. You will also quickly notice that systematically searching for the lowest bidder is rarely a good idea. In truth, although price is very important, it is only one variable in the equation; the engineer's communication, respect for deadlines, and ability to work without compromising the integrity of the project are all important factors to consider.

Over time, they will become familiar with the particularities of your mixing style, while you, in turn, will learn to predict more accurately how your mix will sound once mastered. That kind of rapport will help you bring your projects to completion without surprises and in a climate of trust—to the great satisfaction of your clients!

Consider AI mastering

The range of online AI mastering services is extremely diverse. So much so that more and more plug-in manufacturers and online music distributors now offer their own mastering solution.

The processing choices are also becoming increasingly flexible. Most online solutions allow users to adjust certain mastering parameters, such as the degree of compression, the width of the stereo image, the characteristics of the frequency balance, and, of course, the extent of the dynamic range. Musical style can often be selected as well. Some services also make it possible to provide a reference track in order to obtain a broadly similar result.

Intelligent mastering plug-ins are also available to do the work more or less autonomously. They generally provide more control than online solutions over the starting parameters and offer a processing chain that users can then modify.

The main advantage of AI mastering is, of course, its low cost. In fact, even the most expensive solutions cost about one tenth of the price of a mastering engineer. That low cost also allows us to compare several online mastering sites and choose the service that suits us best.

AI mastering can be an interesting option for projects with tighter budgets.

AI mastering is obviously not suitable for every project. However, it can be an interesting option when budgets are tighter. Many independent artists will indeed prefer to invest the mastering budget in areas where they feel it will have a greater impact. They may use the money saved to improve the production itself or add it to the promotional budget. After all, the best song in the world, even with excellent mastering, will not go very far without at least a minimum of promotion!

15
THE TEMPLATE

Over time, mixers develop an in-depth command of each of their processing tools and of how those tools interact with certain types of tracks. It is therefore no surprise that they often use their favorite plug-ins or devices to build recurring processing chains in their mixes.

We also know that several basic operations are repeated invariably from one mix to the next: putting tracks in order, defining routing, creating subgroups, inserting effects, and so on.

The concept of a template is simple: it is a model project in which most of these routine tasks have already been completed. The audio tracks for the mix at hand are then imported into it. The result is a project with functional organization and routing, where most of the processing chains are already set up and ready to use.

A template is designed to speed up mixing by avoiding the need to repeat certain routine tasks.

15.1 Creating a Template

Creating a template usually begins either with a blank project or with an existing project that serves as a starting point. In the latter case, make sure to delete all the audio tracks and save the project under another name.

Creating and Assigning Tracks

It is of course impossible to know precisely what future mixes will include. We can, however, define the key tracks that will be present in the vast majority of projects. The lead vocal track immediately comes to mind. We may therefore create a mono track to receive it and insert the processing tools we use most often for this type of track. A look at your previous projects will reveal which tools those are. We can also create another empty track to hold a copy of the vocal so we can quickly perform parallel processing if needed.

My template also includes three tracks for the bass: one for the DI, one for the amplifier, and one for saturation. As with the vocal track, I have placed the tools I use frequently on them. A selection of compressors is present in the inserts of the DI track. I can therefore compare them in a few clicks. The amplifier track has two guitar simulators inserted. That way, if I do not receive any amp tracks, I can quickly generate one from a copy of the DI track. A few saturation plug-ins are installed on my last bass track. All of these tracks feed a bass subgroup. We discuss subgroups a little further on.

When creating a template, the idea is not to cover every possible situation, but to address the most common needs.

Acoustic drums obviously require special attention. We generally reserve two tracks for the snare: one for the microphone placed above it (SN Top) and another for the one placed below it (SN Btm). We may also want to add a third track to make it easier to add a sample (SN Add). The same applies to the kick drum (KICK In, KICK Out, and KICK Add).

Although overheads are often recorded with two microphones, it may be useful to provide an additional track for a center microphone. This would give us OH L for the left microphone, OH R for the right microphone, and OH C for the center microphone. Another track is reserved for the hi-hat (HH).

Since the most common drum configuration includes three toms, we can add three mono channels (Tom 1, Tom 2, and Floor). Finally, drum ambience is generally captured with two microphones. We can therefore create one track for each of them: Room L and Room R.

Deploying the Tracks

As we noted in the chapter on preparatory work, it is essential to order tracks the same way from one project to the next. The template is obviously no exception to this rule. In fact, it is a way to ensure that this layout is repeated. In the main project window, we can create folders for each instrument family and assign a color to each one. These very simple operations will make it easier to find our way around.

Routing

One of the main advantages of a template is that it saves us from having to redo routing procedures for every new mix. Thus, we can create a series of subgroups, or auxes depending on your software, to receive instrument tracks such as drums, lead vocal, bass, guitars, backing vocals, synthesizers, and so on. It may also be useful to create a few unnamed subgroups right away, so they are quickly available for other track groupings.

Although it is perfectly legitimate to limit ourselves to the usual subgroups, your working habits may lead you to integrate other routing strategies into your template. For example, the routing for parallel drum compression can be set up. Many mixers also find it useful to route all the tracks in the mix to a premaster, a general subgroup that adds a step before the output bus. This premaster and its routing can be integrated into the template from the outset.

We should avoid overloading a template's routing unnecessarily.

Keep in mind, however, that a template is meant to make the work easier, not more complicated. We should avoid overloading a template's routing, so that it remains both clear and flexible.

Adding Effects

Creating effects tracks is another task that has to be redone for each project. We can therefore do a large part of this work in our template right away.

Your previous projects will naturally reveal recurring patterns in the way you use effects. These are the patterns you should carry over into your template.

Your previous projects will shed light on the processing plug-ins you use and the way you work with effects.

For instance, my template includes six reverbs: one for vocals, one for the snare, one for general ambience, a spring reverb, a chamber, and a plate. For echoes, it includes a slapback, two echoes set to the song's tempo, and a double delay. A doubler and a chorus will cover my modulation needs. Will I use all of these effects on every mix? Probably not. However, all these effects now appear in the sends menu and are ready to be assigned and tested.

Inserting Processing Tools

You may now want to insert your preferred processing tools on the tracks and subgroups you have created. For the kick drum, for example, I often use an emulation of an SSL console channel followed by a four-band parametric equalizer. That is therefore what you will find on that track in my template.

Although it is wise to limit the number of inserts placed on tracks, it is sometimes useful to leave ourselves a few options during mixing. For example, if you use an 1176 compressor as often as an LA-3A on the electric guitar subgroup, it is entirely possible to insert both compressors so that you can compare them quickly and choose the one that best suits the needs of the song.

We may also add plug-ins to the output bus inserts. In my template, you would find a console simulator, an EQ, one or two compressors, a tape simulator, and a frequency analyzer.

Activating the Plug-Ins or Not?

Before finalizing our template, it is worth asking two final questions: should plug-ins be active, and if so, which ones?

Whether plug-ins are active or not influences the way we will work on the project.

If all the plug-ins are active, you will hear a processed version of the song as soon as you press play. That moment may be magical or... disastrous! Hearing this processed version can make the mixing process feel like one large revision operation. That is why many mixers prefer to build the mix gradually, turning on processing plug-ins only as they need them. You simply need to experiment with both approaches and choose the one that best suits your way of working.

In my own template, all effects tracks and output bus inserts are active. Everything else remains inactive and is activated as needed.

Saving the Template

Once the project is complete, it is essential to save it as a template. Depending on the software, this option is available directly in the save menu or through the "save as..." command.

15.2 Importing the Tracks into the Template

15.2.1 INSTRUCTIONS TO CLIENTS FOR SENDING TRACKS

Transferring Project Tracks

It is common for clients' projects to be created in software other than our own, which prevents us from opening them directly. This situation requires our attention.

First, let us point out that even if we work with the same software as the client, different versions can complicate project retrieval. It is also fairly rare for us to own all the plug-ins the client used. In either case, your software will display a warning message.

To avoid this problem, we should ask the client to export each of the project's tracks from the beginning to the end of the song, regardless of where it contains audio. With audio files that all begin at the same point, we can line them up at the beginning of our project and guarantee synchronization.

Your client may have a few questions about how to perform this export. First, they may wonder whether to export the tracks with or without insert processing. As long as the client also sends me a rough mix, I usually prefer to receive the tracks without processing. The same goes for effects. Unless the client has created one they are especially attached to, I prefer to use the rough mix as inspiration for recreating them.

If your client is an experienced professional, it is often much more appropriate to continue the mix from where they left off. In that case, we will suggest that they export the tracks with all inserts active and create stereo tracks of their main effects.

Sample Settings and Tempo

Two other important variables must also be checked before integrating the tracks into our template.

It is essential to check the sampling characteristics of the tracks before integrating them into the template.

We must first determine whether the audio files to be imported and the template use the same sample settings. If not, we will have to either modify the template's sample settings or convert the received files to match them. Fortunately, most software performs this conversion automatically during import or offers this option through a dialog box.

It is also preferable to set the template to the tempo of the song before importing the audio files into it. This will make navigation, editing, and the use of synchronized effects easier. Personally, I ask clients to write the song's BPM in the file name after the song title ("Fall in Summer – 92 BPM").

15.2.2 IMPORTING AUDIO FILES

The way audio files are integrated into a template varies from one piece of software to another. Some allow the template to be applied to an existing mix; others require the files to be imported manually or through a dialog box. Normally, the import procedure places the audio files in the project window by creating a new track for each of them.

Since we have created only a few essential tracks for the vocal, drums, and bass, most elements will not be covered by the template. We therefore simply place each track in the appropriate instrument family and give it the color assigned to that family.

Integrating audio tracks into the template is a task that requires a great deal of attention.

When manipulating tracks, it is essential not to unintentionally change the position of the files in time while moving them. All DAWs provide a keyboard command that lets you preserve the files' origin point while moving them.

Once all the files have found a home in the template, we move on to the cleanup operation. We first delete the empty tracks from the project window. We then remove from the template anything that is not useful for this particular mix. This declutters the mixing console and the project window, making it easier to find our way around.

Of course, we create a backup copy. It is important to check whether your software requires the use of the "save as..." option to prevent the current project from overwriting your precious template!

15.2.3 RECOMMENDATIONS

Build Your Template in Stages

Creating a template is a delicate operation. It requires a minimum of mixing experience and a good knowledge of mixing techniques. A great deal of time and attention is needed to ensure that it is versatile enough to meet your common needs without being unnecessarily complicated. That is, in fact, why I decided to address this subject only at the very end of this book.

Many apprentice mixers fall into the trap of developing a template that is so loaded and complex that it slows down mixing instead of speeding it up. In that regard, many mixers are perfectly satisfied with a template that only sets up routine routing operations. For example, they will implement only the effects, a premaster subgroup, and the inserts on the master bus.

A template is generally the result of several successive improvements.

It should also be noted that a template is generally the result of several successive improvements introduced over months and years. It is therefore a good idea to save it as a new version each time you make a change. This allows you to test it while keeping the option of returning to an earlier version.

Create Variations of Your Template

The genre of music we work on, or the type of sound we are trying to give a project, influences many of our mixing decisions, especially when it comes to selecting processing tools. If the projects entrusted to you fall into a few specific musical genres, it is entirely possible to modify an existing template into an adapted version that reflects your routing and processing preferences for a particular musical style. The goal is always to help you mix the projects entrusted to you more efficiently.

References

Works Consulted

Everest, F. Alton, and Ken C. Pohlmann. *Master Handbook of Acoustics*, 6th ed. McGraw-Hill Education, 2015.

Izhaki, Roey. *Mixing Audio: Concepts, Practices and Tools.* Burlington: Elsevier, 2008.

Massey, Howard. *Behind the Glass: Top Record Producers Tell How They Craft the Hits.* San Francisco: Backbeat Books, 2000.

Massey, Howard. *Behind the Glass, Volume 2: Top Record Producers Tell How They Craft the Hits.* San Francisco: Backbeat Books, 2009.

Massy, Sylvia and Chris Johnson. *Recording Unhinged: Creative & Unconventional Music Recording Techniques.* Milwaukee: Hal Leonard Books, 2016.

Mixerman. *Zen in the Art of Mixing.* Milwaukee: Hal Leonard Books, 2010.

Owsinski, Bobby. *The Mixing Engineer's Handbook. 3rd ed.* Boston: Cengage Learning PTR, 2014.

Senior, Mike. *Mixing Secrets for the Small Studio.* Burlington: Focal Press, 2011.

Sites Web consultés

Audiofanzine. https://fr.audiofanzine.com
Ethan Winer. https://ethanwiner.com/articles.html
Full Sail University. https://www.youtube.com/user/fullsailuniversity
Gearslutz. https://www.gearslutz.com
iZotope Blog. https://www.izotope.com/en/blog

Lavry Engineering. https://www.lavryengineering.com/lavry-white-papers
Mix. https://www.mixonline.com
Mix with the Masters. https://www.mixwiththemasters.com
Pensado's Place. https://www.pensadosplace.tv
Pro Audio Files. https://www.theproaudiofiles.com
Production Advice. https://www.productionadvice.co.uk
Produce Like a Pro. https://www.producelikeapro.com
Progressions: Success in the Music Industry. https://www.progressionspodcast.com
Pro Tools Expert. https://www.pro-tools-expert.com
Puremix. https://www.puremix.net
Record Production. https://www.recordproduction.com
Recording Studio Rockstars. https://www.recordingstudiorockstars.com
SonicScoop. https://www.sonicscoop.com
Sound On Sound. https://www.soundonsound.com
Tape Op. https://www.tapeop.com
Waves Tutorials. https://www.waves.com/videos/tutorials
Working Class Audio. https://www.workingclassaudio.com
Xiph.Org Foundation. https://www.xiph.org

And, of course:
Musiqueprod. https://www.musiqueprod.com

Made in the USA
Las Vegas, NV
05 November 2026

57575819R00162